P9-CLC-636

Uncivil Agreement

Uncivil Agreement

How Politics Became Our Identity

LILLIANA MASON

The University of Chicago Press
Chicago and London

The University of Chicago Press, Chicago 60637
The University of Chicago Press, Ltd., London
© 2018 by The University of Chicago
All rights reserved. No part of this book may be used or reproduced in any manner whatsoever without written permission, except in the case of brief quotations in critical articles and reviews. For more information, contact the University of Chicago Press, 1427 East 60th Street, Chicago, IL 60637.
Published 2018
Printed in the United States of America

27 26 25 24 23 22 21 20 4 5

ISBN-13: 978-0-226-52440-5 (cloth)
ISBN-13: 978-0-226-52454-2 (paper)
ISBN-13: 978-0-226-52468-9 (e-book)
DOI: 10.7208/chicago/9780226524689.001.0001

Library of Congress Cataloging-in-Publication Data

Names: Mason, Lilliana, author.
Title: Uncivil agreement : how politics became our identity / Lilliana Mason.
Description: Chicago ; London : The University of Chicago Press, 2018. | Includes bibliographical references and index.
Identifiers: LCCN 2017046162 | ISBN 9780226524405 (cloth : alk. paper) | ISBN 9780226524542 (pbk. : alk. paper) | ISBN 9780226524689 (e-book)
Subjects: LCSH: Party affiliation—United States. | Political parties—United States. | Political activists—United States. | United States—Politics and government—21st century.
Classification: LCC JK2271 .M312 2018 | DDC 324.273—dc23
LC record available at https://lccn.loc.gov/2017046162

♾ This paper meets the requirements of ANSI/NISO Z39.48-1992 (Permanence of Paper).

CONTENTS

ACKNOWLEDGMENTS

First and foremost I thank the people of the University of Chicago Press for working tirelessly to help this book come into the world. John Tryneski kept this project alive, and Chuck Myers made it real. The anonymous reviewers of the manuscript made it much, much better.

The National Science Foundation funded a portion of my research under grant no. SES-1065054. This made my data collection possible.

None of this work would have happened without the help of my graduate advisors Stanley Feldman and Leonie Huddy, whose continuing advice, support, and faith in me were at times what kept me writing.

My deep and endless thanks go to Rick Lau, who read every chapter of the first draft of this book, providing crucial and insightful guidance and wisdom, and also a desk to write from.

Profound thanks go to many years of attendees of the New York Area Political Psychology meeting, particularly those who commented directly on a distilled version of the theory presented here, including John Bullock, Adam Levine, George Marcus, Tali Mendelberg, Diana Mutz, and Julie Wronski.

To the attendees of the National Capital Area Political Science Association, I thank you for your welcome and your feedback.

For inviting me to their home institutions to present many of these ideas, I am extremely grateful to Nick Valentino, Ted Carmines, Hans Noel, Jon Ladd, Jaime Settle, Carin Robinson, Sean Westwood, Cornell Clayton, and Torben Lütjen.

I would like to thank discussants and reviewers of many versions of the ideas presented here, including those at the University of Göttingen Symposium on the 2016 Elections, the Foley Institute Symposium, the Princeton Center for the Study of Democratic Politics, the University of Michigan

Center for Political Studies, the Indiana University Center on American Politics, the Georgetown American Government Seminar, and the University of Maryland American Politics Workshop.

For being reliable and kind colleagues, I thank my mentors Antoine Banks, Mike Hanmer, and Frances Lee, as well as the rest of the extremely supportive Department of Government and Politics at the University of Maryland.

To Bill Bishop, my fairy godfather, you found my research out in the wilds of academic scholarship and helped me spread the word.

For one surprise email early on in this process, I thank Morris Fiorina, who helped me believe that this whole idea was worthwhile.

To my parents: you are the reason I chose academia, and your continuing encouragement and support make every day possible. To my brothers, Joe and Keith: your talented ears helped me write this book in my own voice.

And beyond all others, I thank the people who truly sacrificed their time and my attention. To my family—Dave, Penny, and Mabel: you are the reason I write and the reason I can. This book is dedicated to you. To my daughters in particular: your curiosity, endless enthusiasm, and faith give me hope for the next generation of Americans. It's up to you to fix this. I can't think of anyone more qualified.

ONE

Identity-Based Democracy

In the summer of 1954, the social psychologist Muzafer Sherif and his colleagues recruited twenty-two fifth-grade boys from Oklahoma City and sent them to two adjacent campsites in Robbers Cave State Park. The boys were carefully selected to be nearly identical to each other in social, educational, physical, and emotional fitness. They were all white, Protestant, and middle class. None had ever met the others before. They were carefully divided into two equal-sized teams, designed to be similar to each other in every possible way. The two teams came to call themselves the Eagles and the Rattlers, and without knowing it they participated in a three-week-long psychological experiment.

During the first week, the teams were kept separate. The boys on each team grew to know each other and to form, from scratch, a sense of being a group. In the second week, each team learned of the other's existence. Having never laid eyes on the other team, the boys on each side immediately began referring to the others as "outsiders," "intruders," and "those boys at the other end of the camp." They grew impatient for a challenge. The experimenters arranged a tournament between the Eagles and the Rattlers. When they came into contact for the very first time—to play baseball—a member of the Eagles immediately called one of the Rattlers "dirty shirt." By the second day of the tournament, both teams were regularly name-calling and using derogatory terms such as *pigs*, *bums*, and *cheaters*, and they began to show reluctance to spend time with members of the other team. Even boys who were compelled to sit out the competitions hurled insults from the sidelines.

In the next few days, the relations between the teams quickly degraded. The Eagles burned the Rattlers' flag. The Rattlers raided the Eagles' cabin in the middle of the night. The Eagles raided the Rattlers' cabin in the middle of the day. Boys from both sides began to collect rocks to use in combat, fistfights broke out, and the staff decided to "stop the interaction altogether to avoid possible injury" (Sherif et al. 1988, 115). They were sent back to their separate camps. By the end of the second week, twenty-two highly similar boys who had met only two weeks before had formed two nearly warring tribes, with only the gentle nudge of isolation and competition to encourage them.

By the start of the third week, the conflict had affected the boys' abilities to judge objective reality. They were given a task to collect as many beans off the ground as possible. Each boy's collection was viewed by both groups on an overhead projector for five seconds. The campers were asked to quickly estimate the number of beans collected by each child. Every boy estimated more beans for their own teammates than for the children on the opposing team. The experimenters had shown them the same number of beans every time.

The Robbers Cave experiment was one of the first to look at the determinants and effects of group membership and intergroup conflict. It inspired years of increasingly precise and wide-ranging research, looking into exactly how our group memberships shape us, affect our relationships with outsiders, and distort our perceptions of objective reality. The following chapters will discuss many of these results. But the simplicity of the Robbers Cave experiment is itself telling. The boys at Robbers Cave needed nothing but isolation and competition to almost instantaneously consider the other team to be "dirty bums," to hold negative stereotypes about them, to avoid social contact with them, and to overestimate their own group's abilities. In very basic ways, group identification and conflict change the way we think and feel about ourselves and our opponents.

We, as modern Americans, probably like to think of ourselves as more sophisticated and tolerant than a group of fifth-grade boys from 1954. In many ways, of course, we are. But the Rattlers and the Eagles have a lot more in common with today's Democrats and Republicans than we would like to believe. Recently, the presidential campaign and election of Donald Trump laid bare some of the basest motivations in the American electorate, and they provide a compelling demonstration of the theory underlying this book.

The Trump phenomenon is particularly rooted in identity and intergroup competition—something that Trump himself often highlights. In September 2015, then-candidate Trump told a crowd, "We will have so much winning if I get elected that you may get bored with the winning" (Schwartz 2015). Trump's ultimately successful rhetoric, while often criticized for its crudeness and lack of ideological coherence, is consistent in its most important message: we will win. The "we" that is promised to win is a crucial element for understanding the election of Donald Trump and, more broadly, recent politics in the American electorate as a whole.

The election of Trump is the culmination of a process by which the American electorate has become deeply socially divided along partisan lines. As the parties have grown racially, religiously, and socially distant from one another, a new kind of social discord has been growing. The increasing political divide has allowed political, public, electoral, and national norms to be broken with little to no consequence. The norms of racial, religious, and cultural respect have deteriorated. Partisan battles have helped organize Americans' distrust for "the other" in politically powerful ways. In this political environment, a candidate who picks up the banner of "us versus them" and "winning versus losing" is almost guaranteed to tap into a current of resentment and anger across racial, religious, and cultural lines, which have recently divided neatly by party.

Across the electorate, Americans have been dividing with increasing distinction into two partisan teams. Emerging research has shown that members of both parties negatively stereotype members of the opposing party, and the extent of this partisan stereotyping has increased by 50 percent between 1960 and 2010 (Iyengar, Sood, and Lelkes 2012). They view the other party as more extreme than their own, while they view their own party as not at all extreme (Jacobson 2012). In June 2016, a Pew study found that for the first time in more than twenty years, majorities of Democrats and Republicans hold *very* unfavorable views of their partisan opponents (Pew 2016). American partisans today prefer to live in neighborhoods with members of their own party, expressing less satisfaction with their neighborhood when told that opposing partisans live there (Hui 2013).

Increasing numbers of partisans don't want party leaders to compromise, blaming the other party for all incivility in the government (Wolf, Strachan, and Shea 2012), even though, according to a 2014 Pew poll, 71 percent of Americans believe that a failure of the two parties to work together would harm the nation "a lot" (Pew 2014). Yet, as a 2016 Pew poll reports, "Most partisans say that, when it comes to how Democrats and Republicans should address the most important issues facing the country, their party should get more out of the deal" (Pew 2016).

Democrats and Republicans also view objective economic conditions differently, depending on which party is in power (Enns and McAvoy 2012). In the week before the 2016 election, 16 percent of Republicans and 61 percent of Democrats believed the US economy was getting better. In the week after the election, 49 percent of Republicans and 46 percent of Democrats believed the economy was improving (Gallup 2016).

These attitudes are all strikingly reminiscent of the relations between the Rattlers and the Eagles. Those boys desperately wanted to defeat each other, for no reason other than that they were in different groups. Group victory is a powerful prize, and American partisans have increasingly seen that goal as more important than the practical matters of governing a nation. Democrats and Republicans do not like each other. But unlike the Rattlers and the Eagles, the Democrats and Republicans today make up 85 percent of the American population.[1]

This book looks at the effects of our group identities, particularly our partisan identities and other party-linked identities, on our abilities to fairly judge political opponents, to view politics with a reasoned and unbiased eye, and to evaluate objective reality. I explain how natural and easy it can be for Democrats and Republicans to see the world through partisan eyes and why we are increasingly doing so. Just like the Rattlers and the Eagles, American partisans today are prone to stereotyping, prejudice, and emotional volatility, a phenomenon that I refer to as social polarization. Rather than simply disagreeing over policy outcomes, we are increasingly blind to our commonalities, seeing each other only as two teams fighting for a trophy.

Social polarization is defined by prejudice, anger, and activism on behalf of that prejudice and anger. These phenomena are increasing quickly—more quickly, in fact, than the level of our policy disagreements. We act like we disagree more than we really do. Like the Rattlers and the Eagles, our conflicts are largely over who we think we are rather than over reasoned differences of opinion.

The separation of the country into two teams discourages compromise and encourages an escalation of conflict, with no camp staff to break up the fights. The cooperation and compromise required by democracy grow less attainable as partisan isolation and conflict increase. As political scientist Seth Masket wrote in December 2016, "The Republican Party is demonstrating every day that it hates Democrats more than it loves democracy" (Masket 2016). That is, the election of Donald Trump and the policy and party conflicts his campaign engendered has revealed a preference for party victory over real policy outcomes that has only been building over time.

The First Step Is to Admit There Is a Problem

In 1950, the American Political Science Association (APSA) assembled a Committee on Political Parties that produced a report arguing for a "responsible two-party system" (American Political Science Association 1950). As they argued, "popular government in a nation of more than 150 million people requires political parties which provide the electorate with a proper range of choice between alternatives of action" (APSA Report 1950, 15). Parties, therefore, simplify politics for people who rightly do not have the time or resources to be political experts. In fact, E. E. Schattschneider argued in 1942 that "political parties created democracy and that modern democracy is unthinkable save in terms of parties" (Schattschneider 1942, 1).

Sean Theriault, in his 2008 book on congressional polarization, described the context of the APSA report this way:

> When the report was released (the 81st Congress, 1950), the average Democrat in the House was less than 3 standard deviations away from the average Republican. In the Senate, the distance was less than 2.25 standard deviations. Little changed in the ensuing 25 years. . . . As a result of both polarization between the parties and homogenization within the parties, by the 108th Congress (2003–4), the average party members were separated by more than 5 standard deviations in the House and almost 5 standard deviations in the Senate. . . . Now, political scientists, in claiming that party polarization has drastic consequences, are offering reforms to weaken the party leadership inside Congress. . . . Although polarized parties may be ugly for the legislative process, they were the prescription for a responsible electorate. No longer are constituents forced to make the complicated vote choice between a liberal Republican and a conservative Democrat. Additionally, voters need not wonder whom to credit or blame for the way that Congress operates. (Theriault 2008, 226)

Political parties are indeed important elements of democracy. Parties simplify the voting decision. The vast majority of American citizens are not, and cannot be expected to be, political experts. They do not read legislation; many do not even know which party is currently in the majority. But most voters have a sense of party loyalty. They know, either through a lifetime of learning, from parental socialization, from news media, or through some combination thereof, that one party is better suited to them. This acts as a heuristic, a cognitive shortcut that allows voters to make choices that are informed by some helpful truth. According to Schattschneider (1942), this is a crucial element of representative democracy.

Even better, when people feel linked to a party, they tend to more often participate in politics, just like sports fans attend a game and cheer. Partisanship, then, is one important link between individuals and political action. It encourages citizens to participate and feel involved in their own democracy.

So why write a book about the problems generated by partisan identity? It should be clarified at the start that this book is not opposed to all partisanship, all parties, party systems, or even partisan discord. There has been, and can be, a responsible two-party system in American politics. Instead, this book explains how the responsible part of a two-party system can be called into question when the electorate itself begins to lose perspective on the differences between opponents and enemies. If the mass electorate can be driven to insulate themselves from their partisan opponents, closing themselves off from cordial interaction, then parties become a tool of division rather than organization. Parties can help citizens construct and maintain a functioning government. But if citizens use parties as a social dividing line, those same parties can keep citizens from agreeing to the compromise and cooperation that necessarily define democracy.

Partisanship grows irresponsible when it sends partisans into action for the wrong reasons. Activism is almost always a good thing, particularly when we have so often worried about an apathetic electorate. But if the electorate is moved to action by a desire for victory that exceeds their desire for the greater good, the action is no longer, as regards the general electorate, responsible.

In the chapters that follow, I demonstrate how partisan, ideological, religious, and racial identities have, in recent decades, moved into strong alignment, or have become "sorted." This means that each party has grown increasingly socially homogeneous. It is not a new finding. Matthew Levendusky (2009) wrote a thorough review of how partisan and ideological identities, in particular, have grown increasingly sorted. Alan Abramowitz (2011) wrote a full summary of the polarization of various demographic groups in the American electorate. Both authors note the increasing divide in the electorate but generally come to the conclusion that, on balance, this sorting or demographic polarization could be read as a source for good, as it has simplified our electoral choices and increased political engagement.

I take a more cautious, even cautionary, view of the effects of the social, demographic, and ideological sorting that has occurred during recent decades. In line with Bill Bishop's (2009) book *The Big Sort*, I argue that this new alignment has degraded the cross-cutting social ties that once allowed for partisan compromise. This has generated an electorate that is more biased against and angry at opponents, and more willing to act on that bias and anger.

There is a very wide line between a political rally and an angry mob. At some point, however, there must be an assessment of how closely a responsible party can or should approach that line. When parties grow more socially homogeneous, their members are quicker to anger and tend toward intolerance. I argue here that, despite clearer partisan boundaries and a more active public, the polarizing effects of social sorting have done more harm than good to American democracy.

Robert Kagan, a prominent neoconservative, wrote in spring 2016, "Here is the other threat to liberty that Alexis de Tocqueville and the ancient philosophers warned about: that the people in a democracy, excited, angry and unconstrained, might run roughshod over even the institutions created to preserve their freedoms" (Kagan 2016).

As American partisans find themselves in increasingly socially isolated parties, it is worth examining what kind of effects this social isolation may have on their political behavior and sense of civic responsibility.

Cross-Pressures

For decades, political scientists have understood that the effects of partisanship are mitigated by what are called "cross-cutting cleavages." These are attitudes or identities that are not commonly found in the partisan's party. If a person is a member of one party and also a member of a social group that is generally associated with the opposing party, the effect of partisanship on bias and action can be dampened. However, if a person is a member of one party and also a member of another social group that is mostly made up of fellow partisans, the biasing and polarizing effect of partisanship can grow stronger.

Since the earliest studies of political behavior, scholars have found that those with "cross-pressures" on their partisanship would be less likely to participate in politics. In 1944, Paul Lazarsfeld and his colleagues and, in 1960, Angus Campbell and his colleagues suggested that partisans who identify with groups associated with the opposing party would be less likely to vote (Lazarsfeld, Berelson, and Gaudet 1944; Campbell et al. 1960). Lipset ([1960] 1963) went so far as to call these cross-pressured voters "politically impotent," suggesting that "the more pressures brought to bear on individuals or groups which operate in opposing directions, the more likely are prospective voters to withdraw from the situation by 'losing interest' and not making a choice" (211). Further research found that these voters would be less strongly partisan (Powell 1976), and that these "cross-cutting cleavages" would mitigate social conflict (Nordlinger 1972).

Berelson, Lazarsfeld, and McPhee (1954), in their seminal book *Voting*, wrote, "For those who change political preferences most readily are those who are least interested, who are subject to conflicting social pressures, who have inconsistent beliefs and erratic voting histories. Without them—if the decision were left only to the deeply concerned, well-integrated, consistently principled ideal citizens—the political system might easily prove too rigid to adapt to changing domestic and international conditions" (316).

While the traditional view of cross-pressured voters is that they are generally uninvolved and uninterested, some of the foundational literature of political behavior suggests that those with cross-cutting social identities are an important segment of the American electorate. Democracy needs these voters. Berelson and colleagues found them to be an important source of flexibility in American policy responses to changing conditions. Not only are cross-pressured voters a source of popular responsiveness, they are also a buffer against social polarization.

Cross-cutting religious, racial, and partisan identities tend to allow partisans to engage socially with their fellow citizens and partisan opponents. On the other end of the social-sorting spectrum, those with highly aligned religious, racial, and partisan identities are less prepared to engage with their partisan opponents.

But we don't have to go back to 1954 to find positive references to cross-pressured partisans. More recently, Lavine, Johnston, and Steenbergen (2012) described another group of responsive voters, looking directly at what happens when a partisan holds some negative opinions about their own party. They call this "partisan ambivalence." In line with prior research, they find that these ambivalent partisans are in fact more likely to defect from the party in voting and, further, that they tend to think more carefully about their political decisions, rather than taking partisan identity as a simple cue. These voters are far more like what is normatively desirable in a voter—they are open to new information. Unfortunately, they are also less likely to participate.

The ambivalent, however, are not the voters I focus on in the current study. Here, rather than looking at a clash between partisans and their evaluations of their own party, I look at the relationship between partisan identities and other social identities that are to greater or lesser degrees associated with the party.

The reason I focus on the clash of identities, rather than the clash between party and attitudes, is that social identities have a special power to affect behavior. First, scholars Betsy Sinclair (2012) and Samara Klar (2014) have found that social environments can dramatically affect partisanship and political behavior. Partisans are responsive to the identities and ideas of the people around them.

Second, and more central to the theme of the book, the identities themselves have psychological effects of their own. Green, Palmquist, and Schickler (2002) make a strong argument for the social elements of partisan identity but explicitly reject the psychological theory of social identity. I believe that this rejection misses out on a wealth of information provided by the social identity literature. I therefore follow in the footsteps of Steven Greene (1999, 2002, 2004), who has repeatedly made the case for using the psychological definition of a social identity to better understand partisanship and political behavior. This is, in fact, the key to truly taking advantage of the cross-cutting-cleavage literature from decades ago. The power of cross-pressures (or the lack thereof) is far easier to see when social-psychological theory is employed to explain it.

This explanation must begin with a look, first, at the psychological effects of holding a single social identity.

The Origins of Group Conflict

> That was the first time we got together and decided we were a group, and not just a bunch of pissed-off guys.
>
> —Mick Mulvaney, Director of the Office of Management and Budget, founding member of the Freedom Caucus (quoted in Lizza 2015)

Humans are hardwired to cling to social groups. There are a few good reasons for us to do so. First, without a sense of social cohesion, we would have had a hard time creating societies and civilizations. Second, and even more basic, humans have a need to categorize (Tajfel et al. 1971). It is how we understand the world. This includes categorizing people. Third, our social categories don't simply help us understand our social environment, they also help us understand ourselves and our place in the world. Once we are part of a group, we know how to identify ourselves in relation to the other people in our society, and we derive an emotional connection and a sense of well-being from being group members.[2] These are powerful psychological motivations to form groups.

However, simple social cohesion creates boundaries between those in our group and those outside it. Marilynn Brewer has argued that as human beings we have two competing social needs: one for inclusion and one for differentiation. That is, we want to fit in, but we don't want to disappear within the group. If we create clear boundaries between our group and outsiders, we can satisfy our needs for both inclusion and exclusion (Brewer 1991). This means that humans are motivated not only to form groups but to form exclusive groups. The exclusivity of group identities isn't necessarily based in animosity. As the psychologist Gordon Allport described in 1954, people automatically tend to spend time with people like themselves. Much of the reasoning for this is simple convenience. He explains, "it requires less effort to deal with people who have similar presuppositions" (Allport [1954] 1979, 17). However, once this separation occurs, we are psychologically inclined to evaluate our various groups with an unrealistic view of their relative merits. This is true of nearly any social group that can exist. One famous experiment makes this abundantly clear.

Minimal Group Paradigm

In the late 1960s, a social psychologist named Henri Tajfel wanted to know more about the origins of conflict between groups. He grew interested in the work of Muzafer Sherif, who, based on his research at Robbers Cave and other experiments, had formed a theory that discrimination between groups naturally arises out of a simple conflict of interest between them. Tajfel and his colleagues wanted to know whether the conflict of interest was necessary for creating discrimination between groups, or whether intergroup discrimination grew out of something even simpler. They ran a number of experiments in order to find a baseline intergroup relationship in which there were two distinct groups with so little conflict between them that they did not engage in discrimination or bias. The design and outcome of these experiments became known as the minimal group paradigm.

The original baseline condition required that subjects in the experiments remain isolated in a laboratory, unaware of who was in their ingroup or in their outgroup, unable to even see or hear any of the other subjects. The groups were designed to be meaningless and value-free—no group was objectively superior to the other. In one experiment, subjects were shown a number of dots on a screen, and asked to estimate the number of dots. Some were then told they were overestimators, some that they were underestimators. In a second experiment, the subjects were shown a number of abstract paintings and asked to choose their favorites. Some were told that they preferred the paintings of Klee, others that they preferred the paintings of Kandinsky. These group labels were, in fact, randomly assigned.

After being informed of their group label, the subjects were then asked to allocate money to other subjects (not to themselves), each identified only by a subject identification number and a group label. They allocated money by writing numbers on a sheet of paper. In one experiment, they were explicitly invited to choose between two scenarios: (1) everyone receives the maximum amount of money; or (2) the subject's own group receives less than the maximum, but the outgroup receives even less than that. They still had never seen another subject's face. They did not stand to gain any benefit themselves.

Tajfel did not expect to find intergroup discrimination in these experiments. He was looking for a design that generated no discrimination and hoping to slowly add conditions until discrimination was achieved (Turner 1996). He expected that with no conflict, no value differences, no contact, and no personal utility gained from group cohesiveness, the group names would not matter in determining the amount of money allocated at the end of the experiment. He expected the common good of the whole to be more attractive than turning the teams against each other. He was incorrect in this expectation.

Even in the most basic definition of a group, Tajfel and his colleagues found evidence of ingroup bias: a preference for or privileging of the ingroup over the outgroup. In every conceivable iteration of this experiment, people privileged the group to which they had been randomly assigned.[3] Ingroup bias emerged even when Billig and Tajfel in 1973 explicitly told respondents that they had been randomly assigned to two groups, because it was "easier this way." The ingroup bias still appeared, simply because the experimenters distinguished two groups. These respondents were not fighting for tangible self-interest, the money they allocated went to other people, not themselves. They simply felt psychologically motivated to privilege members of their own imaginary and ephemeral group—a group of people they had never met and would never meet, and whose existence they had only learned of minutes earlier. People react powerfully when they worry about a group losing status, even when the group is "minimal."

The ingroup bias that results from even minimal group membership is very deeply rooted in human psychological function and is perhaps impossible to escape. Adults, children, and even monkeys have automatic negative associations with outgroup individuals (Greene 2013). Simply being part of a group causes ingroup favoritism, with or without objective competition between the groups over real resources. Even when there is nothing to fight over, group members want to win.

Tajfel points out that one of the most important lessons of the minimal group experiments is that when the subjects are given a choice between providing the maximum benefit to all of the subjects, including those in their own group, or gaining less benefits for their group but seeing their team win, "*it is the winning that seems more important to them*" (Tajfel et al. 1971, 172). This is a crucial discovery for understanding American partisan politics today. The privileging of victory over the greater good is a natural outcome of even the most meaningless group label.

These natural, even primal human tendencies toward group isolation and group comparison open the door to group conflict. The human inclination is to prefer and privilege members of the ingroup. The primary result of group membership is simply to hold positive feelings for the ingroup, and no positive feelings toward outsiders. Even this difference can cause discrimination, but it is not distinctly hostile. Under circumstances of perceived threat or competition, however, the preference for the ingroup can lead to outright hostility toward the outgroup, particularly when the competition is a zero-sum game (Brewer 2001a). The Rattlers and Eagles were involved in a zero-sum competition, as are Democrats and Republicans every election. Only one team can win, and the other team loses. This threat of loss will prove to be an essential ingredient in modern polarization.

Physical Evidence of Group Attachment

It is important to be clear that group identities are not simply factual memberships. Emerging research is finding repeated instances of physical effects of group membership on human bodies and brains. Avenanti, Sirigu, and Aglioti (2010) showed respondents video of hands being pricked by pins. People tended to unconsciously twitch their own hand when watching these videos, except when the hand belonged to a member of a racial outgroup.

Scheepers and Derks (2016) explained that it is possible to observe changes in brain activity within 200 milliseconds after a face is shown to a person, and that these changes depend on the social category of the face. Furthermore, they found that people who identify with a group use the same parts of their brain to process group-related and self-related information, but a different part of the brain to process outgroup-related information.

People learn differently depending on whether an ingroup member or an outgroup member is observing them. Hobson and Inzlicht (2016) found that when learning a new task, a person will learn more slowly if he or she is being observed by an outgroup member.

You can find evidence of group membership in saliva. Sampasivam et al. (2016) found that when people's group identity is threatened, they secrete higher levels of cortisol in their saliva, indicating stress.

Even our emotions are neurally connected to our groups. People's brains respond similarly when people are sad and when they are observing a sad ingroup member, but when they are observing a sad outgroup member, their brains respond by activating areas of positive emotion. As Scheepers and Derks (2016) explain, "favoring the ingroup is not a conscious choice. Instead, people automatically and preferentially process information related to their ingroup over the outgroup" (8).

This is an important point for all of the analyses that follow. Group-based reactions to events and information are not entirely voluntary. A person cannot simply turn off his or her preference for the ingroup. It should not be considered an insult to point out the inherent ingroup bias shared by all humans. Ingroup bias is deeply rooted in the physical body as well as the thoughtful mind, and no person is immune.

Invented Conflicts

Social identities can alter the way people see the world. Zero-sum conflict between groups is easily exacerbated and can be based in both real and invented conflicts. During the Robbers Cave experiment, the boys from both teams began accusing each other of sabotage that had never occurred. The Rattlers accused the Eagles of throwing trash on their beach (they had forgotten that they themselves had left the trash behind the day before). The Eagles erroneously accused the Rattlers of throwing ice and stones into their swimming hole after one of them considered the water to be colder than the day before, and another stubbed his toe.

Allport ([1954] 1979) explains that group members "easily exaggerate the degree of difference between groups, and readily misunderstand the grounds for it. And, perhaps most important of all, the separateness may lead to genuine conflicts of interest as well as to many imaginary conflicts" (19). Allport's words were meant to describe the conflicts between racial, religious, or class-based groups. The previous passage, however, is almost eerily prescient in its descriptions of the current conflict between Democrats and Republicans in American politics. Partisan conflict today is characterized by an exaggerated and poorly understood difference between the parties, based in both genuine and imaginary conflicts of interest.

Political psychologists Milton Lodge and Charles Taber in 2013 wrote a comprehensive review of the effects of motivated reasoning on voters. Motivated reasoning is the process by which individuals rationalize their choices in a way that is consistent with what they prefer to believe, rather than with what is actually true. Lodge and Taber (2013) write that "political behavior and attitudes are very much a function of the unconscious mechanisms that govern memory accessibility" (1). Motivated reasoning is not exactly "inventing" conflicts, but it is the brain's way of making preexisting attitudes easier to believe. This occurs not by choice, but at a subconscious level in the brain, where the things a person wants to believe are easier to locate than the things that contradict a person's worldview. In this way, imaginary and exaggerated conflicts are very difficult to remedy. The human brain prefers not to revise erroneous beliefs about opponents. Eric Groenendyk (2013) suggests that these often-elaborate justifications in defense of the party can occasionally be broken down by reminding partisans of civic values and a desire for accuracy. The tendency toward motivated reasoning, however, remains prominent.

American politics has always been characterized by real differences between the two parties and by true conflicts of interest. As the APSA committee on responsible two-party government explained, the parties should be distinguishable and unique. They should represent real differences in governing philosophy, so that citizens can choose between them. A partisan's natural inclination, once he or she has chosen sides, is to engage strongly in claiming victory for his or her own side. In fact, politics, along with religion, has long been one of the most famous dinner-party topics to avoid if you want the discussion to remain polite. None of this is the major problem with American political identities today.

The trouble arises when party competitions grow increasingly impassioned due to the inclusion of additional, nonpartisan social identities in every partisan conflict. The American political parties are growing socially polarized. Religion and race, as well as class, geography, and culture, are dividing the parties in such a way that the effect of party identity is magnified. The competition is no longer between only Democrats and Republicans. A single vote can now indicate a person's partisan preference *as well as* his or her religion, race, ethnicity, gender, neighborhood, and favorite grocery store. This is no longer a single social identity. Partisanship can now be thought of as a mega-identity, with all the psychological and behavioral magnifications that implies.

American citizens currently believe that they are in a partisan competition against a socially homogeneous group of outsiders, sometimes to an exaggerated degree (Ahler and Sood 2016). At a dinner party today, talking about politics is increasingly also talking about religion and race. They are wrapped together in a new way. Social sorting is not simply a score on a scale, it is a general trend of partisan homogenization. Ironically, politics and religion may be increasingly acceptable topics at a dinner party today, because most of our dinner parties include mainly socially and politically similar people. When we limit our exposure to outgroup individuals, the differences we perceive between parties grow increasingly exaggerated, and imaginary conflicts of interest rival genuine ones.

Why Does This Matter?

> In this binary tribal world, where everything is at stake, everything is in play, there is no room for quibbles about character, or truth, or principles. If everything—the Supreme Court, the fate of Western civilization, the survival of the planet—depends on tribal victory, then neither individuals nor ideas can be determinative.
>
> —Charles Sykes, "Charlie Sykes on Where the Right Went Wrong"

Unlike the Rattlers and the Eagles, the Democrats and Republicans aren't fighting over a simple trophy. Their job, as the only two governing parties, is to enact real policies that benefit or harm real people. When winning becomes as important as or more important than the content of those policies, real people feel the consequences.

As American social identities grow increasingly party linked, parties become more influential in American political decision-making, behavior, and emotion. Two separate factors drive these changes. The first is the effect of partisanship on policy opinion itself. Policy opinion is defined here as the collection of attitudes that an individual holds about how the government should (or should not) address particular public problems. It could be argued that partisanship encourages more consistency in political attitudes and that this helps democracy.[4] However, in the extreme this consistency can also be a signal that American voters are no longer thinking independently, that they are less open to alternative ideas.[5] In the latter case, the policy opinions of Americans become a reflexive response to party cues, and deliberation or reasoned disagreement grows increasingly difficult.

The second effect is the main concern of this book, and that is the power of social identities to affect party evaluations, levels of anger, and political activism, *independently of a person's policy opinions*. When megaparties form, social polarization increases in the American electorate. Both social and issue-based polarization have recently been shown to decrease public desire for compromise (Wolf, Strachan, and Shea 2012), decrease the impact of substantive information on policy opinions (Druckman, Peterson, and Slothuus 2013), increase income inequality (Bonica et al. 2013), discourage economic investment and output, increase unemployment, and inhibit public understanding of objective economic information (Enns and McAvoy 2012), among other things. Polarization is generally not considered to be a helpful political development.

The increase in social and issue-based polarization has been blamed on elected officials, the primary system, gerrymandering, the partisan media, and a host of other influences. This book takes account of these generally structural and outward-looking explanations for social polarization but adds to the discussion the possibility that one source of our polarized politics is a psychological motivation that most Americans share. Social polarization is an increasingly intense conflict between our two partisan groups. It is based in the same impulses that drive racial and religious prejudice. And just as in the case of racial or religious prejudice, there are institutional, outward-looking explanations, as well as individual psychological explanations. These inner sources of social polarization are less visible, but they are Americans' responsibility to observe and understand.

As citizens, we may not be able to change the primary rules or tone down the partisan media, but we can begin to understand how much of our political behavior is driven by forces that are not rational or fair-minded. This book lays out the evidence for the current state of social polarization, in which our political identities are running circles around our policy preferences in driving our political thoughts, emotions, and actions. I explain how this came to be, illustrate the extent of the problem, and offer some suggestions on how to bring American politics back to a state of civil competition, rather than a state of victory-centric conflict.

TWO

Using Old Words in New Ways

The goal of this book is to examine the effect of social sorting on social polarization. In the social-scientific study of politics the term *polarization* traditionally describes an expansion of the distance between the issue positions of Democrats and Republicans. The process of polarization is defined by Democrats acquiring more extremely liberal issue positions and Republicans acquiring more extremely conservative issue positions. In the same vein, *sorting* is usually defined as an increasing alignment between party and ideology, where *ideology* indicates a set of issue positions or values. The process of sorting is traditionally understood as Democrats holding more consistently liberal issue positions and Republicans holding more consistently conservative issue positions.

In this book, one major goal is to make the point that each of these terms—*polarization, sorting,* and *ideology*—include within them both a social meaning and an issue-based meaning. The social definition focuses on people's feelings of social attachment to a group of others, not their policy attitudes. The issue-based definition is limited to individual policy attitudes, excluding group attachments. The fact that these two elements can be separated from each other at all is the basis on which this entire argument rests. In the following pages, I examine literature that supports this division, but for now it is simply important to understand that social attachments and policy preferences, while related, are not the same concept, and can have different downstream effects on political behavior.

Following this principle, I discuss two types of polarization, one that is social (or affective) and one that is issue based. *Social polarization* refers to an increasing social distance between Democrats and Republicans. This is made up of three phenomena: increased partisan bias, increased emotional reactivity, and increased activism. *Issue-based polarization* is closer to the traditional understanding of the term *polarization*, and indicates an increasing distance between the average issue positions of Democrats and Republicans.

Similarly, I discuss two types of ideology, one that is identity based, and one that is issue based. This is described more fully below, but for now it should be made clear that *identity-based* (or *symbolic*) *ideology* is the sense of belonging to the groups called liberal and conservative, regardless of policy attitudes. *Issue-based* (or *operational*) *ideology* is a set of policy attitudes and the extent to which they tend to be on the liberal or conservative end of the spectrum.

Finally, I discuss two types of sorting, one that is social, and one that is issue based. *Social sorting* involves an increasing social homogeneity within each party, such that religious, racial, and ideological divides tend to line up along partisan lines. *Issue-based sorting* is closer to the traditional understanding of sorting, meaning that Democrats hold liberal issue positions and Republicans hold conservative issue positions.

The difference between *issue-based sorting* and *issue-based polarization* is simply that issue-based sorting occurs when partisans hold policy preferences that are increasingly consistent with their party's positions. There are fewer cross-cutting policy attitudes. Issue-based polarization involves the policy preferences of Democrats and Republicans growing increasingly bimodal and moving toward extremely liberal or conservative policy choices. For more than a decade, this distinction has been the subject of debate between, among others, Morris Fiorina (Fiorina, Abrams, and Pope 2005) and Alan Abramowitz (2011), who disagree over whether issue-based sorting or issue-based polarization is occurring in the American electorate at large. I choose here not to engage in this debate but to suggest a new, social-identity-based approach to these familiar ideas.

The common theme here is that in each case—polarization, sorting, and ideology—I am separating the identity-based social elements from the issue-based policy elements. This separation is borne out by the data, and it allows me to explain how American partisans can grow increasingly socially distant from one another even if their policy disagreements are not profound.

A Different Identity Politics

A traditional view of identity politics takes individual social identities such as race or religion and examines how each identity is capable of driving political behavior in relation to that specific group. As Conover (1984, 761) explains,

> Relatively few Americans think "ideologically" in the sense that they order their political beliefs according to certain basic ideological principles. Thus, as Kinder (1982) has pointed out, the key question is no longer "do people think ideologically?" but rather simply, "how *do* people think about politics?" In addressing this question one approach is to return to "basics," to go back to those ideas that originally fueled research on political behavior. *And, one of the more appealing of those is the notion that people's ties to various groups help to structure their political thinking.* (emphasis added)

Using individuals' ties to their distinct social groups has in fact been a productive way to help political scientists understand how Americans organize their political views. Klandermans (2014), for example, explains that "collective identity becomes politically relevant when people who share a specific identity take part in political action on behalf of that collective" (2). In other words, social identities translate into political ones when the group expresses political demands. At times, even as a replacement for ideological sophistication, a strong racial or religious identity can motivate individuals to take political action on behalf of racial or religious issues, respectively. Yet these are inherently limited entries into politics because they force us to consider each identity in isolation from the other identities that compose a person's worldview.

This book represents a revised approach to identity politics in the sense that these single social identities not only have effects on politics in isolation but they have significantly different effects when understood in relation to each other. Imagine how much more intense the Robbers Cave conflict would have been had the Rattlers all been Catholic, northern, and white, while the Eagles were Protestant, southern, and black.

A single group identity can have powerful effects, but multiple identities all playing for the same team can lead to a very deep social and even cultural divide. Those with cross-cutting partisan, religious, and racial identities are more likely than socially sorted citizens to welcome the opposing team into their lives and to consider them as fellow citizens. Identity politics is a far more powerful concept if we consider how a collection of identities is working in concert, rather than isolating each one and examining them in turn. The relationship between identities is also identity politics, and it may be a more powerful way to understand political involvement. Not only do our identities work together in powerful ways but a threat to one identity makes it easier to dislike multiple additional outgroups.

The American electorate has sorted itself into two increasingly homogeneous parties, with a variety of social, economic, geographic, and ideological cleavages falling in line with the partisan divide. This creates two megaparties, with each party representing not only policy positions but also an increasing list of other social cleavages. Parties, then, draw convenient battle lines between an array of social groups. Isolation and competition, the two sources of intergroup conflict in the Robbers Cave experiment, increase between the two parties. Policy preferences, over time, take a back seat to the team loyalty that is bound to grow out of these increasingly homogeneous and isolated partisan collections. Remember that the Rattlers and the Eagles were competing only for a trophy. Neither pursued any agenda but victory.

Identity and Policy

Theoretically, a democracy should represent the will of its citizens. In the most common understanding of American democracy, citizens' opinions regarding policies are related to their own self-interest or values. These citizens evaluate which party is closest to their own position. They support that party through voting or activism and, ideally, change parties when the other party moves closer to their position. V. O. Key, in 1966, described an electorate "moved by concern about central and relevant questions of public policy, of governmental performance, and of executive personality" (7). At the very least, according to E. E. Schattschneider ([1960] 1975), democracy is defined as a "competitive political system in which competing leaders and organizations define the alternatives of public policy in such a way that the public can participate in the decision-making process" (141). Informed public choice over policies is an ideal element of a well-functioning democracy. But it isn't exactly how American democracy works. In fact, this view of American democracy is what Christopher Achen and Larry Bartels (2016a) call the "folk theory" of democracy.

Self-interest and political values do enter into policy opinions, but they are not the only ingredients. Quietly, behind the scenes of reasoned, analytical thought, some subtle but powerful forces are at work. Primal psychological influences such as motivated reasoning and social identity are capable of shifting and sometimes entirely determining the policies that citizens support. As Achen and Bartels (2016b) explain, "Decades of social-scientific evidence show that voting behavior is primarily a product of inherited partisan loyalties, social identities and symbolic attachments. Over time, engaged citizens may construct policy preferences and ideologies that rationalize their choices, but those issues are seldom fundamental."

Partisans edit their list of reasons for holding particular attitudes in order to defend the position that is faithful to the party. More often than not, citizens do not choose which party to support based on policy opinion; they alter their policy opinion according to which party they support. Usually they do not notice that this is happening, and most, in fact, feel outraged when the possibility is mentioned. All citizens want to believe that their political values are solid and well reasoned. More often, though, policy attitudes grow out of group-based defense. Partisanship muddies the folk pathway from interests to outcomes, sometimes sending a person in a wrong direction or further down a path than self-interest and values alone would dictate.

In this identity-based democracy, arguments over policy are partly about important issues of the day and partly about which side is winning. Political action is driven not only by policy concerns but also, powerfully, by the need to feel victorious. Parties and their policies are evaluated unfairly, with a biased and distorted eye. Citizens are easily angered, somewhat by policy defeats but more intensely by party defeats. In American politics, individual interests and partisanship have always vied for influence in determining political behavior. Recently, however, political identities have been increasingly dominant.

Identity and Ideology

Importantly, the distinction between social identity and policy preference does not mean that ideology cannot have a social component. There is a difference between a Democrat who holds increasingly liberal policy positions and a Democrat who increasingly self-identifies as a liberal. In the first case, the Democrat's policy positions are changing. He or she is changing his or her mind about whether affirmative action is fair, welfare is helpful, or health care should be supported by government. This is a policy-driven change.

In the second case, when a Democrat increasingly identifies with a group called liberals, the individual's group identity shifts. The individual's policy opinion might also shift, although not necessarily. This seems counterintuitive, but it is a concept key to the entire scheme of the book and must therefore be made very explicit. Feeling more strongly connected to a group called conservatives does not automatically mean that a person holds more conservative policy positions. In a study of Americans that I conducted in 2011 (described more fully in chapter 3), conservative identification was correlated with conservative policy positions at only $r = 0.24$, suggesting that there is a weak positive relationship between the two. In other words, those with intense conservative identities do tend to have more intensely conservative policy positions, but one value cannot be precisely predicted from the other. Similarly, liberal identification was correlated with liberal policy positions at r = 0.25.[1]

These are significant correlations, but they leave a great deal of wiggle room between identifying with an ideological group and holding ideologically extreme or consistent policy positions. Ideology is not simply a system of values and preferences that constrain policy positions. It is also an identity that, like party identity, can guide political behavior without relying on policy preferences.

Other scholars have found this to be the case. Christopher Ellis and James Stimson in their 2012 book discuss the difference between what they call symbolic ideology and operational ideology. The first is an identification with liberals or conservatives, and the second is a list of policy positions and values. Americans, it seems, are generally liberal in our policy positions and values, but generally conservative in what we like to call ourselves. Going back to the classic work of Philip Converse in 1964, American policy attitudes are relatively unrelated to each other, in the sense that there is little understanding of what ideological consistency, or constraint, requires. It is important to understand that American ideological *identities* are not synonymous with policy preferences. Identities function as the boys at Robbers Cave demonstrated, by affecting prejudice, emotion, and collective action. Policy positions, on the other hand, are caught up somewhere between individual values and interests, the policies that our group leaders demand, and whatever misunderstandings emerge between the two.

In the following pages, when I discuss partisan, religious, or racial identities, the meaning of each will be clear. These are all simple identifications with a group. However, the meaning of ideological identities can easily be confused. Ideology has, in fact, been an embattled concept essentially since its first definition. However, as Frances Lee said in 2009, "The difficulty in devising operational definitions of ideology has not prevented the concept from becoming central to political science" (50). The key point of this book depends upon a clear divide between ideological identity and the collection of policy positions and values that is often referred to as ideology. When I refer to ideology, it will be in reference to ideological identity, or the intensity with which individuals identify with the groups that are labeled liberals or conservatives. This is distinct from the set of individual policy preferences that each person holds, which will generally be referred to as policy attitudes or issue positions. The fact that the two can be separated is a large part of why American partisans have become more biased, intolerant, angry, and politically active than their policy disagreements can explain.

As American partisan and ideological identities have grown more sorted, partisans have grown more intolerant of their political opponents. This new prejudice and distrust does not come simply from more extreme and intense policy disagreements. It comes out of the simple power of two or more social identities lining up together. The Catholic Rattlers and Protestant Eagles would fight harder for the trophy, even though the trophy remained the same. This is what has happened to American politics. The Rattlers and the Eagles have grown racially, religiously, geographically, and ideologically divided. They now have more to fight for, not in terms of the trophy itself, but in terms of their own commitment to the group and the stakes of losing. These stakes include the potential sense of humiliation in seeing your group be the loser. As multiple groups line up behind one party or the other, they all win or lose together. The humiliation of loss is amplified. Victory, then, becomes more important than policy outcomes. Even when both sides hold the same policy positions, the priority is often to make sure the "dirty shirts" don't win.

Three Elements of Social Polarization

Social identities generate distinct psychological and behavioral outcomes. Three of these make up social polarization.

First, in line with Tajfel and Turner's social identity theory, when two groups are in a zero-sum competition, they treat each other with bias and even prejudice. The first element of social polarization is therefore partisan prejudice.

Second, those who identify with a social group are more likely to take action to defend it. When a group's status is threatened, a strongly identified group member will fight to maintain the status of the group. This group member's individual sense of esteem is tied to the group's status, and therefore any reduction in that status would be painful to experience. In other words, when a party might lose, a strongly identified partisan will take action to defend the group. This political action is the second element of social polarization.

Third, one outgrowth of social identity theory is intergroup emotions theory, which specifies that group members can and do feel emotions on behalf of the group (Mackie, Devos, and Smith 2000). In particular, the most strongly identified group members will feel heightened anger in the face of a threat to the group and greater enthusiasm when the group is victorious. This emotional reactivity is the third element of social polarization. Through the remainder of this book, I explain how a well-sorted set of social and partisan identities are uniquely capable of motivating these three types of polarization.

THREE

A Brief History of Social Sorting

> The chief oppositions which occur in society are between individuals, sexes, ages, races, nationalities, sections, classes, political parties and religious sects. Several such may be in full swing at the same time, but the more numerous they are the less menacing is any one. *Every species of conflict interferes with every other species in society at the same time, save only when their lines of cleavage coincide; in which case they reinforce one another.* . . . A society, therefore, which is riven by a dozen oppositions along lines running in every direction, may actually be in less danger of being torn with violence or falling to pieces than one split along just one line.
>
> —Edward Alsworth Ross, *The Principles of Sociology*

For the past hundred years, sociologists such as Edward Alsworth Ross (1920) have understood that a society is sewn together by the complexity of its social divisions. Though the nature of humans is to categorize themselves into self-contained groups, and the nature of those groups is to produce division and conflict, societies are stabilized by the great number and diversity of group divisions. The more divisions there are, and the less organized those groups are around any one division, the more peaceful and cooperative a society can be. Each group conflict is tamped down by a separate group allegiance. A wealthy Republican can find common ground with a working-class Democrat by joining together at a Protestant church. Once the chaotic mess of group loyalties begins to organize itself around a single line of cleavage, however, society is in danger of "falling to pieces," according to Ross's 1920 account.

Political scientists have agreed with this view of the roots of a stable society, using the concept to explain the unique stability of the American political system. Seymour Lipset argued in 1960 that "the available evidence suggests that the chances for stable democracy are enhanced to the extent that groups and individuals have a number of cross-cutting, politically relevant affiliations" (77). In his 1981 analysis of the American political system, Robert Dahl described the "Normal System" of democracy as one of "crosscutting cleavages and low polarization" (284). He praised this system's democratic cooperation and compromise as being assured by two conditions. First, party loyalties are not related to social, economic, or geographical differences. Second, party loyalties are not consistently related to policy opinion differences.

Unfortunately, the conditions for political and social stability that characterized the last century are increasingly unmet in American politics today. The sorting of American social groups into two partisan camps has intensified in recent decades, leading to a distinct decrease in the number of cross-cutting cleavages. Social cleavages today have become significantly linked to our two political parties, with each party taking consistent sides in racial, religious, ideological, and cultural divides.

Decades ago, social divisions between Americans over party, ideology, religion, class, race, and geography did not align neatly, so that particular social groups were friends in some circumstances and opponents in others. In the South, strong geographical attachments to the Democratic Party were unaligned with ideological differences, so that southern, Democratic, and conservative identities were tied together for many Americans. These alignments pitted the generally more liberal Democratic identity against a strong conservative identity, allowing southern Democrats to feel some compassion and understanding for both Republicans and liberals. Similarly, those holding liberal, northern, and Republican identities were motivated to cooperate occasionally with Democrats and conservatives. After all, they often needed to work together with them, sometimes within their own parties, in order to accomplish their goals.

In the 1950s, when the APSA commission called for two responsible parties, the Democrats and Republicans in government were sending mixed messages to the electorate. To be clear, this was not a time of social peace. McCarthyism, the red scare, and fights over civil rights were only a few of the decade's major conflicts. But due to the parties' many cross-cutting cleavages, the voters received ambiguous cues, making it more difficult to make clear electoral choices. The upside of this, however, was that since voters did not receive clear cues about their partisan ingroups and outgroups, they did not treat their fellow citizens as enemies simply because of their party affiliation. Plenty of racial and anticommunist animosity existed, but these did not perfectly match partisan lines. Voters, therefore, could engage in social prejudice and vitriol, but this was decoupled from their political choices.

The 1950s, while certainly not a golden era of social justice, were a time of less social polarization between American partisans. Cross-cutting cleavages, or conflicting party-linked affiliations, aligned partisans with people not entirely like themselves. Conservative Democrats were on the same team as liberal Democrats. Though their ideological identities, and also policy platforms, were in distinct opposition, they were all Democrats, and their party won or lost together. They had superordinate goals. They also had a number of psychological motivations to be charitable to one another, which are elaborated in chapter 4.

The social cleavages between the parties during this time were messily arranged. Not only did party and ideology conflict in the 1950s, but party did not align with class in the South—upper-class southerners were most likely to be Democrats. In the nonsouthern states, the opposite was true—upper-class northerners were more likely to be Republican (Nadeau and Stanley 1993). Since then, the relationship between class and party in the South has come to match and even surpass the class-party alignment in the rest of the country. By 2000, class-party alignment had increased in all of the American states, but the largest increase has been in the South, leading to a highly class-consistent set of parties (Nadeau et al. 2004).

Today, Democrats and Republicans have a lot more information about who their social and partisan enemies are, and have little reason to find common ground. They have become increasingly homogeneous parties, with Democrats now firmly aligned with identities such as liberal, secular, urban, low-income, Hispanic, and black. Republicans are now solidly conservative, middle class or wealthy, rural, churchgoing, and white. These identities are increasingly aligned so that fewer identities affiliated with either party are also associated with the other side. White, religious, and conservative people have little incentive to reach across to the nonwhite, secular, and liberal people in the other party. What superordinate goals do they have? In which places do they mix with opposing partisans? Few of today's salient social groups help either party to reach across the aisle.

Ideological Sorting

The first thing that pops into most political scientists' minds when they hear the word "sorting" is specifically issue-based partisan sorting. Democrats have become more liberal and Republicans have grown more conservative in their policy preferences. Confusingly, this type of sorting is typically described with a measure that asks survey respondents to place themselves

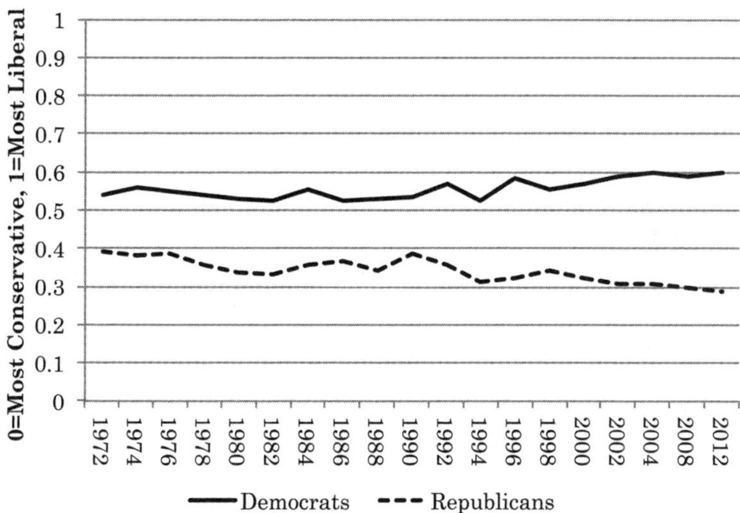

Figure 3.1. Traditional measure of ideology
Note: Data drawn from the American National Election Studies cumulative file 1948–2008 (fully weighted) and the 2012 file (fully weighted). Ideology item available from 1972 and later. Democrats and Republicans include independents who lean toward one party.

on a seven-point scale, ranging from extremely conservative to extremely liberal. Pamela Conover and Stanley Feldman found in 1981 that this measure largely assesses ideological identification, but it nonetheless remains the most common measure of ideology, whether understood as an identity or a set of issue positions. It is therefore useful to examine trends in this variable before attempting to break ideology down into its identification and issue-based elements. Figure 3.1 illustrates the self-reported ideology of Democrats and Republicans in the American electorate over time. Ideological sorting among legislators has increased substantially more than in the electorate as a whole, but the sorting I am most interested in is that of the general population. These are the people who ultimately have the power to change American politics. Whether they wish to do so is partially determined by the sorting I describe here.

In figure 3.1, Democrats and Republicans in the American National Election Studies (ANES) have been growing increasingly ideologically distinct since at least 1972, when ideology was first included in the study. As noted above, ideology is measured as a seven-point scale allowing respondents to identify themselves as extremely conservative, conservative, slightly conservative, moderate, slightly liberal, liberal, or extremely liberal (recoded to range from 0 to 1). The score of 0.5 on the ideology scale marks the purely moderate partisans. Since 1972, Democrats have grown about 7 percentage points more liberal on the total ideology scale, while Republicans have grown about 10 percentage points more conservative. Republicans have also been more distinctly ideological than Democrats during the entire span of time, with scores farther from the moderate midpoint of the scale. This type of figure, though, does not clarify whether partisans are talking about their ideological identities or their policy positions—two separate phenomena. Fortunately, the ANES provides evidence that allows for separating these two types of ideology.

Figure 3.2 demonstrates what happens when, instead of placing themselves on a seven-point ideological scale, partisans are asked whether they feel particularly close to liberals and conservatives. They are asked whether liberals and conservatives are "people who are most like you in their ideas and interests and feelings about things." This comes as close as possible in the ANES data to a measure of a social identity. Unfortunately this measure was available only in select years, but can be examined in 1972, 1992, and 2000. When measured this way, Democratic social identification with liberals increased by about 24 percentage points between 1972 and 2000, while Republican social identification with conservatives increased by about 35 percentage points. Here again, Republicans are more strongly socially identified with conservatives than Democrats are identified with liberals, and the Republican increase in ideological identity strength over time is substantially larger than that of Democrats. Among Republicans in 2000, more than 60 percent of them point to conservatives as the people most like them. In 1972 and 1992, this figure was only around 25 percent. Among Democrats, a similar pattern has occurred, though on a smaller scale. By 2000, 35 percent of Democrats point to liberals as the people most like them, compared to 11 percent in 1972. By 2000, Republicans are nearly twice as likely as Democrats to feel socially connected to their ideological group.

Specifying ideology as a social identity makes it clear that identity-based ideological sorting is increasing more robustly than the traditional measure of ideology can indicate. Democrats and especially Republicans are feeling closer to liberals and conservatives, considering them to be groups of people that are most like them "in their ideas and interests and feelings about things." To a much larger extent than in 1972, partisans in 2000 had found their ideological clans.

In comparison, considering ideology as a set of issue positions also shows a growing partisan divide, though a smaller one. Figure 3.3 depicts

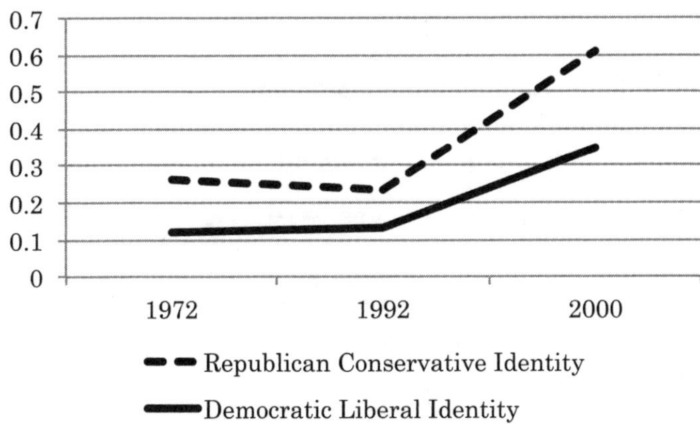

Figure 3.2. Identity-based ideology
Note: Data drawn from the American National Election Studies from 1972, 1992, and 2000. Democrats and Republicans include independents who lean toward one party. Vertical axis represents the percentage of Democrats/Republicans who identify with liberals/conservatives, respectively.

the difference between the average Democratic and Republican positions on a variety of issues, with all available issues combined into a single scale at the bottom of each graph. Unfortunately, only three of the six issues are available in 1972. The difference between the three-issue scale in 1972 and the six-issue scale in 2012 is an increase of about 15 percentage points in the difference between Democratic and Republican policy positions in the electorate at large. A more fair assessment is to compare the six-item scale in 1982 with the same six-item scale in 2012, indicating a 16 percentage point increase in the difference between the two parties' policy positions. These partisan policy differences are not much different from the partisan-ideological differences as measured with the seven-point ideology measure. Both measures, however, produce significantly smaller effects than the identity-based ideological differences between the parties. The increase in partisan-ideological-identity differences is more than twice as large as the increase in partisan policy differences.

The concept of ideology as a set of policy preferences or a placement of a person on a seven-point scale obscures the depth of the increasing ideological divide between Democrats and Republicans. The average opinions of the two parties have certainly diverged. A much larger division, however, is growing between them in their sense of themselves as liberals and conserva-

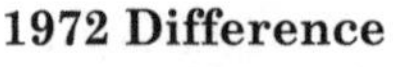

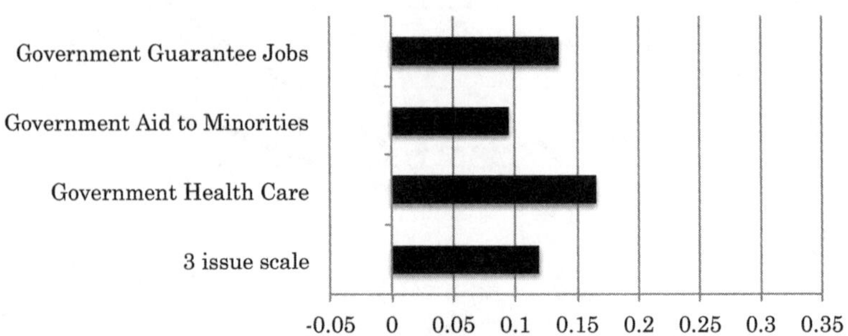

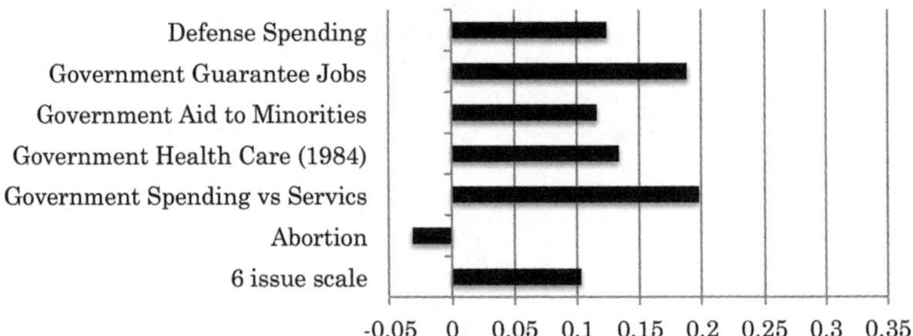

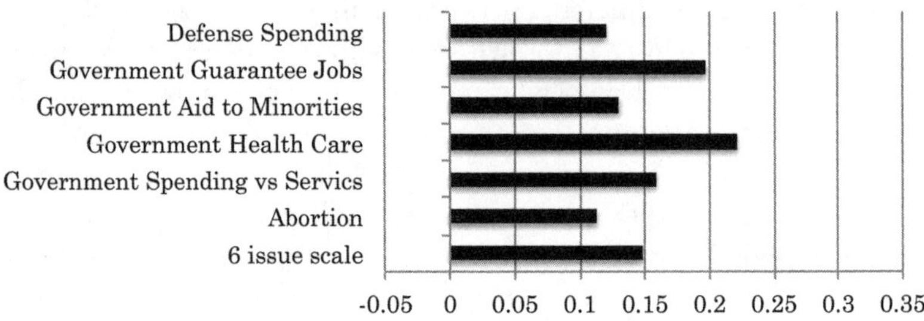

Figure 3.3. Difference between the average policy positions of Democrats and Republicans
Note: Data drawn from the American National Election Studies cumulative file 1948–2008 (fully weighted) and the 2012 ANES file (fully weighted). Democrats and Republicans include independents who lean toward one party. Values represent the difference between the mean Democratic and mean Republican position on each issue. Bars to the left of zero indicate that Democrats and Republicans differ in a party-inconsistent direction.

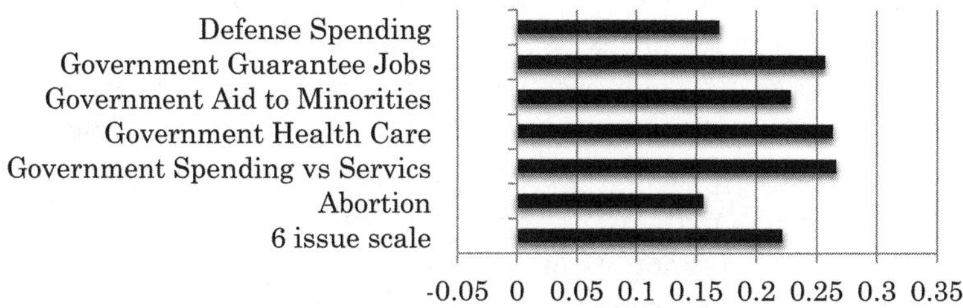

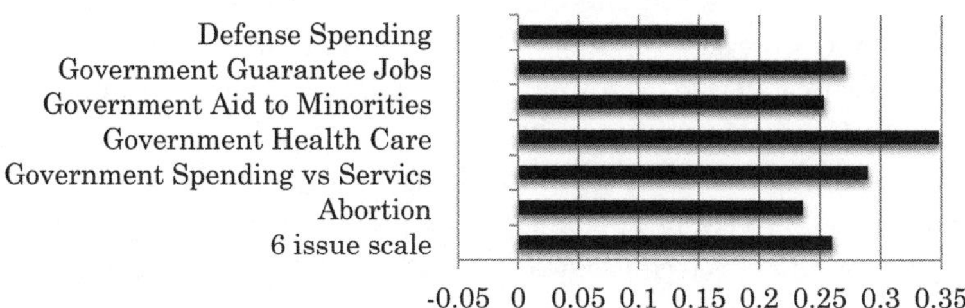

Figure 3.3. (continued)

tives. Democrats and Republicans have chosen ideological teams, and their sense of belonging to one side has divided them more powerfully than their policy differences have. This sense of social division is one that radiates out to many other social cleavages between the parties. More than simply disagreeing, Democrats and Republicans are feeling like very different kinds of people.

Theories of Sorting

The explanations for the increase in ideological sorting (vaguely defined, but generally referring to issue-based polarization) in the American electorate are varied and have been widely examined. A number of theories attempt to explain issue-based sorting, beginning with an issue-based story and ending with a more complete sorting of multiple social identities along partisan lines.

The most popular explanation for issue-based sorting involves the changes in the Democratic Party that occurred as a result of the civil rights movement, culminating in the Civil Rights Act of 1964. James Sundquist, in his study of partisan realignments in America, argues that the transition of the South from Democratic to Republican began "on the day in 1948 that President Truman sent Congress his civil rights proposals, reversing the moderate policy of his predecessor, Franklin Roosevelt" (Sundquist 1983, 353). This caused a deep division within the Democratic Party, which was papered over for a few years but reopened in 1954 after the Supreme Court ruled against segregation in *Brown v. Board of Education*. The northern Democrats strongly supported this decision and demanded that it be carried out, while the southern Democrats engaged in "massive resistance." By the time of the 1960 Democratic convention, the pro–civil rights forces were loudly advocating for reform. President Kennedy remained relatively centrist to placate the intransigent southern contingent of the Democratic Party. After Kennedy's death, however, Lyndon Johnson, the first president from a southern state, chose to align the Democratic Party with the northern contingent on the issue of civil rights.

As a result, the southern states voted heavily for Republican Barry Goldwater in the 1964 election. Stanley, Bianco, and Niemi (1986) point out that, though this was technically a policy difference, the timing of partisan changes by blacks and southern whites in the 1960s "suggest[s] a racially inspired shift in the group basis of the Democratic party" (975). The new alignment of the Democratic Party with the rights of blacks caused vast numbers of conservative white southern Democrats to move gradually to the Republican Party, leaving average Democrats more liberal and average Republicans more conservative. This racial-policy shift in the Democratic Party and subsequent realignment of conservative southern Democrats is generally understood to be one major reason that Democrats and Republicans today are more ideologically pure than they were in 1950. In this explanation, a racial-policy change in the Democratic Party is the root of all of today's partisan polarization. In some sense, this may be true. Without the civil rights policy change, nothing that came later would likely have happened in the same way. But if a policy change started the path to a more socially sorted nation, the effects of that change drew American politics further away from policy and toward an increasingly social partisan divide.

Social Sorting

During this time of change in the Democratic Party, the Republican Party experienced major changes as well. Not only were southern whites leaving the Democratic Party, white citizens all over the country were growing more Republican. As Carmines and Stimson said in 1982, "The 1964 presidential election not only widened the gulf between the Republican Party and the

Democratic Party on a number of policy issues, but it drove a wedge between the parties on issues of race for the first time in this century" (6). By 1988, 49 percent of northern whites identified with the Republican Party, a 17 percentage point increase in the Republican partisanship of northern whites since 1972 (Carmines and Stanley 1992). In places where race was highly salient to white voters (like the heavily black South), they changed their partisanship to match their race (Giles and Hertz 1994).

After the civil rights debates of the 1960s, black voters had clear policy reasons to be loyal to the Democratic Party, and racially biased white voters had clear reasons to prefer the Republican Party. But this policy-based affiliation has since grown into a distinctly social partisan divide. As of 2013, party identity is strongly predicted by racial identity, not racial-policy positions (Mangum 2013). The parties have grown so divided by race that simple racial identity, without policy content, is enough to predict party identity. The policy division that began the process of racial sorting is no longer necessary for Democrats and Republicans to be divided by race. Their partisan identities have become firmly aligned with their racial identities, and decoupled from their racial-policy positions.

As this process of racial sorting was in full swing, another social cleavage lined up along the partisan divide. The formerly nonpolitical religious right found common cause with the Republican leadership. In 1989, after a failed presidential bid by televangelist Pat Robertson, a group that called itself the Christian Coalition emerged. It was made up of conservative Christians, many of whom identified as evangelical or fundamentalist (Schnabel 2013). The Christian Coalition grew steadily in support and influence in the following years. By 1995 they had publicly paired with prominent Republican senators and congressmen, including the Republican Speaker of the House, Newt Gingrich, to announce the Contract with the American Family, which sought the legislation of Christian morality. All of the Contract with the American Family goals were incorporated into the Republican Party platform by 2000. The Republican Party became firmly affiliated with conservative Christianity. A new religious/nonreligious gap between the Republicans and Democrats grew as their activist bases responded to the new religious difference between the parties, leading candidates to take more extreme positions on religious issues and, thus, changing the public perceptions of the two parties (Layman 2001). Once the public was aware of a religious divide between the parties, their electoral composition changed, divided by religion-linked issues and images that both reflected and reinforced religious identities. Gradually, the religious/secular divide was added to the growing list of social cleavages drawing the parties apart.

The changing social alignments in the Democratic and Republican parties are clearly visible in figure 3.4. This figure uses ANES data to tell the story of how the two parties have changed and grown increasingly socially distinct. To do this, I first identify the percentage of each constituent group in each party (e.g., union members made up 31 percent of the Democratic Party in 1952 but only 22 percent of the Republican Party). Each bar represents the difference between the two parties on this measure (in the union example, I subtract 0.22 from 0.31 and end up with −0.09). To the right of the zero line, the Republican Party has a higher percentage of group members than the Democratic Party, and the degree of the difference is represented by the length of the line. To the left of the zero line, the Democratic Party has a higher percentage of group members than the Republican Party. Figure 3.4 presents these partisan social differences every twenty years, beginning in 1952.

1952

Though I argue that social sorting has increased in recent decades, it does not mean there were no sociopartisan alignments in the past. In 1952, the two parties were each affiliated with different social groups. Republicans were significantly more Protestant than Democrats, and Democrats were more strongly southern,[1] Catholic, and union affiliated. To a small degree, Republicans were more white and Democrats were more black. The difference between then and now is that although the parties did attract separate social groups, the extent of the partisan division between these groups was relatively small in 1952. With the exception of the partisan affiliations of southerners and Protestants, no group saw more than a 10 percentage point difference in the percentage of its members represented within each party.

1972

By 1972, two years before *Roe v. Wade* and less than a decade after the Civil Rights Act of 1964, partisan-group affiliations were not significantly different from those of 1952, with the exception of racial-group and southern affiliations. In comparison with 1952, Republicans had grown slightly more Protestant and wealthy, and Democrats slightly more Catholic and union affiliated. Racial sorting, however, had significantly increased, with Republicans now about 13 percentage points more white than Democrats, and Democrats about 11 percentage points more black than Republicans (in comparison, these racial differences were only 6 points and 6 points respec-

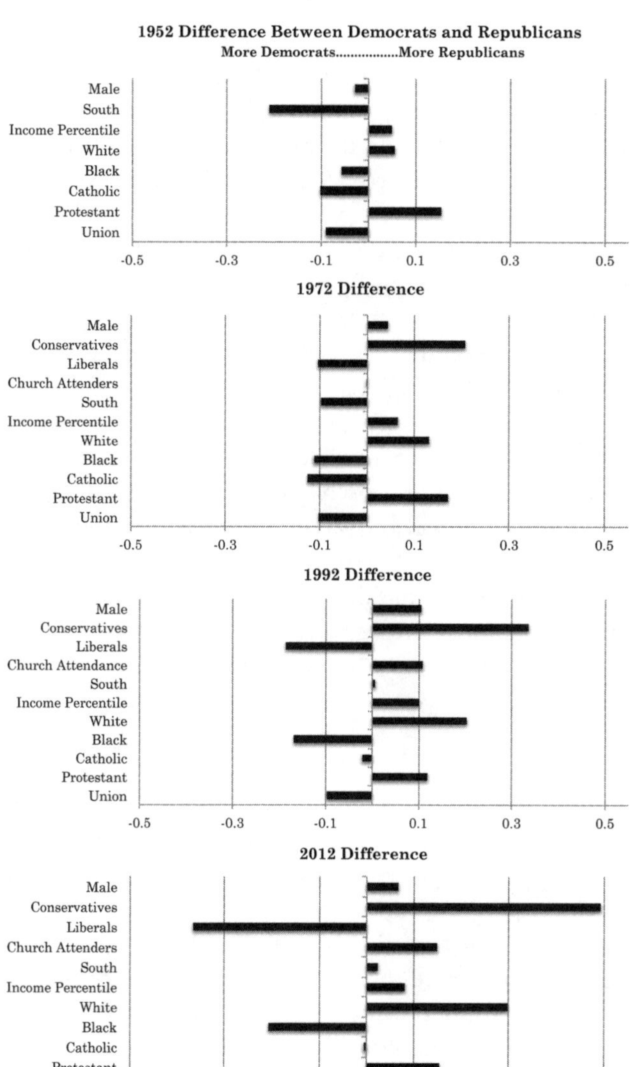

Figure 3.4. Social-group sorting

Note: Bars represent the difference between the percentage of group members in the Republican Party and the percentage of group members in the Democratic Party (including partisan leaners). Income percentile is the difference between the mean income percentile of Republicans and Democrats. Data are drawn from the ANES cumulative data file for the 1952, 1972, and 1992 graphs (fully weighted) and from the 2012 ANES (fully weighted) for the 2012 graph. There is also a gender gap between the parties, but this does not follow a clear pattern over time. Though Democrats were slightly more male (by 3 points) in 1952, Republicans have been consistently more male ever since, with a partisan gap of 4 points in 1972, 10 points in 1992, and 7 points in 2012.

tively in 1952). The data revealed another marked change in the percentages of each party that were southerners. In 1952, Democrats were 21 percentage points more southern than Republicans. This difference had decreased to 10 percentage points in 1972. In the twenty-year span between 1952 and 1972, the racial differences between the parties doubled while the southern divide was cut in half.

The ANES also added measures of ideology and church attendance in 1972, which are included in the figure from 1972 through 2012. In 1972, 10 percent more Democrats than Republicans called themselves liberal, but 20 percent more Republicans than Democrats called themselves conservative. The difference between the parties on conservatism is the largest difference in 1972. The lopsidedness of the difference between liberalism and conservatism is not surprising, considering that the Democratic Party still contained a large number of conservative southern Democrats, while the Republican Party, by comparison, was far more ideologically coherent.

The religious difference between the parties, however, was still Protestant versus Catholic. In fact, this divide had even grown slightly since 1952. There was, however, no difference whatsoever between the parties in levels of weekly church attenders in 1972. Though the racial divide had started to grow, the religious/nonreligious divide had not yet begun.

1992

Twenty years later, by 1992, the religious divide had cracked open, and the beginnings of our current state of sorting had become evident. The difference between the parties on the percentage of weekly churchgoers had increased to an 11 percentage point gap, with Republicans more churchgoing than Democrats. Connected to this new divide, Democrats in 1992 were only 2 percent more Catholic than Republicans. Twenty years earlier the difference had been 13 percentage points. The conservative religious were moving toward the Republican Party. The difference between the parties in the number of Protestants decreased from 17 percentage points in 1972 to 12 percentage points in 1992, as simply identifying as a Protestant was no longer a cohesive partisan indicator. A partisan rift was occurring among Protestants, splitting the traditional, conservative Protestants from the more progressive, liberal, mainline Protestants. As the conservative Christians became affiliated with the Republican Party, many liberal, mainline Protestants felt alienated by the new Republican identity and moved toward the Democrats. Many moved away from religion entirely, though still identified themselves as Protestants. While the Republican Party still remained more

Protestant than the Democratic Party in the aggregate, this difference began to diminish as Protestants themselves divided politically.

In many other ways, the parties were becoming increasingly divided by 1992. The difference between the parties in the percentage of liberals had nearly doubled, moving from 10 percentage points to nearly 19 percentage points. In the number of self-identified conservatives, the parties were now nearly 34 points apart.

Geographically, the defection of southern Democrats finally tipped the partisan balance, so that by 1992, Republicans had become 2 percentage points more southern than Democrats. Racial differences were also growing rapidly. Republicans in 1992 were 20 percent more white than Democrats, and Democrats were 17 percent more black than Republicans. In the twenty years between 1972 and 1992, the parties had again almost doubled the racial divide between them. Also in 1992, the income differences between the parties began to grow. In 1952, the two parties were only 5 percentage points apart in average income percentile, by 1992 this gap had doubled in size. The Republicans were increasingly the party of the wealthy.

2012

By 2012, the old Protestant/Catholic, southern/nonsouthern, and union/nonunion divisions between the parties had largely disappeared. The differences between the parties in southern residency and Catholic religion had faded entirely. The previous 10 percentage point difference between the parties in union membership declined to barely 4 percentage points. But these old divisions had been firmly replaced by much larger ideological, religious, income, and racial differences. This was not simply a matter of swapping one set of partisan alignments with another. The new partisan alignments divided the parties far more powerfully than the divides of the 1950s had. The partisan difference in the percentage of liberals had again doubled, from 18 percentage points in 1992 to a 37-point difference between Democrats and Republicans in 2012. The difference between the parties in the number of constituents self-identifying as conservative rose from 34 percentage points in 1992 to nearly 50 points in 2012.

The parties differed by 14 percentage points in how many attend religious services each week. Levels of income continued to divide the parties, with the influence of wealth slightly increasing in its power to divide the wealthy Republicans from the less-wealthy Democrats. But by far the most powerful social divide between the parties, rivaling the difference in ideology, was race. By 2012, Republicans were, on average, 30 percentage points more white than Democrats. Democrats were, on average, 21 points more black than Republicans. Racial, religious, and ideological divisions separated the parties, and these divisions ran far deeper than in the previous sixty years.

Identity-Based Social Sorting

The partisan shifts shown in figure 3.4, however, cannot tell the story of how closely American partisans feel affiliated with their various groups. Many of the social groups represented in figure 3.4 are essentially ascribed groups: race, southern residence, and income percentile are objective facts about a person. For the remaining groups—ideology, church attendance, religion, and union affiliation—a respondent has some leeway in deciding whether or not to identify him or herself as part of that group, but, in a response to a yes-or-no item, many people will simply provide the generally true response—that they are technically group members. They were raised Catholic. They are union members. They attend church once a week. These types of identities are also often considered objective group identities, ones to which members are assigned based on objective criteria, and with which they do not necessarily identify.

People, however, can also associate with a group on a subjective basis, by feeling some psychological sense of attachment to the group. These subjective group identities have been found to generate more loyalty from group members than objective group memberships, and therefore to have greater effects on individual behavior and intergroup relations (Huddy 2001).

The survey items that generated the outcomes in figure 3.4 do not allow respondents to explain to what degree they *feel* like they are connected to the other members of the group, how similar they are to other members of the group, in short, how strongly they identify with each group label. Fortunately, the ANES items used in figure 3.2 were also used to measure identification with other social groups. In comparison with a simple "Are you Catholic or Protestant?" prompt, these items ask respondents to specify who they feel close to, providing much more insightful evidence of a distinctly psychological partisan sorting.

Figure 3.5 includes these items, indicating the difference between the two parties in the percentage of partisans who felt psychologically identified with each group. The results, though limited in time, still provide a solid picture of the trend in social sorting in recent decades. The trend echoes that seen in figure 3.4, and additionally allows some insight into the group-based feelings in each party.

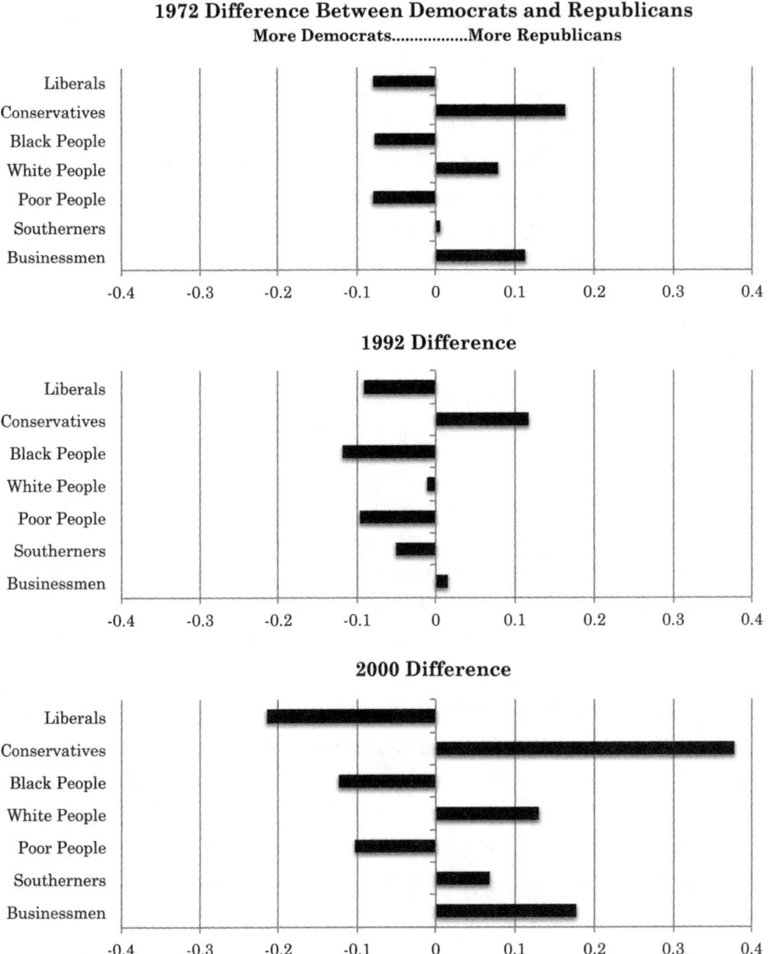

Figure 3.5. Identity-based social sorting
Note: Bars represent the difference between the percentage of Republicans who claimed to feel identified with each group minus the percentage of Democrats who did so (including partisan leaners). Data drawn from the ANES data files of 1972, 1992, and 2000.

The ideological-identity differences reiterate the data shown in figure 3.2 and indicate, again, a strengthening of both liberal identity among Democrats and conservative identity among Republicans, with a distinctly larger increase in ideological identity among Republicans. By 2000, Republicans overwhelmingly felt that conservatives were their kind of people. Democrats felt this way about liberals as well, but not to the same degree.

In addition to these very large differences in ideological identity, figure 3.5 indicates a steadily growing increase in racial identity differences between the two parties. Between 1972 and 2000, the percentage of people in each party who felt close to black people increased from an 8 percentage point difference to a 12 percentage point difference between the two parties. Likewise, respondents who claimed to feel particularly close to white people grew increasingly Republican, with an 8 percentage point difference between the parties in 1972 growing to a 13 percentage point difference in 2000.

There was also a growing income disparity, not only in objective income levels but also in the extent to which people identified with certain income levels. The difference between the parties in the percentage of people identified with poor people remained relatively steady between 1972 and 2000, with Democrats consistently more strongly identified with the poor. In the number of people who identified with "businessmen," the difference between the parties increased from 11 percentage points in 1972 to 18 percentage points in 2000. Democrats consistently identified with poor people, while Republicans felt more and more like businessmen.

Finally, in comparison with the objective measure of southern residence, the percentage of each party that *felt* like a southerner was about the same in each party in 1972. In 1992, 5 percentage points more Democrats than Republicans felt connected to southerners as a group, suggesting that even as the Republican Party became more geographically southern than the Democratic Party, many Democrats still felt connected to the South. This is likely reflective of the southern provenance of the Democratic presidential candidate, Bill Clinton. But by 2000, 7 percentage points more Republicans than Democrats felt particularly close to southerners. The southern partisan reversal was firmly under way, and it was occurring on a psychological level as well as a purely geographical level.

These subjective feelings of attachment are important indicators in the trend of social sorting. It might have been possible for the parties to grow objectively sorted into observable but psychologically unimportant groups. This, however, did not happen. As the parties became more homogeneous in ideology, race, class, geography, and religion, partisans on both sides felt increasingly connected to the groups that divided them. As I explain in the following chapters, the psychological identifications with groups that divide along partisan lines have serious implications for the thinking, behavior, and emotions of American partisans.

Sorting Made Easy

One important final element in the history of sorting is the role of non-policy-based phenomena that eased the way along the path toward American partisan division. Though a racial-policy divide may have started the trend in social sorting, it was not the sole culprit. Social sorting has its roots in a few separate developments.

First, the issue-based division of the Democratic Party was accompanied by a providential change in American civil society. As Bill Bishop argues in his book *The Big Sort* (2009), the 1960s and 1970s saw a large decline in trust in government among both Democrats and Republicans—so large that it encouraged citizens to detach from their parties. Political scientists responded to this with declarations of the end of partisanship, writing articles with titles like "The End of American Party Politics" (Burnham 1969). This detachment, however, was part of a larger trend. Not only did Americans lose trust in their parties, they lost trust in all institutions, resulting in a decline in civic engagement. As Robert Putnam (2000) has observed, Americans had previously associated in bowling leagues, civic organizations such as the Grange, the Elks, and the Scouts, professional organizations, parent-teacher organizations, and politically diverse churches and neighborhood communities. During the 1970s and the 1980s, however, membership in all of these organizations declined sharply. Americans began to grow more isolated and independent, and their political ties loosened.

This social loosening freed Americans to rearrange their partisan, social, and civic affiliations. It also, however, led Americans to feel increasingly detached from their communities and country, and compelled them to seek comfort in increasingly homogeneous neighborhoods, towns, and churches, causing American citizens to sort themselves into geographically isolated groups that shared their culture, values, race, and politics. They disengaged from their old, community-centered groups and formed new affiliations, tailored exactly to meet their needs.

Unattached and increasingly mobile Democrats and Republicans moved into increasingly homogeneous communities. White urban residents moved to the suburbs while urban areas grew increasingly populated by black residents (Frey 1979). Roof and McKinney (1987) described a post-1960s religious environment that included "greater choice in religious affiliation" and a "heightened religious individualism" that allowed religious Americans to detach from old mainline churches and move to churches more precisely suited to their specific social requirements. The partisan segregation of US counties increased by 26 percentage points between 1980 and 2000 (Bishop 2009). Andrew Garner and Harvey Palmer in 2011 described American residential neighborhoods as "increasingly balkanized by political attitudes as well as . . . race, education, and income" (230). Much of this was due to Americans choosing to live in more homogeneous communities and surrounding themselves with people who felt familiar. As Gordon Allport explained in the 1950s, it simply takes less effort to surround yourself with people similar to you.

The second force to contribute to social sorting, however, was the relationship between citizens and their party leaders. While citizens had been disengaging and socially segregating, the Democratic and Republican parties had been changing to provide clearer partisan, ideological, and social cues to the electorate, particularly on the Republican side. Kyle Saunders and Alan Abramowitz looked at American political activism from 1972 to 2000 and found that, as the parties' ideological cues grew more distinct and more potent, more partisans were motivated to participate, particularly within the Republican Party (Saunders and Abramowitz 2004). The Republican Party did a better job of organizing sympathetic social groups behind it. So, although social sorting may have begun with a split in the Democratic Party, it was the solidification of the Republican Party into religious, middle-/upper-class, and white categories that increasingly led to a more socially sorted and divided electorate. Due to the clearer distinction between the parties, Americans had far more simple cues to follow. These cues helped citizens to understand that a highly religious Christian who is also wealthy and white will feel most at home among Republicans. Similarly, a secular, less-wealthy, black person will feel more comfortable surrounding herself with Democrats. The parties, by providing increasingly clear cues, have helped Americans to know which party is their own.

A third stimulus toward social sorting was a growing diversity of media sources. The increasingly clear partisan cues have been reinforced by an increasingly diverse set of media sources, many of which are overtly partisan and/or misleading. Partisans are now able to protect themselves from any exposure at all to the arguments and opinions of the other side. Already geographically and culturally isolated, these citizens are also informationally isolated. Americans are not only sorted into homogeneous parties, they have diminishing opportunities even to hear the arguments of their political opponents. The news media allow voters to listen only to the narratives of their own side, causing them to become increasingly consistent in understanding whose team they are on, and which other teams are on their side. Though the audience for this type of media represents a small portion of the

American population, Matthew Levendusky (2013) has found that "partisan media have multiplier effects that allow a relatively limited medium that speaks to a narrow segment of the market to have an outsize influence on American politics" (7). The isolating effects of this segmented media environment make very clear where the partisan boundaries are between social groups. The news about which groups belong in each party spreads widely, allowing individual citizens to understand better which party is their home, and which party is their adversary.

All of these forces have worked to encourage social sorting far beyond the effects of simple policy positions. We have gone from two parties that are a little bit different in a lot of ways to two parties that are very different in a few powerful ways. These underlying social shifts have put the American population into a partisan team-based mindset, through which the country has split itself into us and them, the Rattlers and the Eagles. Democrats and Republicans have become different types of people, and not only in terms of the groups that can be measured by the ANES.

Cultural Differences

Democrats and Republicans come from and create different kinds of families. The national decline in fertility and increase in the age of marriage that has occurred since the 1950s has been limited mostly to the "Blue" states. The "Red" states have comparatively higher levels of fertility and are married at younger ages (Cahn and Carbone 2010). Research has found a strong relationship between fertility rates among white voters and Republican voting that stands even when controlling for urbanization, wealth, female education, Evangelism, Mormonism, Catholicism, and geography (Lesthaeghe and Neidert 2006).

The parties are divided in what they watch on television. In 2012, TiVo Research and Analytics matched television viewing data with voter registration information from 186,000 American households (Carter 2012). They sorted television programs by how popular they were with members of each party, listing the top twenty shows for Democratic and Republican viewers. Not a single network show appeared on both lists. A 2016 *New York Times* study found an urban/rural cultural divide in television watching that matched partisan voting patterns. The correlation between Trump votes and "fandom" for the show *Duck Dynasty* (a Christian-value-based hunting show) was higher than for any other show. In fact, *Duck Dynasty* viewing was more predictive of a Trump vote in 2016 than it was of a Bush vote in 2000 (Katz 2016). *Family Guy*, an animated sitcom, was more correlated with 2016

Hillary Clinton support than any other show. According to Katz (2016), this pattern was consistent with most satirical comedy shows popular in cities, where Clinton tended to receive the most votes. What this means is that, even when we sit down to relax and watch TV, Democrats and Republicans are different kinds of people. Increasingly, we cannot even connect at the water cooler to discuss last night's shows.

This type of cultural difference is pervasive. Thomas Edsall (2012) explained the campaign strategy of "nanotargeting," a method that is only possible because Democrats and Republicans can be found purchasing and enjoying categorically different things. They receive news from different sources (Democrats like the *Washington Post*, Republicans like the *Washington Times*); they eat at different restaurants (Democrats like Chuck E. Cheese's, Republicans like Macaroni Grill); they drive different cars (Democrats like hybrids, Republicans like Land Rovers); they drink different alcohol (Democrats like Cognac, Republicans like Amstel Light). These are cultural differences so notable that campaigns rely on them to target advertising at the voters they are most likely to attract.

The makeup of the two parties has changed a great deal in the past sixty years, increasing the social distance between them. Partisans have less and less in common. Fewer cross-cutting cleavages remain to link the parties together and allow the understanding, communication, and compromise necessary to fuel the American electorate, and, by extension, the American government. Democrats and Republicans have grown so different from each other that cooperation is receding as a perceived value. When two teams grow so distinct and isolated from each other, the status of the teams themselves grows in importance. The functional outcomes of governing matter less. The sorting of our identities into partisan camps has allowed these identities to increasingly drive polarized political behavior, thought, and emotion.

FOUR

Partisan Prejudice

> Elections aren't just about policy choices. They're status competitions. When the polls swing your way, you feel a surge of righteous affirmation. Your views are obviously correct! Your team's virtues are widely recognized! You get to see the humiliation and pain afflicting your foes.
>
> —David Brooks, "Poll Addict Confesses"

Social sorting affects political relations by a simple, powerful effect. Being a member of a group tends to change our perception of the world and bias our relationships with others. Any group member who feels connected to the group is powerfully motivated to evaluate other ingroup members more positively than nonmembers, to be more generous with ingroup members, in short, to show bias in favor of the ingroup. This effect is magnified when multiple group memberships coincide, which is why the sorting of multiple identities into two parties can exacerbate the general effect of a single identity. However, to explain the results of sorting, it is important to take a step back and begin by looking more closely at the effects of a single group identity.

Group identities, particularly partisan identities, have been well studied, and, before presenting my own analyses here, I provide a short summary of the work done to date.

What Is Partisanship?

In political science, the understanding of partisanship has undergone a significant evolution. In the middle of the last century, political scientists and sociologists tended toward the idea of partisanship as a distinctly social phenomenon. Lazarsfeld, Berelson, and Gaudet (1944) wrote, "A person thinks, politically, as he is, socially" (27). In 1960, Angus Campbell and his colleagues at the University of Michigan published *The American Voter*, which described partisan identification as a "psychological identification" and an "affective orientation." They believed that identifying with a party was not simply a record of past voting or an indicator of future vote choice. It was not only a list of issue positions that a voter attempted to match to one party or the other. Instead, they thought that the psychological and emotional sense of belonging to a party was capable of altering the thoughts, feelings, and actions of partisans. This "Michigan model" of partisanship was one of the first to discuss the real and apparent psychological effects of being part of a partisan group.

In later years, however, the Michigan model of partisanship began to meet challenges. A new wave of research suggested that party identity was more likely an endpoint—a reasoned decision based on a person's political opinions and rational evaluations of the performance of political leaders. In 1977, Morris Fiorina described candidate evaluations as being made up of two main elements: past political evaluations and current issue concerns. He explained, "Party ID combines additively with current issue concerns. But party ID at any given point is a function of issue concerns prior to that point" (611). Party identity, he explained in 1981, was a "running tally" of issue considerations. This literature viewed voters as information-based decision makers, more like bankers choosing an investment than like sports fans cheering for a team.

Since then, a more social approach to partisan identity has seen a resurgence. Between the 1970s and the 2000s, partisan voting markedly and significantly increased, as did the number of strong partisan identifiers (Bartels 2002). In 2002, Green, Palmquist, and Schickler likened partisan identity to religious identity, a social-group membership that is acquired early in life and acts as an organizing force in an individual's sense of identity and self, driving action and decision-making. Steven Greene, in three separate papers (1999, 2002, 2004), described and measured partisanship as a social identity in the classic, psychological sense of the term.

My own work with Leonie Huddy and Lene Aarøe in 2015 demonstrated the powerful effect of partisan social identity in driving emotional reactivity and political activism, independent of the effects of instrumental policy concerns. McConnell et al. (2016) have even found effects of partisanship on nonpolitical outcomes, such as willingness to engage in economic transactions with outgroup partisans.

The current climate in political science is one that generally accepts the social nature of partisan identity but also allows for the ability of individuals to understand some issues and apply this knowledge to their political choices. For example, Bullock (2011) found that among people who possess policy information (an admittedly small group), many are capable of applying their policy preferences to political decisions without being unduly influenced by partisan bias. Similarly, Carsey and Layman (2006) found that individual partisan identification can be influenced by particular issues that are salient to the voter and on which the voter is aware of party differences (again, a limited domain).

Other research attempts to combine the instrumental model of partisanship and the social, expressive models. The work on ambivalence by Lavine, Johnston, and Steenbergen (2012) allows for partisans to dislike their own party for a variety of reasons, weakening the bond between party and partisan. Groenendyk's 2013 book contributes to this synthesis of the instrumental and expressive models of partisanship, as he identifies the motivations that may lead partisans to avoid partisan bias.

Ultimately, however, partisanship itself is an undeniable psychological force in modern American politics. As Iyengar, Sood, and Lelkes observed in 2012, Democrats and Republicans have grown to "dislike, even loathe" each other, and this emotional partisan loathing is only minimally due to differences in policy opinions. There is a power that partisanship exerts on individual partisans in the way they see the world, and in the way they think about other citizens. Much of the current partisan loathing grows out of the enduring effects of partisan and other social identities.

The Psychological Effects of Party Identity

Democrats and Republicans compete for the power to implement very different policy platforms, affecting the entire nation. Political victory provides power in government and increased freedom to enact real policy outcomes that often directly benefit the members of the winning party in the form of tax policies, welfare policies, business regulation, or social programs. However, as Tajfel and Turner (1979) explain, "It is nearly impossible in most natural social situations to distinguish between discriminatory intergroup behavior based on real or perceived conflict of 'objective' interests between the groups and discrimination based on attempts to establish a positively valued distinctiveness for one's own group" (46). In other words, though the parties are competing for real interests, they are also competing because ust feels good to win. Distinguishing between those motivations is not simple matter, but it is important to remember that both motivations are eparately present in any political competition.

One powerful example of these tangled motivations is visible in the government shutdown of 2013. In October of 2013, the federal government shut down for sixteen days. According to the Office of Management and Budget (2013), the shutdown was "the second longest since 1980 and the most significant on record, measured in terms of employee furlough days." Their most conservative estimates found that the shutdown lowered GDP growth by $2 billion to $6 billion, led to 120,000 fewer jobs created, hindered trade, disrupted private-sector and federal lending to businesses and individuals, cost Alaskan fisherman thousands of dollars per day, reduced small-business contracts with the government by a third, delayed approval of important drugs, and deprived businesses of information about the state of the economy. Federal employees lost $2.5 billion in compensation for their furloughed work time. The shutdown delayed tax refunds, prevented sick patients from enrolling in clinical trials, closed Head Start daycare centers to 6,300 children, delayed home loans for 8,000 rural families, and delayed food-safety inspections.

What was worth so much damage to the economy and the nation as a whole? House Republicans insisted that they would not pass a spending bill required for government operation unless the Affordable Care Act (ACA, also known as Obamacare) was defunded or otherwise derailed. The ACA was Democratic president Obama's signature achievement during his first term. It was a health-care reform bill that represented a massive victory for the Democratic Party and an infuriating loss for the Republicans. Republicans had challenged the act before the Supreme Court, and the act was upheld. Legislatively, judicially, and executively, the act was approved and was moving ahead. Logistically and by all rational measures, there was no way to stop it.

Prior to the government shutdown, Republicans in the House of Representatives had voted forty-one times to repeal the ACA, knowing each time that these bills would never pass the Senate. The forty-second vote to repeal the ACA was tied to the approval of the spending bill in October. Though Democrats in Congress and the president himself had assured them that this type of brinksmanship would have no effect on the ACA, Republicans in the House went ahead with their demands, costing the nation billions of dollars, thousands of jobs, and untold opportunity costs. By the time the shutdown ended, nothing had been gained for the Republican Party, and the American taxpayers had seen billions of dollars squandered. When asked why Republicans had gone ahead with a hopeless cause that did so much damage, Republican representative Jack Kingston from Georgia replied, "I think it was important to us to reestablish our brand as being against Obamacare" (*All In with Chris Hayes*, 2013). Members of the Republican Party were willing to significantly damage the greater good of the nation in order to improve their partisan "brand." It seems crazy, but it's not. Henri Tajfel could have predicted this kind of behavior decades ago. The Republicans had an identity to defend. As long as the ACA goes forward, Republicans will be reminded of a massive group loss. Standing against the ACA is like pushing back against defeat. Republicans, particularly strongly identified ones, must defend their group against losing, at nearly any cost.

The example of the 2013 government shutdown is not notable in the damage done to the nation in pursuit of partisan goals. Certainly partisans in government have supported or opposed legislation that would ultimately damage the nation, on behalf of strongly held values or beliefs, or for strategic purposes. What distinguishes the 2013 shutdown is the hopelessness of the cause, and the knowledge on the part of Republicans that their actions would not change any policy. The goal of the shutdown was not, in reality, to prevent the enactment of the ACA. It was, as many representatives suggested, to enhance their brand. As an identity grows increasingly central, and increasingly encompassing as an element of any individual's self-concept, the status of that identity grows more important. Even in the face of defeat, the shutdown was a way to say to supporters, "We are not entirely powerless, we still have status." It was an act of reassurance for partisans whose sense of self had been damaged. It was a way to repair the damaged egos of a team who had just suffered a massive loss. It was a way to hold the team together, and heal the wounds of defeat. The damage caused to the nation by shutting down the government was, from an identity standpoint, justified. Millions of strongly identified Republicans needed to know that they were not losers. Their party had to deliver that message. It cost a great deal, but it was necessary for protecting the group.

The work of Tajfel and Turner (1979) has grown into what is now known as social identity theory. They describe a social identity as "those *aspects of an individual's self-image* that derive from the social categories to which he perceives himself as belonging" (40; emphasis added). Being part of a group informs each person's self-image. Part of the reason for the deep and enduring existence of ingroup bias and the quest for group victory is that people are compelled to think of their groups as better than others. Without that, they themselves feel inferior. According to social identity theory, group members, at a very primal level, are powerfully motivated to see outgroups as different from them and to view the world through a competitive lens, with importance placed on their own group's superiority. This is crucial to keep in mind in the pages that follow. There is something inherent in a group identity that causes group members to be biased against their opponents. All of the political arguments over taxes, welfare, abortion, compassion, responsibility, and the ACA are built on a base of automatic and primal feelings that compel partisans to believe that their group is right, regardless of the content of the discussion. A partisan prefers his or her own team partly for rational, policy-based reasons but also for irrational, automatic, self-defensive reasons. This can cause irrational behavior in the search for victory. It can also cause very deep feelings of prejudice toward other partisans.

The term *prejudice* is used here interchangeably with the concept of ingroup bias. Ingroup bias is an essential element of any group identity, including a partisan identity, and it means essentially that a person prefers their own group to the outgroup, for no reason other than that they are part of the ingroup, as was so well demonstrated by the minimal group paradigm experiments. I call this prejudice because it is the element of the group identity that is the most visceral and tribal, and in this sense it is indistinguishable from the base motive that drives racial prejudice or religious prejudice. Partisan bias has been experimentally demonstrated in grading (Musgrave and Rom 2015), college admissions (Munro, Lasane, and Leary 2010), and among survey interviewers (Healy and Malhotra 2014)—with copartisans given preferential treatment and judged superior to outgroup partisans. This is similar to the racial bias found by Bertrand and Mullainathan (2003) in the evaluations of resumes in a job search. If racial bias in hiring could be called prejudice, then the motive driving partisans to prefer their own kind can also be understood to be a type of prejudice. It is something that Cass Sunstein (2015) has labeled "partyism." In defending the use of the term *prejudice*, Sunstein writes, "A degree of antipathy—at least if it is not personal—may reflect principled disagreement, not prejudice at all. But there is a large difference between a degree of antipathy and the forms of partyism we are now observing" (10).

The analyses that follow provide evidence that current levels of partisan antipathy have moved beyond pure disagreements of principle. Partisans dislike each other to a degree that cannot be explained by policy disagreement alone.

Warm Feelings

Every election year, the American National Election Studies (ANES) ask respondents to rate the two parties on a "feeling thermometer," essentially gauging how "warm" or "cool" the respondents feel toward Democrats and Republicans. Figure 4.1 shows mean levels of the difference between the two party-feeling thermometers, what I call "warmth bias," over time, compared against the average extremity of Americans' positions on six prominent policies.[1] The partisan preference for one party over the other has been steadily increasing, adding a 10 percentage point difference in feelings toward the two parties since 1984. At the same time the overall extremity of American policy positions has not seen the same increase. In fact, between 2008 and 2012 the two trends significantly diverged—our feelings toward the par-

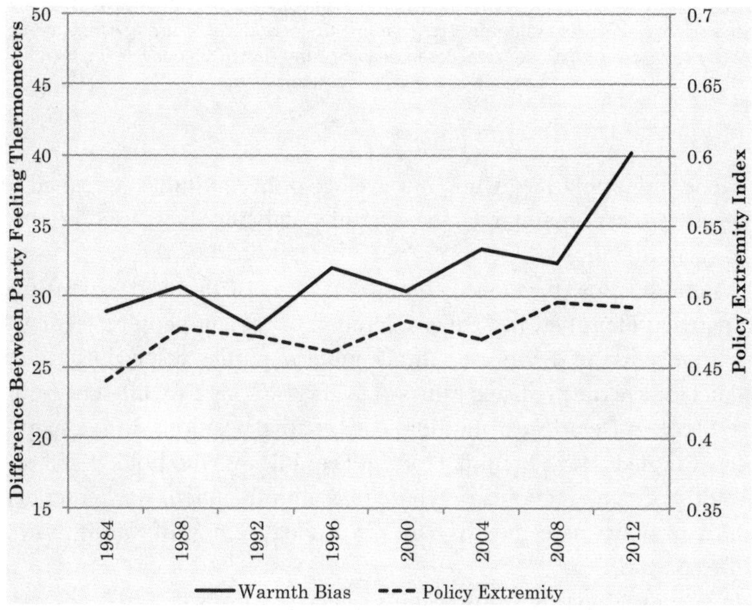

Figure 4.1. Warmth bias and policy extremity over time

Note: Warmth bias is the absolute difference between each respondent's thermometer rating of the Democratic and Republican parties. Policy extremity is an index of six issues including abortion policy, government services versus spending, government health insurance, government aid to minorities, government employment protections, and defense spending. Each issue is folded in half so that higher scores represent more extreme positions on both ends of the spectrum. The six folded issue scales are then combined into an index. Data are drawn from the ANES cumulative file through 2012 (fully weighted), using only observations for which answers are available for all six issues.

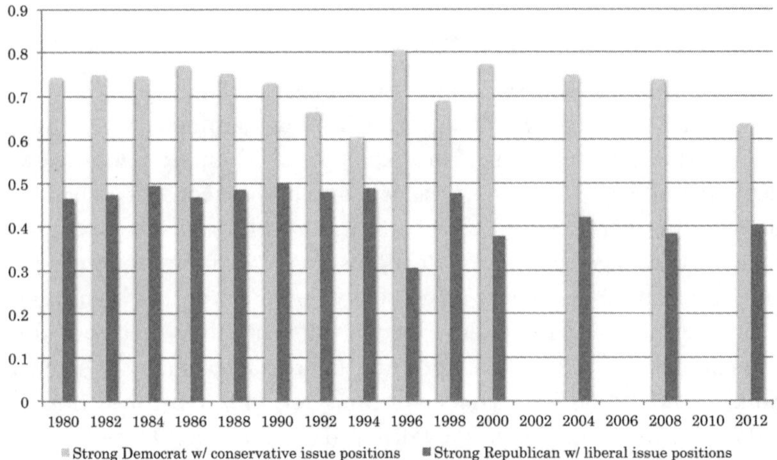

Figure 4.2. Predicted feelings of warmth toward the Democratic Party
Note: Data drawn from the ANES cumulative file (fully weighted) and the ANES 2012 file (fully weighted). Predicted values are derived from OLS regressions, controlling for education, sex, race, age, southern residence, urban residence, and church attendance. For the full regressions, see appendix table A.1a.

ties grew more polarized while our average policy attitudes remained unchanged. Partisans maintained the extremity of their policy preferences, and liked each other less.

Where did this divergence come from? Part of the story comes from our partisan identities. In figures 4.2 and 4.3 I look at people's feelings of warmth toward the Democratic and Republican parties, respectively. In particular, I look at the predicted values of feelings among two different groups. First, I look at Democrats who hold conservative positions on the six policies mentioned above. Second, I look at Republicans who hold liberal positions on the same six policies. What I'm examining, then, is whether party identity or policy agreement is better at driving feelings of warmth toward the two parties.[2]

In every year, partisanship trumps policy positions in determining our feelings toward the two parties. Even if we agree with the opposing party on most policies, we still feel most warmly toward our own party. Democrats who hold consistently conservative policy positions generally report feelings between 60 and 80 degrees (out of 100) for the Democratic Party. However, Republicans who agree with Democrats on most issues rate the Democratic Party between 30 and 50 degrees, depending on the year. This difference has fluctuated since 1980, the earliest point available in the series. The small-

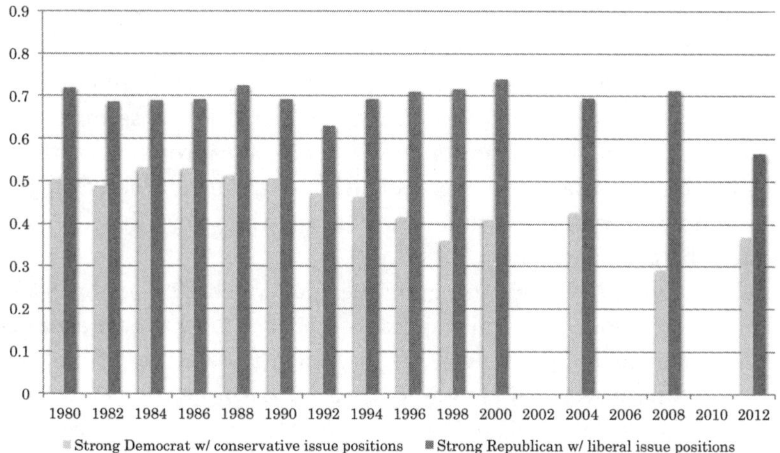

Figure 4.3. Predicted feelings of warmth toward the Republican Party
Note: Data drawn from the ANES cumulative file (fully weighted) and the ANES 2012 file (fully weighted). Predicted values are derived from OLS regressions, controlling for education, sex, race, age, southern residence, urban residence, and church attendance. For the full regressions, see appendix table A.1b.

est difference between these cross-pressured partisans occurred in 1994, when only 11 degrees separated their evaluations. The very next election year, in 1996, the two cross-pressured partisans rated the Democratic Party 50 degrees apart.[3] The difference between these cross-pressured partisans, although slightly volatile, exists in every year going back to 1980.[4]

The same basic pattern occurs in our feelings toward Republicans. Republicans whose policy attitudes rightly belong with the Democratic Party report feelings of warmth toward Republicans of around 60 to 70 degrees across time. At the same time, Democrats who agree with most of the Republican positions on policies feel between 30 and 50 degrees or warmth toward Republicans, mostly on the "cool" end of the thermometer spectrum. The difference between these cross-pressured partisans was smallest in 1984, when their ratings were about 16 points apart, and largest in 2008, when their ratings were about 42 points apart.

This is not a picture of a nation that is choosing its parties based entirely on its policy attitudes. Simply being a member of one party can cause significant differences in our preferences for the two parties, even when our policy positions conflict with those of our own party. These conflicted partisans are still very loyal to their partisan teams, despite a consistent disagreement with their goals.

Rather than holding parties responsible for their policy positions, partisans are inclined to cling to their own party, seeing it through rose-colored glasses. The real outcomes of government, and a person's opinions about those outcomes, take a back seat to the central importance of seeing the inparty as better than the outparty. As long as the inparty is winning, partisans will have little motivation to stray. As Tajfel found, and the House Republicans demonstrated in 2013, winning is often more important than the good of the population as a whole.

This is part of the reason that even when policy debates crack open and an opportunity for compromise appears—a chance to increase the greater good—partisans are psychologically motivated to look away from that possibility and instead to find a way for the team to win, even if it means that we all receive less than we could have won together. In the 2013 debate over expanding background checks for gun purchases, 83 percent of Democrats and 81 percent of Republicans personally supported a law expanding background checks in a Pew poll. But only 57 percent of Republicans supported the Senate passing a background check bill, an action that would have been a victory for Democrats (Pew 2013). On this issue, Republicans and Democrats in the electorate clearly and massively agreed on what they wanted as the outcome. However, when it came to the moment of public partisan competition, party victory trumped preferred policy for many Republicans. Party affiliation today means that a partisan cares a great deal about one party being the winner. Policy results come second.

Friends and Neighbors

Sadly, this natural bias against the outparty does not end at the gates of policy and governance. According to the 2016 Pew poll, when asked about a hypothetical person moving into their neighborhood, 61 percent of both Democrats and Republicans thought it would be easier to get along with the new person if that person were a member of the same party. Data that I collected from a national sample in 2011[5] confirm this type of social discomfort between partisans in the electorate. I asked a sample of Americans how willing they would be to spend time with Democrats and Republicans at four different levels of social intimacy. These included spending occasional social time, being next-door neighbors, being close friends, and marrying a partisan from each side. The items were drawn from a social-distance scale originally used by the sociologist Emory Bogardus (1925) to gauge racial prejudice in the 1920s and 1930s. I suspected that these prompts might reveal a distinctly social difference between contemporary Democrats and Republicans.

Figure 4.4 shows mean levels of willingness to engage in social contact with ingroup partisans and outgroup partisans. The results follow what Gordon Allport would likely have predicted in 1954. Democrats and Republicans would much rather spend time with people from their own party. On the full range of willingness,[6] Americans are 19 percentage points less willing to spend occasional social time with outgroup partisans than with ingroup partisans. They are 13 percentage points less willing to have an outgroup partisan as a next-door neighbor. They are 17 percentage points less willing to be close friends with a person from the opposing party, and they are 36 percentage points less willing to marry a political opponent than a political comrade. These results are nearly identical for Democrats and Republicans (though Democrats are slightly less willing to be close friends with Republicans than Republicans are with Democrats in this sample). These are all statistically significant differences. Partisans in America would prefer to spend time with their own kind. In 2011, 52 percent of American partisans said that they definitely or probably would not marry a member of the opposing party. As a point of comparison, when Bogardus asked these questions of white Protestant Americans in 1928, he found that 10 percent would not marry a Canadian or northern European, but 90 percent would not marry a southern or eastern European (Triandis and Triandis 1960). In their suitability for marriage, therefore, outgroup partisans today rank somewhere between Canadians and Italians in the early twentieth century. These results echo those found in 2012 by Shanto Iyengar and colleagues, in which nearly 50 percent of Republicans and 30 percent of Democrats in 2010 reported that they would feel somewhat or very unhappy if their child chose to marry an outgroup partisan.

Figure 4.4 reveals that American partisans are not simply unhappy with their political choices in government, they dislike their political opponents in the electorate as well. This is where the social element of social polarization becomes clear. Partisans prefer to spend time with members of their own party. In a purely rational view of partisanship, this could be explained by a general reluctance to encounter social disagreements. Perhaps Democrats and Republicans don't wish to spend time together simply because they want to avoid awkward political discussions. However, policy-based disagreements do not explain the entire effect seen in figure 4.4. One easy way to see this is to combine all four of these social domains into one measure and examine it at varying levels of partisanship and issue positions.

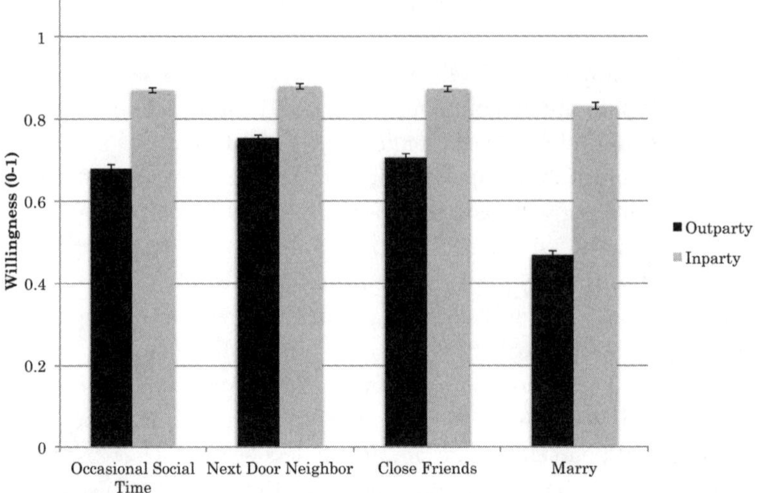

Figure 4.4. Social distance between Democrats and Republicans
Note: Data are drawn from an adult sample collected by YouGov Polimetrix, using funding from the National Science Foundation under grant no. SES-1065054. Bars represent mean levels of reported willingness among self-identified Democrats and Republicans, including independent leaners. Ninety-five percent confidence intervals around mean values shown to indicate significant differences.

In figure 4.5, I plot predicted values of the difference between the two parties' scores on this aggregated social-distance measure. I refer to this difference as social-distance bias—the relative willingness to spend time with members of the inparty versus members of the outparty in all four domains. Measuring social distance this way controls for people who simply don't like to spend time with any partisan. If this partisan bias against outparty friends and neighbors is due largely to an avoidance of policy arguments, a person's policy positions should drive most of the bias. However, if simple group identity drives a biased evaluation of the two parties, strong partisanship should play an independent role.

Figure 4.5 reveals almost exactly what Tajfel would have predicted. Real conflicts and partisan identities are both driving ingroup bias. In this case, they are doing so to a relatively equal extent. The measures used here are superior to the ANES measures, with a four-item measure of social identity used to gauge partisan identity,[7] and an issue-position measure that includes respondents' sense of whether each issue is important and how consistently liberal or conservative those issues are (see figure note for details).

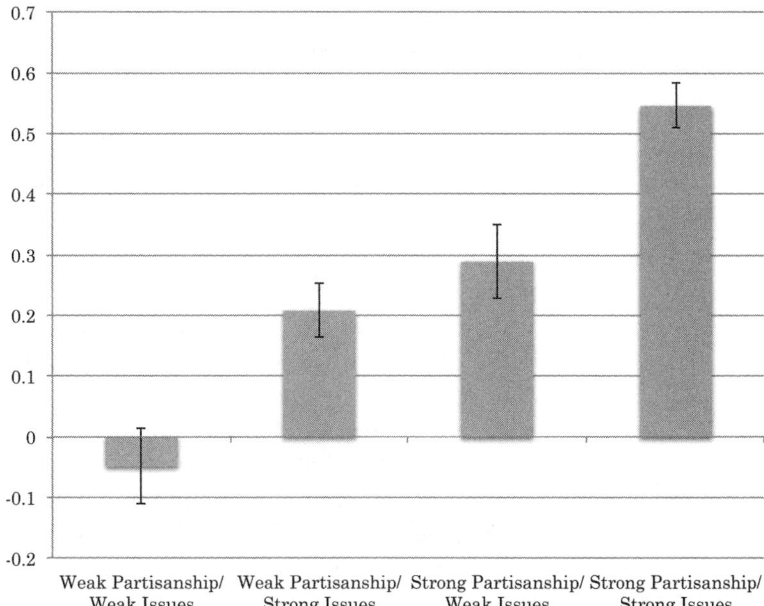

Figure 4.5. Predicted difference in social distance between ingroup and outgroup partisans
Note: Predicted values drawn from an OLS regression controlling for education, political knowledge, race, gender, income, age, and church attendance. Ninety-five percent confidence intervals shown. Originating regressions are shown in appendix table A.2. Data are drawn from the 2011 Polimetrix sample. Sample includes only those respondents who have indicated preference for one party (N = 774). Partisanship is a scale introduced and tested by Huddy, Mason, and Aarøe (2015), based on items often found in social-psychological identity scales (Luhtanen and Crocker 1992; Crocker et al. 1994). Issues are an index of five generally salient political issues, weighted by the rated importance of each one, as well as a measure of issue constraint. Social-distance scale ranges from 0 (no difference in willingness to interact socially with members of the two parties) to 1 (maximal difference in willingness to interact socially with members of the two parties).

The regression model predicting social-distance bias (SDB) is as follows:

$$\text{SDB} = a + B_1(\text{PID}) + B_2(\text{IE}) + B_3(\text{IC}) + B_4(\text{IE*IC}) + B_i(\text{controls}) + e.$$

In this linear regression model, social-distance bias is a function of partisan social identity (PID), issue extremity (IE), issue constraint (IC), and the interaction of the two issue measures (as well as control variables listed under the figure). The reason for interacting the two issue measures is to account for two particular types of people who are often difficult to measure.

First, those people who may hold a host of extreme issue positions but who are ideologically inconsistent (a mix of liberal and conservative extreme positions). The second type is a person who is consistently either liberal or conservative but never holds an extreme position (always just barely on one side of the central/moderate response). The interaction allows for extremity to be separated from constraint and for the power of the combination to be more precisely examined.[8] In figure 4.5, I only examine the effects of both measures at low or high levels together.[9]

In the first column of figure 4.5, the level of social-distance bias is estimated for a very weakly identified partisan with (a) the most moderate positions on immigration, health care, gay marriage, abortion, and the deficit, (b) very little sense that those issues are important, and (c) no particular tendency toward either the liberal or conservative end of the spectrum. This person is predicted to exhibit no social-distance bias whatsoever. That is, he or she does not care about the partisanship of their social contacts and may, in fact, prefer outgroup partisans (though this is not statistically distinguishable, as the confidence interval includes zero).

In the second column, the weakly identified partisan is given very strong positions on all five issues, a sense that all of those issues are highly important, and a consistently liberal or conservative answer to all questions. This person is about 21 percentage points more willing to spend time with ingroup partisans than outgroup partisans. This is the element of social-distance bias that comes from policy-based disagreement. It is not based in strong partisanship.

In the third column, however, social-distance bias is predicted for a very strongly identified partisan with the most moderate and unconstrained issue positions, and the sense that these issues are unimportant. This person is predicted to exhibit slightly more social-distance bias than the weak partisan who cares a great deal about issues. Even when policy does not matter at all, a strong partisan is still about 29 percentage points more willing to spend time with ingroup partisans than with outgroup partisans, an 8 percentage point increase over the weak partisan who feels strongly about issues (though this difference does not reach statistical significance). This is the portion of social-distance bias that is not entirely based in policy. A person who doesn't care at all about issues is unlikely to be worried about starting a political argument with an outgroup partisan. She or he simply does not want to spend time with someone outside the group.

The fourth column predicts the social-distance bias of a strong partisan with very strong, important, and constrained issue positions. This person is 55 percentage points more willing to spend time with ingroup partisans than with outgroup partisans. The combined effect of partisanship and issue positions is larger than the additive effect of each one taken separately. When strong rational disagreements are combined with a strong group-based psychological bias, people begin to demonstrate the "loathing" that Iyengar, Sood, and Lelkes (2012) have described. This social distance between Republicans and Democrats, however, is not entirely seated in policy disagreement. To a large extent, simply feeling part of a partisan group is driving people apart. The discriminatory intergroup behavior is partly based, as Tajfel predicted, on "real conflict of 'objective' interests between the groups" but also driven by "attempts to establish a positively valued distinctiveness for one's own group." Partisans prefer their own kind. It just feels right.

Of course, American politics wasn't always quite so reactive to these deeply rooted identities. There was a time when partisans found paths toward compromise, despite their natural inclinations toward ingroup triumph. Though partisan identity has always driven partisans to want to win, this victory hasn't always been such a powerful motivator of political behavior. And though partisans have always preferred their own party, they have not always felt as socially distant from outgroup partisans as they have in recent years. Iyengar, Sood, and Lelkes (2012) showed that less than 5 percent of partisans in 1960 were opposed to their children marrying outgroup partisans. Part of the reason for the subsequent increase is that the number of strongly affiliated partisans has risen. In 2012, 38 percent of Americans called themselves strong partisans versus 22 percent in 1974. But partisans today are not only more strongly affiliated. They are also, as I discussed in chapter 3, more socially similar to other members of their own party than they have been in decades. It is reasonable to expect that, as long as there are parties, partisans will want their party to win. The extent of that desire, and the extent to which it eclipses concrete policy outcomes, depends on not just party identities but the other social identities that have gathered around our two parties. The simple effects of partisan identity on our political perceptions are amplified when those party identities are joined by other social-group divisions.

A Frightful Despotism

George Washington, in his farewell address of 1796, warned the new nation about "the expedients of party." He was concerned that if the nation divided itself into distinct parties, the priorities of the new government would focus on those parties, rather than on loyalty to the nation itself. He called this partisan loyalty "a frightful despotism." Washington's worry grew out of his experience observing human nature, and noting the natural inclination toward factionalism that seemed to be always close to the surface of political interaction. He warned that this factionalism, once set in motion, could cause citizens to misrepresent the opinions of other citizens, and could cause fellow citizens to consider each other as enemies, even as the nation itself was struggling to form.

The data presented in this chapter would do little to reassure Washington that partisanship has not done exactly what he predicted. However, while American partisanship has existed since Washington left office, the current brand differs in nature from what Washington may have expected. This is because the factionalism that Washington feared is not only applicable to partisan teams. People form factions in all sorts of dimensions. We have long known that religion, race, and even sports-team affiliations have driven people into factions, set against each other along a dividing line. Partisanship may be necessary for government to organize and assist its citizens in decision-making. The problem arises when partisanship implicitly evokes racial, religious, and other social identities. As the sorting of the previous chapter occurs, parties become increasingly socially homogeneous. It is this social dimension of the partisan divide that makes it far easier for individual partisans to dehumanize their political opponents.

Social contact and shared social identities are the things that allow individuals to understand each other and tolerate differences in opinion. As those connections grow scarce, the effects of party no longer affect parties alone. Partisan battles become social and cultural battles, as well as political ones. The social homogenization of parties reduces room for compromise and increases the importance of simple party victory. The brand matters more than the good of the nation. This is what George Washington was concerned about, and it is now increasingly visible as American social identities reinforce the partisan divide.

FIVE

Socially Sorted Parties

The recent increases in levels of partyism shown in the previous chapter are not rooted solely in increasing practical disagreements. Partisans do not need to hold wildly extreme political attitudes in order to grow increasingly biased against their opponents. Partisanship alone cannot tell the whole story either. It turns out that one essential factor driving partisan prejudice is a set of well-sorted political identities.

The social psychologist Marilynn Brewer and her colleagues noticed a few years ago that, while there was plenty of evidence of the psychological effects of a single social identity, little research existed that explained how exactly our social identities work *together*. After all, none of us has just one social identity. A strongly identified Democrat or Republican is also a member of any number of other social groups. Each partisan could also identify as a woman, a conservative, a Christian, a runner, a football fan, a graduate of their particular college or high school; the list is endless. Brewer and her colleagues therefore decided it was important to examine the psychological effects of holding multiple social identities (Roccas and Brewer 2002).

When they asked people to think about how much their various social identities overlapped, they found a large difference between the thinking of people with highly aligned identities and the thinking of people with very unaligned identities. Identities are aligned when a large portion of the members of one group are (or are believed to be) also members of the other group. When multiple identities align, Brewer and her colleagues found, people are less tolerant, more biased, and feel angrier at the people in their outgroups. As an example, people who are Irish and Catholic (highly aligned national and religious identities) are more likely to be intolerant of non-Irish people than are people who are Irish and Jewish (relatively unaligned national and religious identities).

This is because a person with two highly aligned social identities sees outsiders as very different from herself. Her understanding of who she is will be constrained, and the list of the identities that define her feels smaller. On the other hand, when a person holds two social identities that are unaligned, outside groups seem more approachable. A person with cross-cutting identities feels that she is defined by a broad range of groups, and this makes her more tolerant toward groups that aren't exactly like her. An Irish-Jewish person will feel closer to non-Irish people than an Irish-Catholic person will.

The intolerance generated by a set of aligned identities can also come simply from lack of exposure to people unlike oneself. According to Allport's intergroup contact hypothesis, interaction between members of different groups can, under the right circumstances, reduce prejudice against those outgroups. A homogeneous set of social identities reduces the chance for that outgroup exposure. In fact, Diana Mutz found in 2002 that cross-cutting political identities *do* reduce intolerance toward outgroups by giving people the "capacity to see that there is more than one side to an issue, that a political conflict is, in fact, a *legitimate* controversy with rationales on both sides" (Mutz 2002, 122). Without this exposure to members of the political outgroup, it becomes far easier to view opponents with prejudice and their values as illegitimate. Thus, even as increasing numbers of Americans call themselves political independents, they tend to maintain partisan allegiances, as the social identities connected to the parties remain intact (Klar and Krupnikov 2016).

A lack of exposure to other ideas and people can make other ideas seem extreme and other people seem totally foreign, even when they are not. This includes both an intolerance of the policy positions of the other side and, more basically, an intolerance of the increasing strangeness of the outsiders. It can make a relatively moderate person intolerant of other views. The response is based on the strength and alignment of the identities, not the content of the identity-linked issue positions. This type of intolerance does not require partisan identities to correspond to highly extreme policy opinions. Even when our policy opinions remain relatively moderate, the alignment between our partisan and other identities can drive us toward prejudice against our opponents.

Magnified Ingroup Bias

The gradual sorting of partisans into the "correct" parties during the last fifty years has transformed a nation of cross-cutting partisan identities into a nation of increasingly aligned partisan identities. As Democrats and Republicans grow socially sorted, they have to contend not only with the natural bias that comes from being a partisan but also with their own growing intolerance, sharpened by the shrinking of their social world. A conservative Democrat will feel closer to Republicans than a liberal Democrat would. A secular Republican will feel closer to Democrats than an evangelical Republican would. The sorting of our parties into socially distinct groups intensifies the partisan bias that we've always had. This is the American identity crisis. Not that we have partisan identities, we've always had those. The crisis emerges when partisan identities fall into alignment with other social identities, stoking our intolerance of each other to levels that are unsupported by our degrees of political disagreement.

In the previous chapter, I looked at feelings toward the two parties as an example of the emergence of partisan prejudice. Partisanship alone, in those models, was capable of driving identity-based prejudice. Independent of policy positions, partisans like their own party better than the other party. This is not surprising, but it is also not an unbiased choice.

In this chapter, however, I look at the added effect of a well-sorted partisan identity. As other identities fall into alignment with party, partyism only grows stronger. The other party seems more distant to a partisan, and it becomes easier to dislike them. I use the same measures of partisan prejudice—warmth bias and social-distance bias—so that the contribution of sorting will be clear. Sorting can be thought of in two different ways. The traditional understanding in political science is that sorting is simply the alignment between party and ideology. I argue that a number of additional social identities can be involved as well, as was demonstrated in chapter 2. In order to provide a thorough picture of the effects of sorting, I include both types of sorting here—simple ideological sorting and the more complex social sorting.

Warmer Feelings

In order to look at the added effect of sorting, I first examine only strong partisans. Although most people are not strong partisans, those who are most committed to their parties provide the strongest test for the effects of sorting. We know that strong partisans will be the most biased against the outgroup party, but if their ideological or other social identities are aligned with that strong partisan identity, can their partisan bias grow even larger? It turns out that it can.

In figure 5.1, I show the predicted difference in feeling-thermometer ratings between the two parties, controlling for political knowledge, education, race, gender, income, age, and church attendance.[1] Importantly, the regres-

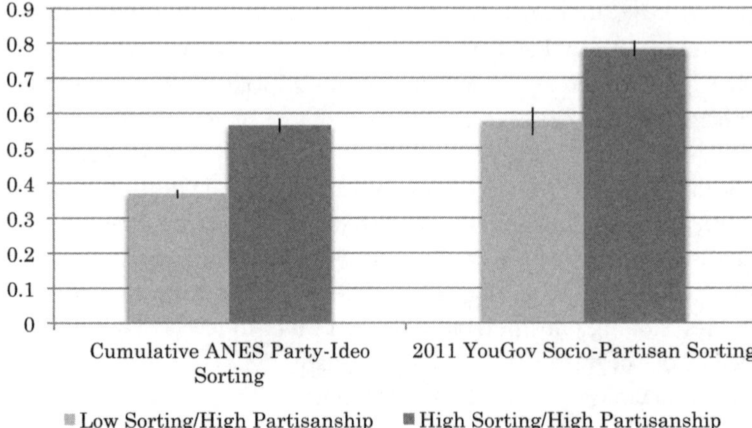

Figure 5.1. Predicted values of partisan prejudice (warmth bias) among strong partisans across levels of sorting

Note: Bars represent predicted values of warmth bias at varying levels of partisan-ideological sorting in the ANES models and social sorting in the YouGov model, controlling for issue extremity and constraint, political knowledge, education, race, gender, income, age, and church attendance. Originating regressions are shown in appendix table A.4. Ninety-five percent confidence intervals are shown. ANES samples are fully weighted. The low sorting score in the ANES models is not zero but 0.0857, the lowest sorting score possible given a strong partisan identity. In the YouGov sample, the lowest possible value of the social-sorting scale among strong partisans is 0.4286, and this is therefore the low sorting value used.

sions used to generate these predicted values also control for the extremity and constraint of policy positions,[2] so the intensity of policy attitudes about abortion, gay marriage, health care, race, immigration, defense spending, government spending in general, the importance of the deficit versus unemployment, and the degree to which they are all ideologically consistent is unchanging. I also constrain partisan identity to be as strong as it can be. The two bars in each cluster, therefore, are demonstrating the difference between a strong partisan with cross-cutting identities and a strong partisan with well-sorted identities. The only difference between the two bars is the level of sorting. This way, the added effect of sorting, above the regular effects of partisanship, is made clear. The two clusters of columns show the difference between sorted and unsorted partisans in two separate data sets.[3]

ANES Results

In the first column of figure 5.1, all of the American National Election Studies data from 1972 to 2012 are combined, showing a general picture of partisan prejudice averaged over the last few decades. In these data, sorting is measured as the alignment between party and ideology, both measured using the seven-point scale traditionally used in the ANES.[4] The partisan-ideological sorting score is calculated by taking the difference between the party and ideology scores, reverse-coding that difference, then multiplying it by the rated strength of each identity (i.e., lean, weak, strong). The sorting variable is coded to range from 0 (weakest and least-aligned identities) to 1 (strongest and perfectly aligned identities). In the cumulative file sample, a strong partisan with a cross-cutting ideological identity is predicted to rate the two parties about 37 degrees apart. However, add a strong and matching ideological identity, and the two parties all of a sudden have 56 degrees of warmth separating them. On a scale of 0 to 100, this is a large difference, and it is also statistically significant (the 95 percent confidence intervals are shown). Once the predicted difference between the two parties' feeling thermometers rises above 50, the respondent must be, to some extent, feeling coolly toward one party and warmly toward another. Even if one party is given a thermometer rating of zero (coldest), a 51 degree difference would put the other party at 51 degrees (on the warm side of the scale). There is no room for analogous feelings when the two parties are separated by more than 50 degrees. The addition of a sorted ideological identity, even when nothing else changes, causes a strong partisan to prefer his or her own party by 20 more degrees than partisanship alone can account for.

YouGov Results and the Social-Sorting Measure

The second cluster of bars is drawn from the 2011 YouGov study, which included the four-item social identity scale to measure partisan identity (described in chapter 4) and social-identity-based measures of six other identities, including liberal, conservative, secular, evangelical, black, and Tea Party.[5] This is a far more powerful measure of sorting than the simple partisan-ideological sorting used in the ANES analyses[6] and a far more powerful measure of partisan identity. It is created to assess the feeling described as early as 1961 by V. O. Key, who said, "A person may have so intimate an identification with the Republican Party that when it is assaulted he cringes as if he had been attacked personally" (219). This type of attachment is assessed by the social identity measure, and it is assessed for all of the identities listed.

The sociopartisan sorting scale is designed to (1) assess the objective alignment between a respondent's social identities, while (2) accounting for the subjective strength of those identities. This is done because the alignment between identities means nothing if a person does not identify with one or more groups. The objective alignment of these various identities is determined by linking each nonparty identity to one of the two parties according to connections found in prior research and verified by examining the mean level of each identity for each party separately in the data. Aligned identities are found to be, for the Democratic Party, liberal, secular, and black identities, and, for the Republican Party, conservative, evangelical, and Tea Party identities.

The social-sorting scale is constructed so that, for each party, aligned identities are coded with positive values while unaligned identities are coded negatively. The mean of the identity scores is then taken for each party, with aligned identities increasing the total value and unaligned identities decreasing the final score. The party-specific scores are gathered into one measure, recoded to range from 0 to 1, with 0 representing consistently weak or totally unaligned identities, and 1 representing the strongest, most consistently aligned identities.[7] This is an additive scale, rather than an interactive model, because here I am not interested in what happens when one identity moves while the others are held constant. Instead, this measure is constructed to allow all of the identities to move in relation to each other, generating varying sorting scores.

Using the social identity scale generates stronger results than the seven-point scales available in the ANES. In figure 5.1, the strong partisan in the YouGov data whose ideological, racial, and/or religious identities are in conflict with his or her party still feels 58 degrees of difference between the inparty and the opposing party. This person already feels warmly toward one party and coolly toward the other. Even this powerful effect of partisanship, however, can be strengthened by adding a set of well-sorted social identities. Once this strong partisan is socially well sorted, the difference between the two parties rises to 78 degrees. This means that, even if the inparty is placed at the warmest possible location on the thermometer, the opposing party is nearly 30 degrees colder than a neutral evaluation.

The effect of sorting across both data sets is to increase the biasing effects of partisan identity, even when nothing else changes, including policy extremity and constraint. This means that as the country grows more sorted, our ability to judge each other fairly is diminished. Even if we can find realistic policy solutions that we could all agree on, the alignment of our social identities behind our parties can generate its own animosity and partisan bias.

The Role of Issues

In figure 5.1, issue positions were held constant, but what role do issues play as our identities pull us apart? In figure 5.2, I look only at the YouGov data, due to their superior measurement possibilities, and I replicate the sorting effects versus the partisanship effects across three levels of issue-position extremity.[8] At low issue extremity, people have consistently moderate policy attitudes, and they consider those issues to be unimportant. At mean issue extremity, people are generally representative of the average American's policy attitudes and their sense of the importance of those policies. At high issue extremity, people have very extreme policy attitudes that they consider to be highly important.

Again, when partisanship is strong but combined with cross-cutting social identities, levels of bias are significantly lower than when a strong partisan identity is well aligned with other party-linked identities. But even more importantly, this is true across all three levels of issue-position extrem-

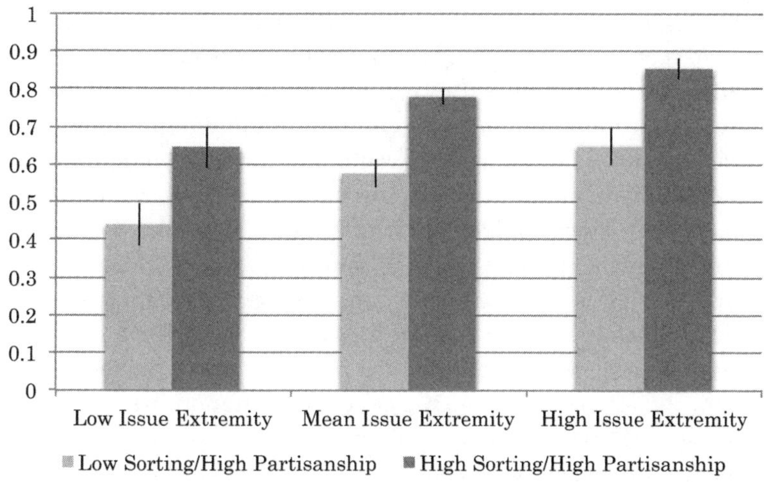

Figure 5.2. Predicted values of partisan prejudice (warmth bias) among strong partisans across levels of sorting and issue polarization

Note: Bars represent predicted values of warmth bias at varying levels of social sorting in the YouGov 2011 sample, across three levels of issue extremity, controlling for issue constraint, political knowledge, education, race, gender, income, age, and church attendance. Originating regression is shown in appendix table A.5. Ninety-five percent confidence intervals are shown. The lowest observed value of the social-sorting scale among strong partisans is 0.4286, and this is therefore the low sorting value used. The mean value of issue extremity is 0.65 (the median, not shown here, is 0.67).

ity. At every level of issue extremity, a cross-cutting set of identities reduces the partisan bias of a strong partisan by about 20 degrees on the feeling thermometer. Though overall bias is lower when issue extremity is low compared to when issue extremity is high, the difference between sorted partisans and unsorted partisans is significant no matter whether issue positions are extreme or moderate. This means that even in the moderate center of the electorate, where partisans from both sides find common ground on issues, a sorted identity is capable of driving citizens to feel increasingly warmly toward their own party and coolly toward their partisan opponents. The moderation of their policy attitudes does not protect them from the biasing effects of social sorting. However, a cross-cutting set of identities combined with a moderate set of issue positions does appear to be the only condition in which a strong partisan might place both parties on the same end of the feeling thermometer.

Matching

The previous tests looked at the effect of sorting among strong partisans. But this doesn't demonstrate the full effect of sorting in the electorate as a whole. Most citizens, after all, are not strong partisans. Another way to look at the effect of sorting on feelings of warmth is to account for the full range of sorting and to test it very strictly using a method called matching. Matching is a particularly strong test of the effect of sorting because it takes a large sample of people (here the full cumulative ANES file including 2012) and simulates the random assignment of sorting[9] to the population. In essence, this method makes it possible to pretend that each respondent is part of an experiment in which they are randomly assigned to a level of sorting. It does this by matching as many respondents as possible so that they are nearly identical in their ideology, issue extremity, political knowledge, education, age, sex, race, geographical location, and religiosity. This group of matched respondents is then divided into two groups, with the only measured difference between them being the level of sorting, either low or high, depending on whether respondents score above or below the median value of sorting.[10]

Once the matched sample is divided into low and high levels of sorting, I look at the differences between them in how warmly they feel toward the two parties. Because of the exact matching, a simple difference in means on the matched data can reveal whether sorting has a measurable effect on partisan prejudice. Little else can influence changes in partisan prejudice because the respondents are constrained to be essentially identical in all other aspects observed.

To find any effect of sorting at all on people who are identical in their education, political knowledge, age, sex, race, location, religiosity, issue-position extremity,[11] and ideological identity would be a powerful outcome, particularly because people who are highly sorted are generally demographically *different* from those who are unsorted. It would be unlikely to find, in the general population, people who are identical in these multiple demographic and social domains divided evenly between cross-cutting and sorted identities. More likely is that the types of people who hold well-aligned ideological and partisan identities are similar to each other in levels of education, knowledge, religiosity, and issue-position extremity and different from those with cross-cutting identities. These other social similarities would likely drive sorted individuals to hold even more partisan bias than what is observed here. If sorting has any effect on the partisan feelings of these matched and evenly divided individuals, it is likely an underestimate of the effect in the population as a whole.

In figure 5.3, the samples are matched on ideology (and the abovementioned variables), while the extent to which partisan identity is aligned with that ideological identity is varied. Ideologically identical people (in both identity and issue positions) are significantly more biased in their assessments of the two parties when their partisan identity is strong and in line with their ideological identity. The mean warmth bias score for a person with an inconsistent partisan identity is a difference of 27 degrees between

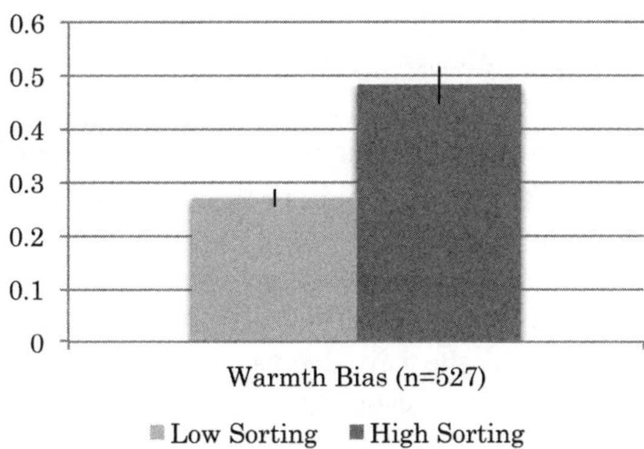

Figure 5.3. Difference in warmth bias by sorting in matched samples
Note: Respondents are matched on ideology, issue extremity, political knowledge, education, age, sex, race, geographical location, and church attendance. The only observed difference between the two bars is the degree to which party identity aligns with ideological identity. Bars represent the mean level of warmth bias for each group. Ninety-five percent confidence intervals are shown.

the two parties, while an otherwise similar person with a consistent partisan identity rates the parties 48 degrees apart. Moving from unsorted to sorted increases the difference in feelings toward the two parties by 20 degrees, even among people who are otherwise identical in multiple domains.

As partisanship moves into alignment with ideological identity, even when little else changes, partisan prejudice increases. People who are identical in their demographics, knowledge, issue positions, and ideological identity become significantly more biased when their party is aligned with their ideology. As the partisan rift in the American electorate falls into line with an ideological rift, average citizens are finding the opposing party increasingly different, unlikeable. Even when these citizens have a great deal in common, sorting alone is able to drive their opinions of the two parties apart.

Friends and Neighbors

It isn't only our feelings of warmth toward the political parties that are polarized by sorting. As the previous chapter showed, our feelings toward our fellow citizens are just as vulnerable to the prejudice that comes out of a highly sorted set of political identities. And again, just as in the case of warmth bias, our social bias against spending time with outgroup partisans is only strengthened by adding a set of sorted identities to our partisan loyalties. Figure 5.4 uses the YouGov data again to demonstrate the effects of social sorting, issue extremity, and constraint on individuals who are already strong partisans. Once again, though the level of policy-attitude extremity and constraint does make a difference in general levels of social-distance bias, it cannot eliminate the socially divisive effects of social sorting.

In figure 5.4, partisans with cross-cutting identities who care little about policy outcomes and have no ideological constraint (but are nonetheless strong partisans) are predicted to report a 21 percentage point difference in their willingness to be socially involved with members of the two parties (first set of bars). However, if that same strong partisan—the one who doesn't care much about any issues—also identifies with racial and religious social groups aligned with the party, that partisan is predicted to be 36 percentage points more willing to spend time with members of their own party than with members of the outgroup party. This is a person who holds moderate positions on abortion, gay marriage, immigration, health care, and the deficit and unemployment, considers all of these issues to be unimportant, and demonstrates no ideological bent one way or the other. Party-matched racial and religious social identities make a 15 percentage point difference in the social tolerance of ingroup and outgroup partisans. This social dis-

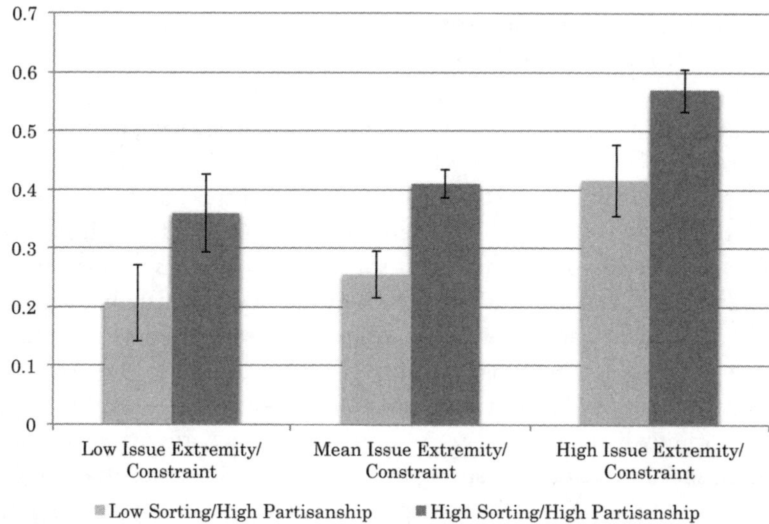

Figure 5.4. Predicted social-distance bias by social sorting
Note: Bars represent predicted values of social-distance bias at varying levels of social sorting in the YouGov 2011 sample, across three levels of issue positions, controlling for political knowledge, education, race, gender, income, age, and church attendance. Originating regression is shown in appendix table A.6. Ninety-five percent confidence intervals are shown. The lowest observed value of the social-sorting scale among strong partisans is 0.43, and this is therefore the low sorting value used. Social distance scale ranges from 0 (no difference in willingness to interact socially with members of the two parties) to 1 (maximal difference in willingness to interact socially with members of the two parties). There is a significant interaction between issue extremity and constraint in this model, so both variables are included, both set at their minimum, mean, and maximum values for each set of predicted values.

comfort is unlikely to be due to worries about policy arguments, these individuals do not have strong opinions about any of the issues measured here. When issues don't matter, the alignment of racial and religious social identities behind a partisan identity can make the difference between a welcoming neighbor and a hostile one.

Even when a person cares somewhat about the issues measured, when they hold a set of well-aligned identities they are still less comfortable around outgroup partisans. In fact, those with mean levels of issue extremity and constraint are not statistically different from those who do not care about issues. These moderate partisans with cross-cutting identities (in the second set of bars) are about 15 percentage points more comfortable spending time with outparty (versus inparty) members than are the partisans with well-aligned social identities. A moderate involvement with policy outcomes generates the same social distance as nonengagement with these policies; the major effect is between those partisans who hold cross-cutting identities and those who are socially sorted. Almost regardless of policy attitudes, social sorting is associated with a social distancing of outgroup partisans.

Among those who hold consistently extreme and constrained issue positions that they consider to be extremely important (the third set of bars), the difference between an unsorted and a sorted set of identities has essentially the same effect that it has at other levels of issue engagement, but general levels of social distance are higher. The difference between cross-cutting and socially sorted identities increases social distance by about 15 percentage points, once again. This 15 percentage point difference, however, begins at a significantly higher level of social distance. Strong partisans with cross-cutting social identities but strong and constrained issue positions prefer to spend social time with the inparty rather than the outparty by about 41 percentage points. Add a set of well-sorted racial and religious social identities, and this preference difference increases to 57 percentage points. The effect of strong and constrained issue positions, then, is to increase the total level of social distance between partisans but not to alter the effect of social sorting at all.

All of this means that highly sorted partisans will be biased against their outparty friends, neighbors, and romantic interests no matter what they think about political issues. Not only that, but strong partisans with cross-cutting identities will demonstrate the most tolerance toward their political opponents. If any grounds can be found for political harmony in American politics, it will not be the common ground of shared policy opinions. One robust force for political harmony appears to be an increasingly rare set of cross-cutting political identities rather than a moderate set of issue positions. Even in a group of partisans who all hold moderate, conflicting issue positions, a set of sorted identities will drive them to dislike and avoid contact with their friends and neighbors from the outgroup party. And even among those strong partisans who care a great deal about issues, they are more likely to be socially tolerant of other partisans if their racial and religious identities do not match their party. The increasing levels of social sorting described in chapter 3 are encouraging Americans to avoid social contact with members of the opposing party. The more socially sorted American partisans become, the more they will want to pull away from one another. This outcome goes beyond the simple effect of partisan identity. Partisanship can drive significant levels of partisan prejudice, but, when our social identities line up behind our parties, our prejudices expand beyond what partisanship can do on its own. Social sorting, in other words, links our racial and religious prejudice directly to our partisan preferences and allows our political opinions to be driven by increasingly social divides.

This is one source of the political acrimony that characterizes so much of contemporary American politics. We are not dealing with normal partisan bickering. The sorting of American social identities into partisan teams has magnified the effects of ingroup bias and pulled American partisans apart. This social sorting has created, in essence, two megaparties, whose members dislike and avoid their political opponents, even when they live next door. While partisanship is not new in American politics, the social sorting that magnifies partisan prejudice is changing the power of partisan identity.

Sorting and Policy Bias

> The White House press starts from the premise: Is the President up or down today? Is this good politically or not good politically? There's far less interest in the substance of policy.
>
> —Mike McCurry, White House Press Secretary, 2014

The primacy of social sorting as a driver of partisan prejudice is not consistent with a common view of politics. The folk theory of representative democracy, named by Achen and Bartels (2016a), assumes that individual citizens choose to vote for a party because it best represents their own interests and values. The classic Downsian view of voting assumes that parties compete, in their policy positions, for the approval of the median voter, who is always voting in his or her self-interest (Downs 1957). In this view, the party that comes closest to the median policy attitude among all voters will win the majority of the votes. This premise requires that voters make choices based mainly on the policy positions of parties and their proximity to voters' own positions. Davis, Hinich, and Ordeshook, in 1970, wrote that "the fundamental process of politics is the aggregation of citizens' preferences into a collective—a social—choice . . . in which the social choice is a policy package which the victorious candidate advocates" (426). The "social choice" is seen as policy-based. Policy positions are, in this traditional view, the fundamental basis of politics and of voter decision-making.

This view of the centrality of policy attitudes among the citizenry is a highly optimistic view of American political thought. A large body of literature has found Americans' understanding of political policy debates to be sorely lacking.[12] Still, this is the way that many Americans tend to understand electoral contests and political battles. Democrats and Republicans are in a battle over health care, over abortion, over tax policy. The political fights in American politics are supposed to be *about* something.

An abundance of evidence, however, contradicts this view. Geoffrey Cohen, in 2003, found issue positions to be highly dependent on group and party cues. In an experiment in which he varied the policies of the two parties, liberals expressed support for a harsh welfare program and conservatives expressed support for a lavish welfare program when they were told that their ingroup party supported the policy. Notably, these respondents did not believe that their position had been influenced by their party affiliation. They were capable of coming up with explanations for why they held these beliefs. This result, in particular, casts doubt on the general perception expressed among partisans and pundits that our political evaluations are drawn entirely from the conviction of our issue opinions. In fact, issue positions appear to be quite slippery.

A Pew poll from June 2013 found that, under Republican president George W. Bush, 38 percent more Republicans than Democrats believed that NSA surveillance programs were acceptable, while under Democratic president Barack Obama, Republicans were 12 percent *less* supportive of NSA surveillance than Democrats. The question prompt was identical, the only difference was the party of the president. As in Cohen's experiment, it is likely that these voters, if asked, would have provided logical reasons for their change of heart. But, as Cohen experimentally demonstrated, the influence of party loyalty is capable of reversing a single person's well-argued issue position without them even realizing it.

Part of the reason that policy opinions are so vulnerable to partisan cues is that partisans tend to engage more in motivated reasoning when their social settings are more homogeneous (Klar 2014)—a condition that is more likely in more highly sorted groups (Mutz 2002). As we sort ourselves into socially uniform parties, we lose perspective on what we really believe and begin to simply defend the positions that our party takes. It is a self-defense mechanism that takes hold when our parties take up larger and larger parts of who we think we are. The more parts of our identities that are linked with our parties, the more the success of our parties becomes more important than any real policy outcomes.

This is why, when we judge the Democratic and Republican parties, our issue positions have become less consequential than our identities. In figure 5.5, predicted values of warmth bias are shown at varying levels of policy extremity[13] and constraint and then, separately, at varying levels of sociopartisan sorting. The difference between the two panels is telling. The bars repre-

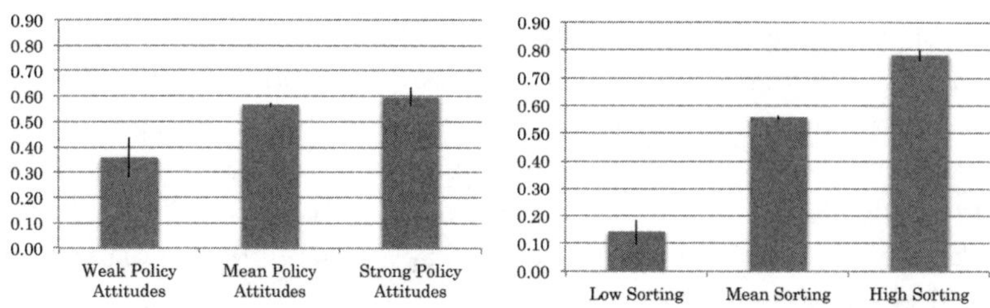

Figure 5.5. Predicted warmth bias by levels of social sorting and policy attitudes
Note: Bars represent predicted values of warmth bias (the difference between Democratic and Republican feeling thermometers) at varying levels of social sorting in the YouGov 2011 sample, controlling for political knowledge, education, race, gender, income, age, and church attendance. Originating regression is shown in appendix table A.7. Ninety-five percent confidence intervals are shown. Mean value of policy extremity is 0.66, of policy constraint is 0.56, and of social sorting is 0.71 out of 1.0.

sent the predicted distance between the Democratic and Republican feeling thermometers. In the first panel, levels of issue extremity and constraint are varied while all other variables are held at their means or modes. Policy attitudes do have a significant effect on feelings toward the two parties. People with the most extreme and constrained policy attitudes place the two parties 60 degrees apart, while those with the most moderate and unconstrained policy attitudes place the parties 36 degrees apart. The difference in our feelings toward the two parties grows by 24 degrees when we move from a total moderate who cares little about issues to an extreme ideologue who cares a great deal about issues.

This effect, however, is noticeably different from the effect of sorting shown in the second panel of figure 5.5. Those people with the most cross-cutting racial, religious, and partisan identities (and average policy attitudes) are predicted to place the two parties 14 degrees apart on the feeling thermometer. This is less than half the size of the partisan gap seen among those with the most moderate policy attitudes. A set of cross-cutting identities is much better than moderate issue positions at equalizing feelings toward the two parties. All else equal, the most moderate and unconstrained policy attitudes still allow a strong preference for one party over the other, while a set of cross-cutting identities is a truly moderating force in driving feelings toward the two parties. At the other end of the spectrum, a very well sorted person places the two parties 78 points apart. The difference in feelings toward the two parties grows by 64 degrees when we move from a set of cross-cutting identities to a set of well-sorted identities. The effect of sorting is nearly three times larger than the effect of issue extremity.

It shouldn't be much of a surprise that policy attitudes are less effective at changing feelings toward the two parties, considering that they seem to be relatively unreliable and vulnerable to identity-based influences. Since identity is at least partially responsible for the effect of policy attitudes on party evaluations, it makes sense that a direct measure of multiple party-linked identities would be a more direct way to determine the polarization of citizens' feelings toward the parties.

This does, however, fly in the face of the folk narrative about political polarization. Many media stories focus on the policy elements of partisan battles and present elections as referenda on public opinion about policies. Polls are examined to see what percent of America agrees with policies X, Y, and Z. Citizens assume that we have reasons for our opinions, and that parties win or lose based on our thoughtful choices. In fact, the data presented here reliably show that partisan identities and the social identities that line up behind them have a significant effect on our political judgments. Political scientists have long known that partisan identities can affect our policy attitudes and our feelings about political contests. What is new here is the idea that partisan identities are only part of the story. The sorting that has often been recognized as a simple realignment of identities has in fact been able to motivate substantially larger levels of partisan bias than partisanship alone could do.

When Americans decide how they feel about the Democratic and Republican parties, they only partially turn to an assessment of their own policy opinions. They are driven, substantially, by a need to maintain a positive distinctiveness for their own team. And as their team grows increasingly socially homogeneous, it becomes even more important for it to be the best. The opposing party becomes more distant and unfamiliar as our social identities line up behind our partisan identities. This makes it all the more important for partisans to see their own party as better than the other. Unfortunately, this is not normatively useful for democratic representation. The American system of democracy, as it grows increasingly socially polarized, will rely less on policy preferences and more on knee-jerk "evaluations" that should rightfully be called partisan prejudice.

Is This Polarization?

In the study of partisan polarization, a debate continues between two camps of political scientists. On one side, scholars such as Alan Abramowitz argue that the American electorate is polarizing at the level of the mass electorate and that this polarization is defined by American policy attitudes. On the other side, scholars such as Morris Fiorina claim that the American electorate is not exceptionally polarized in their policy preferences and that American polarization is therefore limited to our highly policy-polarized elites. What this debate overlooks is the behavior, emotions, and actions of the electorate, aside from their policy attitudes. This chapter demonstrates the robust presence of an ingrained prejudice that grows out of the increasing alignment between our partisan, ideological, racial, and religious social identities. This is a distinctly social phenomenon, unbound by the extremity of policy attitudes, but undeniably a sign of a polarizing electorate. Political scientists can disagree until we are blue in the face over the extent of America's policy polarization, but are citizens prejudiced in their evaluations of political opponents? Absolutely. Even when they can agree with them.

Looking at partisan polarization in a less policy-focused way allows us to discover many areas of American political life, including our political judgment, emotion, and actions, that don't necessarily correspond to policy extremism or polarization but are nonetheless present. Policy attitudes are said to be polarized when they can demonstrate an extreme and bimodal distribution of policy positions, with Democrats clustered on the extreme liberal end of the spectrum and Republicans clustered on the extreme conservative end of the spectrum. Abramowitz and Fiorina have been going over this territory repeatedly in the last few decades, so I will not enter this particular debate here. However, it is possible for Americans to be socially polarized even when their policy positions are not, or when those policy attitudes are relatively less polarized. A distinctly social type of polarization that includes political prejudice, anger, enthusiasm, and activism does exist, and it is being driven by political and social identities. An electorate that increasingly treats its political opponents as enemies, with ever-growing levels of prejudice, offensive action, and anger, is a clear sign of partisan polarization occurring within the citizenry. If issue positions do not follow precisely this pattern of behavioral polarization, it does not make those increasingly tribal partisan interactions irrelevant.

SIX

The Outrage and Elation of Partisan Sorting

> Trump has gotten voters who are so angry that they are willing to put their ideological concerns aside. We have never seen voters do that to this extent. They're saying, "We're so ticked off that that's the only message that matters."
>
> —Patrick Murray, pollster, 2016 (quoted in Goldmacher 2016)

In April of 2014, the federal Bureau of Land Management (BLM) attempted to round up and repossess a herd of cows belonging to a man named Cliven Bundy. Bundy grazed his cattle on federal land in Nevada, for which he was legally required to pay grazing fees. He had refused to pay these fees since 1993, claiming ownership of the land. By 2014, the BLM estimated that Bundy owed the federal government $1 million. As members of the BLM began to round up Bundy's cattle, some members of Bundy's family began protesting and confronting federal officials. Within days, a protest camp formed at Bundy's farm with a sign at the entrance reading "MILITA SIGHN IN" (Fuller 2014). Hundreds of self-identified members of armed militias gathered on Bundy's land, preparing for a violent battle against the federal employees. They dressed in paramilitary gear, set up illegal checkpoints, aimed their weapons at law-enforcement officials and federal employees, and threatened to bomb and kill people at local businesses (MacNab 2014). The story exploded in the national media, with conservative news sources praising Bundy as a hero, and liberal news sources calling him a terrorist and a "big fat million dollar welfare dead beat" (Vyan 2014).

Conservatives were outraged at the federal government's treatment of Bundy. And, with guns drawn, hundreds of militiamen joined Bundy in expressing their anger, if not outright rebellion, against the government. An attorney named Larry Klayman wrote in support of Bundy:

> Before these government goons do come back, let this message go forth. Barack Hussein Obama, Harry Reid and the gutless Republican establishment leaders in Congress who roll over to and further this continued government tyranny, We the People have now risen up and we intend to remove you legally from office. This country belongs to us, not you. This land is our land! And, we will fight you will [*sic*] all legal means, including exercising our legitimate Second Amendment rights of self-defense, to end your tyranny and restore freedom to our shores! (Klayman 2014)

The case of a local rancher who hadn't paid his taxes was quickly turned into a national fiasco, and a source of potent outrage among conservatives. How did Cliven Bundy so quickly become a national conservative icon? The answer—as Paul Waldman (2014) put it in the *Washington Post*—was that "when conservatives looked at Bundy . . . everything about him told them he was their kind of guy."

Bundy checked off many of the boxes that make up the Republican Party. A strong conservative, a white man, a rural southerner, he represented the convergence of the social identities that hold the Republican Party together. This convergence of identities made it much easier for Republicans to get angry on his behalf, and for Democrats to get angry at him. Conservatives, as they defended Bundy, did focus on a policy aspect of the conflict—the overreach of the federal government. But for many conservatives, particularly under Democratic president Barack Obama, the federal government, as Larry Klayman decried, had become more of an enemy—a set of "goons"—than the foundation of a policy position.

This sort of intense anger is not rare in modern American politics. In 2009, when Congress was debating what would eventually become the Affordable Care Act, town hall meetings across America erupted with angry outbursts. *Politico* reported, "Screaming constituents, protesters dragged out by the cops, congressmen fearful for their safety—welcome to the new town-hall-style meeting, the once-staid forum that is rapidly turning into a house of horrors for members of Congress" (Isenstadt 2009). At the same time, members of the Tea Party held angry protests in Washington. In 2011, in New York City, a liberal group calling themselves Occupy Wall Street protested against a number of economic, political, and social injustices. The New York protests spread to dozens of other cities and were described by the *New York Times* as "Countless Grievances, One Thread: We're Angry" (Lacey 2011). Turn on almost any cable news station during the last ten years, and you can find a political pundit expressing anger at a new political development.

Perhaps the pinnacle of all of this anger has been the unexpected success of the 2016 presidential campaign of Donald Trump. According to a 2016 Pew poll, the Americans who expressed anger at the government tended strongly to be Trump supporters. Trump is a fascinating case because, as a candidate, his policy positions were well known to be quite flexible, if not nonexistent.

In a 2016 *Washington Post* article, Philip Rucker and Dan Balz wrote, "Donald Trump fits no simple ideological framework. The presidential candidate collects thoughts from across the spectrum. Added together, however, his ideas represent a sharp departure from many of the Republican Party's values and priorities dating back half a century or more. . . . Trump's presidential candidacy has been described as a hostile takeover of the Republican Party. In reality it appears more a movement that threatens to subsume the GOP behind a menu of ideas and instincts that might best be described as 'America Wins.'" In this sense, the Trump candidacy distilled perfectly what Tajfel found in his minimal group paradigm experiments. Winning grows increasingly important as identities grow stronger. To this point, Trump's support was also strongest among those voters who shared multiple Republican-linked identities (Mason and Davis 2016). These particularly include white and Christian identities. Trump's campaign did not tear the Republican Party apart; he spoke directly to the social groups that have aligned with the Republican Party in recent years, and he did so with little real policy content.

The alignment of multiple social identities can directly affect the degree of anger with which individuals respond to identity threats. As identities have moved into alignment in recent years, levels of anger at outgroup candidates have also increased. Though these are simply correlational trends, they serve to set up the story to come.

One crude way to examine average levels of anger over time is to look at one question asked by the American National Election Studies every year beginning in 1980. The item asks respondents whether each presidential candidate "has—because of the kind of person he is, or because of something he has done—made you feel angry." I coded this item so that it refers only to people's feelings of anger toward the outgroup candidate. The numbers in figure 6.1 represent the percentage of people who have reported feeling angry at the outgroup candidate in each presidential election year.[1]

This is a rough measure and fluctuates widely depending on the context of the election. For example, Barack Obama's 2008 Yes We Can campaign was generally oriented toward hope and change and was the first election

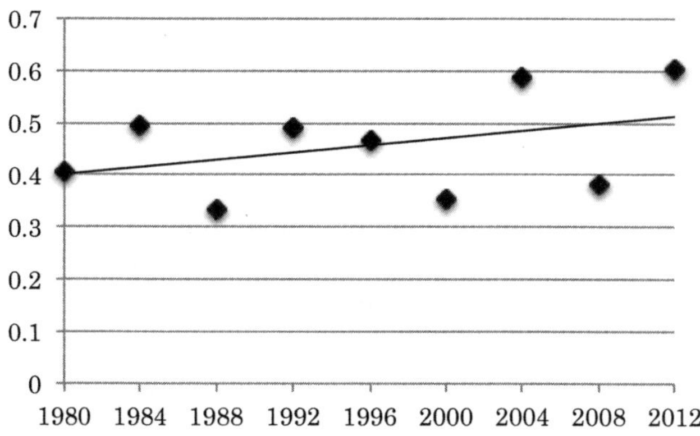

Figure 6.1. Anger toward the outgroup presidential candidate
Note: Data drawn from the weighted ANES cumulative data file, 1948–2012. Numbers represent the percentage of people who reported feeling angry at the outgroup presidential candidate, coded as a presidential candidate of the party that the respondent does not belong to. Question was first asked in 1980. Pure independents are excluded.

in which an African American was elected president. Republicans (those for whom Obama was the outgroup candidate), had little to openly express anger about. Not only did social norms against racism briefly tamp down open partisan rancor, but it was, after all, a Republican president who had only months before presided over one of the greatest financial disasters in national history. Republicans may have been angry, but in that moment they were not angry at the relatively unknown Barack Obama. (That would come later.)

In the same election, John McCain, the Republican, had a reputation as a centrist, party-bucking politician who could be relied upon to make compromises. Democrats (those for whom McCain was the outgroup candidate) therefore had little to hold against him personally. Their ire was reserved for the sitting president, George W. Bush, who held some of the lowest approval ratings of all time.

An earlier drop in anger had registered in the election of 2000, when voters famously saw little difference between the two major party candidates. But these relatively low-anger elections did nothing to reduce anger in the following elections. If anything, the low-anger elections worked as slingshots, pulling levels of anger down, only to shoot them back up in the following elections to unprecedented levels. Voters in recent years, when they do feel angry, feel angrier. In both 2004 and 2012, levels of anger reached 60

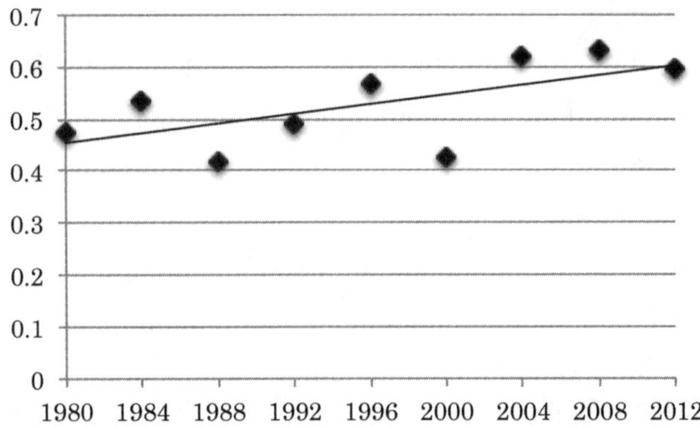

Figure 6.2. Enthusiasm for the ingroup presidential candidate
Note: Data drawn from the weighted ANES cumulative data file, 1948–2012. Numbers represent the percentage of people who reported feeling proud of the ingroup presidential candidate, coded as a presidential candidate of the party that the respondent does belong to. Pure independents are excluded.

percent of the partisan population for the first time since the measure was introduced in 1980.

In figure 6.1, the general trend over time is drawn as a straight line, which is moving upward, toward more anger. In 1980, 40 percent of partisans felt anger toward the opposing presidential candidate, and by 2012 that number had increased to 60 percent. Even accounting for fluctuations, the trend line indicates a 10 percentage point average increase in the proportion of people reporting angry feelings at their party's main opponent since 1980. The anecdotes of partisan rancor and vitriol don't seem to be simply isolated events. There has been a modest but increasing trend toward angrier American politics.

This is not the entire story, however. Americans are not only angrier at their political opponents, they are also happier with their own team's candidates. Figure 6.2 shows trends in the percentages of Americans who claim they have felt "proud" of their ingroup presidential candidate.

Just as in the case of anger toward the outgroup candidate, pride for the ingroup candidate is steadily, if noisily, rising. The general trend from 1980 to 2012 is a mean increase in pride of 12 percentage points. In the three presidential elections since 2000, around 60 percent of partisans felt proud of their presidential candidate, compared to numbers hovering around 50 percent in the decades before. So, just as Americans are growing increasingly angry at their opponents' candidates, they are growing increasingly enthusiastic about their own.

Combine this anger and pride in every presidential election, and we see a picture of an electorate that is increasingly emotionally reactive. As time progresses, American partisans are more likely to feel angry at their opponents and proud of their own candidates. We are priming the pump for a very energetic battle.

Why Are We So Emotional?

Where is all this emotion coming from? In fact, anger and enthusiasm can be understood as very natural reactions to the group-based competition and threats that partisans face on a regular basis. As elections grow longer—and political media coverage explains governing as a constant competition between Democrats and Republicans—partisans are inundated with messages that their group is in the midst of a fight for superiority over the outgroup. Every vote in Congress, then, has the potential to feel like a threat to an attentive partisan. These party threats are capable of motivating significant levels of both anger and enthusiasm in party identifiers, driven not simply by a dissatisfaction with potential policy outcomes or a potential policy victory, but by a much deeper, more primal psychological reaction to group competition.

Intergroup emotions theory (an outgrowth of social identity theory) has found that strongly identified group members react with stronger emotions, particularly anger and enthusiasm, to group threats (Mackie, Devos, and Smith 2000). According to this theory, group-based partisan bias leads strongly identified partisans to believe (correctly or not) that their party is the generally favored party—that Americans like them the best. The sense that the party is strong, enjoying collective support, increases their ability to feel anger and engage in confrontational behavior. This is because when the ingroup is perceived to be stronger than the outgroup, anger results from intergroup competition, while the perception of a weak ingroup leads to anxiety in the face of group competition. These are natural psychological reactions to group competition, driven not by practical thoughts about the concrete outcomes of an intergroup competition but by evolutionarily advantageous reactions to group competition and threat. A strong group is in a powerful position to react to threat with anger and offense, while a weak group is not. A weak group is expected to react to the same threat with anxiety. Partisan anger therefore is not only driven from a loss of tangible resources but also an outgrowth of natural offensive behavior that emerges from faith in the power of the ingroup and the aggressive tendencies that group allegiance allows.

Importantly, this emotional reaction depends on a threat to the status of the group. As identities grow stronger, anger only increases if the group is perceived to be under some kind of threat from the outgroup. Kevin Arceneaux and Martin Johnson in their 2013 book remind us that personalities on cable news shows "raise their voice in outraged frustration, badger hostile guests, and hurl insults at the other side. . . . The apparent goal is to steel and energize the in-partisans while taunting the out-partisans" (75). These types of partisan threats are present on cable news shows, in political commercials, in print media, and even, during election seasons, in simple polls. Status threats are potent emotional catalysts. Pierce, Rogers, and Snyder (2016) found that, in the week following the Democratic presidential victory in the 2012 election, Republicans felt significantly sadder than they had the previous week. But they weren't simply sad. They felt sadder than American parents felt in the week after hearing about the Newtown Shootings. They felt sadder than Bostonians in the week after the Boston Marathon bombing. Republicans, because their party had lost, reported feeling some extremely powerful negative emotions.

These negative reactions can, however, help to generate positive emotions as well. In 1994, Nyla Branscombe and Daniel Wann conducted a study in which they asked people to watch the movie *Rocky IV*. For some respondents, they altered the movie so that, in the end, Rocky is defeated by the Russian fighter, Ivan Drago. In this condition, those people who felt most closely identified with being American took severe hits to their own self-esteem. They felt very negatively about themselves after watching Rocky lose. But they were then given a chance to express their levels of distrust and dislike of Russians in general. Those who did this, who expressed many kinds of negative feelings about Russians, restored their self-esteem. These people felt better about themselves by making insulting judgments about their Russian outgroup. Imagine these effects, now, in terms of partisan competition. When partisans lose an election, they take a hit to their self-esteem, which is wrapped up in their partisan identity. One effective way of soothing this damage is to lash out at partisan opponents. It is this threat to self-esteem that drives partisan insults and rage, which lead to a consequent improvement in self-esteem. This is a cycle, in which threats to group status lead to angry and insulting reactions, which then lead to higher assessments of group status, which cause threats to have even larger effects. Our anger and enthusiasm are fueling each other.

Not only do strong identities push partisans to react to threats with anger and excitement but aligned identities add even more anger to every threat response. Sonia Roccas and Marilynn Brewer (2002) raised the possibility that those with highly aligned identities may be less psychologically equipped to cope with threats to group status. This is because a person with a highly sorted set of identities is more socially isolated and therefore less experienced in dealing with measured conflict. This can lead to higher levels of negative emotions when confronted with threat.

When multiple identities are strongly aligned, a threat to one identity affects the status of multiple other identities. The possible damage to a person's self-esteem grows as more identities are partnered with the damaged group. While stronger identities motivate increased anger and excitement in the face of group threat, more sorted identities have an even larger effect. We have more self-esteem real estate to protect as our identities are linked together.

Although anecdotal stories of political anger and fervor appear to be provoked largely by issues such as health-care reform, gay marriage, abortion, and taxation, social sorting can powerfully drive emotion, contrary to the popular perception that only practical disagreements trigger higher levels of political rancor. Because a highly sorted set of identities increases an individual's perceived differences between groups, the emotions that result from group conflict are likely to be heightened among well-sorted partisans, regardless of policy opinions.

Why Do Emotions Matter?

Before delving into the evidence for the social roots of emotions, it is important to examine why emotions matter in the first place. Anger and enthusiasm seem like politically important emotions, but why? And why focus on these two emotions in particular?

The study of emotion in political science is relatively new, and only recently has it been studied using rigorous empirical methods. One of the better-known theories of emotion in politics is affective intelligence theory, introduced by Marcus, Neuman, and MacKuen (2000). This theory argued that it was not sufficient to study the simple difference between positive and negative (valence) emotions and that far more information could be obtained if researchers looked at different types of emotions within each category—particularly in the category of negative emotions. They determined that the difference between anger and anxiety was significant, especially when looking at political behavior. The two types of negative emotions, in fact, can have opposite effects on judgment and action. Anxiety was found to lead to more thoughtful processing of information, while anger led to more reliance on easily available cues such as social identities. More recent research on anxiety by Albertson and Gadarian (2015) has found that anxious citizens do in fact search out more information, but they do so in a biased way, looking especially for threatening information. In any case, while anxious citizens tend to look for new information, angry and enthusiastic citizens do not.

A related body of research has found anger and enthusiasm to be particularly good at driving action. In 2011, Valentino and colleagues found that those who were angry were more inclined to sign political petitions, register other people to vote, participate in political protests, volunteer for a campaign, and donate money. Van Zomeren, Spears, and Leach (2008) discovered that a strong group identity increased collective-action tendencies via group-based anger. That is, when members of a social group (students) were presented with a threat (rising student fees), they reacted with anger, and this anger precipitated collective political action. Furthermore, Groenendyk and Banks (2014) found that feelings of enthusiasm increased citizens' likelihood of urging others to vote for a particular candidate, wearing a campaign button, attending political rallies, and donating to a candidate or party. Banks (2016) has found fascinating evidence that feelings of anger in white Americans push them to think in more racial terms. In other words, the anger that Banks observes is directly linked to (and occurs prior to) racial divisions into ingroup and outgroup categories. Nonracial anger pushes racially conservative individuals to think about race.

Combined with intergroup emotions theory, all of this research points to the idea that strong group identities and intergroup divisions facilitate increasingly angry and enthusiastic responses to group threats. While political enthusiasm is not usually thought of as problematic, it, along with anger, leads to increased political activity based not on policy goals but on knee-jerk identity-defense responses. The key point, for the purposes of this book, is that anger and enthusiasm are the primary emotional drivers of political action, and they are not drivers of thoughtful processing of information. The following chapter addresses the direct effects of social sorting on activism, but these emotions are important to examine on their own, as they are capable of provoking much of the action and judgment that contributes to current levels of social polarization. The difference between anxious and angry responses (though they are highly correlated in any given event) helps to explain how it is that partisans can grow increasingly divided even when their policy positions do not diverge. Anger is a powerful emotion that can drive group identifiers apart, reflexively. It is therefore important to examine the group-based drivers of both anger and enthusiasm, the two emotions that lead to relatively thoughtless political action.

Evidence from a Panel Study

Between 1992 and 1996, when partisan sorting was in flux, the ANES ran a panel study—interviewing the same people in 1996 that they had interviewed in 1992. In figure 6.3, I compare changes in anger at the outgroup candidate and issue intensity[2] among three groups of citizens—those whose level of partisan-ideological sorting increased, those whose level of sorting did not change, and those whose level of sorting decreased between 1992 and 1996.

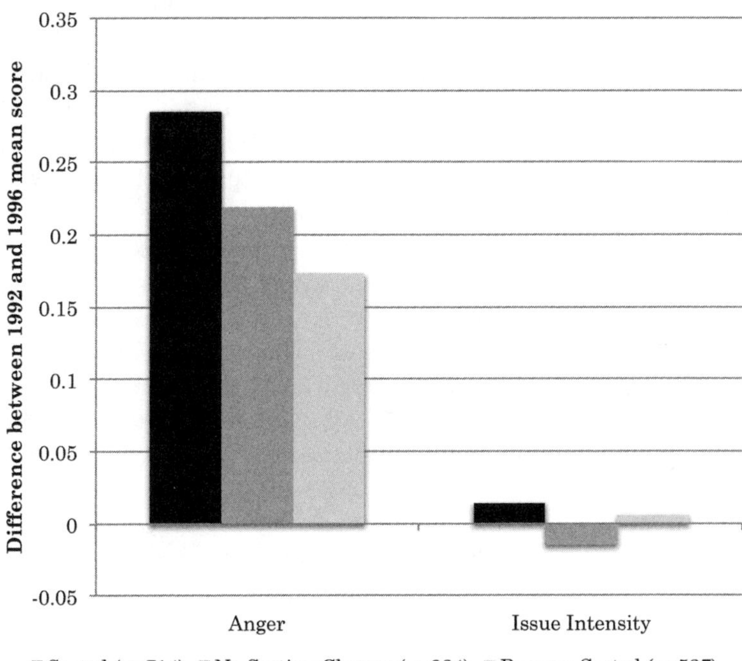

Figure 6.3. Change in anger and issue extremity between 1992 and 1996 by sorting
Note: Data drawn from the ANES 1992–1996 Panel Study. Demographic controls are not necessary as this is a reinterview of the same individuals. Sorting is limited to the partisan-ideological sorting measure, due to data limitations.

Among those people who became increasingly sorted between 1992 and 1996, reported anger at the outgroup candidate increased by 28 percentage points. In comparison, among those whose sorting did not change, anger increased by 22 percentage points, and those whose level of sorting decreased reported a 17 percentage point increase in feeling angry at the outgroup candidate. All three groups reported an increase in anger, which is at least partly contextual. In the intervening four years, Republicans had taken the majority of the House of Representatives for the first time in forty years, and a new partisan conflict between the Democratic president and the Republican House had heated up to the point of a government shutdown in 1995. There was a general feeling of mounting partisan discord. But, importantly, Americans didn't all get angry in the same way. The people whose partisan and ideological identities had moved into alignment were the ones whose anger increased the most. In comparison, when partisan and ideological identities had not moved toward alignment, people were less readily angered.

Was this anger all due to more potent policy attitudes among the increasingly sorted? Apparently not. Among the increasingly sorted, as their levels of anger increased by 28 percentage points, the intensity of their policy attitudes increased by only 1 percentage point. Not only did issue intensity remain essentially the same, its change was barely different from the issue-intensity changes of those whose sorting levels decreased. Those whose levels of sorting remained the same grew less intense by about 1 percentage point. The difference in anger between the sorted and reverse-sorted was 11 percentage points, while the difference in issue intensity between these two groups was less than 1 percentage point.

This pattern holds for both Democrats and Republicans. The only minor difference is that sorted Republicans grew more issue intense (increase of 0.12) than did Democrats (decrease of 0.05), but they also grew slightly less angered than Democrats did. Again, this does not support the idea that anger comes from issue intensity.

This is a picture of a nation whose partisan teams are raring to fight, despite an almost total lack of any substantive policy reasons to do so. It should be reiterated that the changes depicted here are changes among *the same people* over time. When a single person went through a process of aligning their partisan and ideological identities, they came out the other end angrier than they entered. More so than other Americans. Partisan-ideological sorting, without affecting policy extremism, generated significant changes in anger.

Sorting or Party Identity?

Is it possible that these effects of sorting on emotion can be explained by the effects of partisan identity alone? Not likely. Figure 6.4 looks once again at strong partisans in the cumulative ANES data, predicting their probability of feeling angry using logit models (see originating models in the appendix). Among these intense partisans, those who have cross-cutting ideological identities are certainly angry at the outgroup candidate. There is a 66 percent probability that a cross-pressured but strongly committed partisan will report feeling anger. However, once that strong partisanship is accompanied by a strong and well-aligned ideological identity, there is an 86 percent probability that they will report feeling anger. These are substantively and statistically significant differences.[3]

In an emotionally charged election, a simple change in the alignment of partisan and ideological identities has the power to increase the potential for anger by 20 percentage points. These models also are drawn from regressions in which race, gender, education, age, southern origin, urban origin, church attendance, and issue extremity and constraint are all held constant. Without any change in any of these characteristics, and even among the

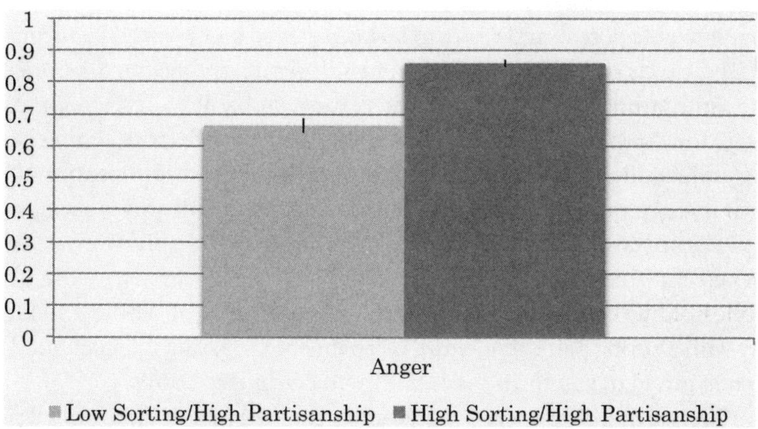

Figure 6.4. Predicted probability of feeling anger at the outgroup candidate
Note: Predicted probabilities drawn from a logit model using weighted ANES data from the cumulative file through 2012. Controls are included for issue extremity and constraint (and their interaction), education, sex, race, age, southern location, urban location, and church attendance. Originating regression is shown in appendix table A.8. Ninety-five percent confidence intervals shown.

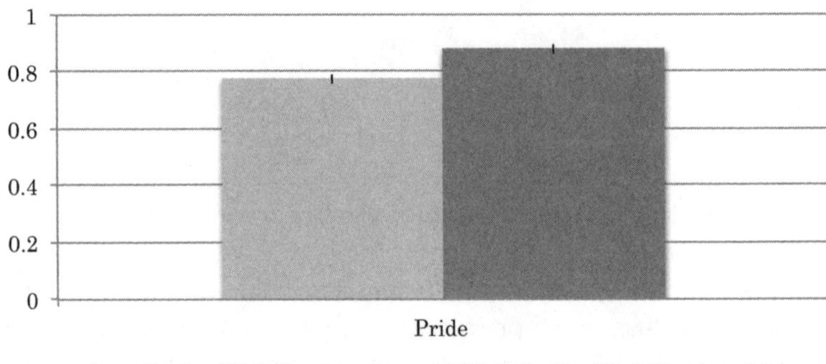

Figure 6.5. Predicted probability of feeling proud of ingroup candidate
Note: Predicted probabilities drawn from a logit model using weighted ANES data through 2012. Controls are included for issue extremity and constraint, education, sex, race, age, southern location, urban location, and church attendance. Originating regression is shown in appendix table A.8. Ninety-five percent confidence intervals shown.

strongest partisans, simply moving from a cross-cutting ideological identity to a sorted ideological identity can drive a significant increase in feelings of anger. This is a psychological response to the feeling that the party makes up a larger part of a person's social world. Once an ideological identity lines up behind a partisan identity, it becomes harder to understand opponents as reasonable people and easier to feel threatened and angered by them.

The effects on pride are smaller but still significant. Figure 6.5 presents the same strong partisans but predicts their probability of feeling proud about their own candidate. Among intense partisans with cross-cutting ideological identities, there is a 77 percent probability that they will feel proud of their ingroup candidate. However, once an ideological identity is strong and well aligned with this strong partisan identity, that probability increases to 88 percent. This difference, again, is statistically significant. Therefore, even while holding issue positions constant, simply aligning an ideological identity with a strong partisan identity is capable of increasing the likelihood of feeling proud of your own candidate by 10 percentage points.

Although the differences between cross-cut partisans and well-sorted partisans are relatively small in magnitude, they are significant, and they suggest something real about American politics. Even our strongest partisans have emotions that are kept slightly in check when their ideological identities are unaligned with their party. Once party and ideology move into alignment, as they have across large swaths of the American electorate, the likelihood that partisans are feeling angry and proud increases significantly. Sorting is pushing us into emotional territory that partisanship alone cannot.

Matching

Another way to examine the effect of sorting on emotion is to go back to the matched sample used in chapter 5. Using the same sample—comprising members nearly identical in ideological identity, issue extremity, education, age, sex, race, geographical location, and religiosity—I again split the sample into low and high levels of sorting. This time I looked at the differences between the groups in their reported levels of anger at the outgroup candidate. This is a challenging test because, although the people are constrained to be matched, the political context in each year is drastically different, causing a large variance in anger across the cumulative ANES sample, which spans from 1972 to 2012. Despite the contextual variation, these highly similar individuals, when averaged across time, tend to be significantly angrier at the outgroup candidate when their ideological identities are aligned with their partisan identities. This is true despite large confidence intervals. Figure 6.6 presents the results of this matching test.

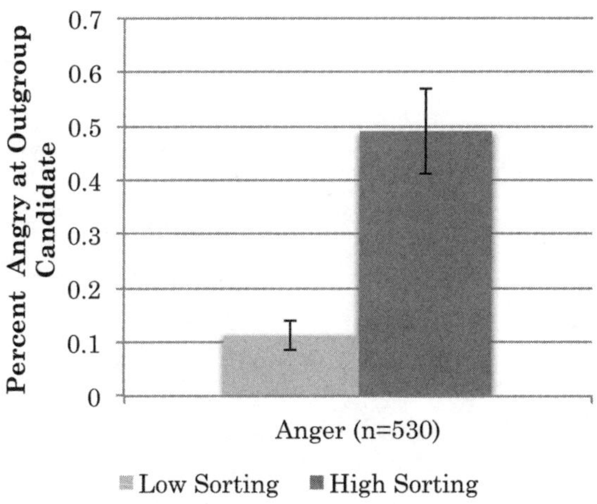

Figure 6.6. Percent angry at the outgroup candidate in matched sample
Note: Data drawn from ANES cumulative file through 2012. Ninety-five percent confidence intervals shown. Respondents matched on ideological identification, issue extremity, education, sex, race, age, southern location, and church attendance. Low sorting and high sorting are divided by cutting the sorting score at its median.

In this figure, ideologically matched people are significantly angrier at the outgroup candidate when their partisan identity is strong and aligned with their ideological identity. About 11 percent of people with cross-cutting partisan identities feel angry at the outgroup candidate, while 49 percent of the well-sorted sample reports feeling angry. This is a significant difference. Although they are quite similar in their characteristics, ideology, and political attitudes, those whose partisan identity is aligned with their matched ideologies are angrier, across the decades, than those whose partisan identities are unaligned with their matched ideologies. The alignment of these two identities is driving people to feel angrier, despite their agreement on policy outcomes and their similarity in every other measured way.

Looking at pride for the ingroup candidate offers a similar picture. In figure 6.7, the same matched sample is compared across levels of sorting. Once again, we see that across the years those individuals who are similar to each other in many ways, and differ in their level of partisan-ideological sorting, feel very differently toward their own party's candidates. Among those with cross-cutting partisan and ideological identities, only 14 percent report feeling proud of their own party's candidate. Move that party into alignment with ideology (again, an ideology matched across conditions), and 55 percent report feeling proud.

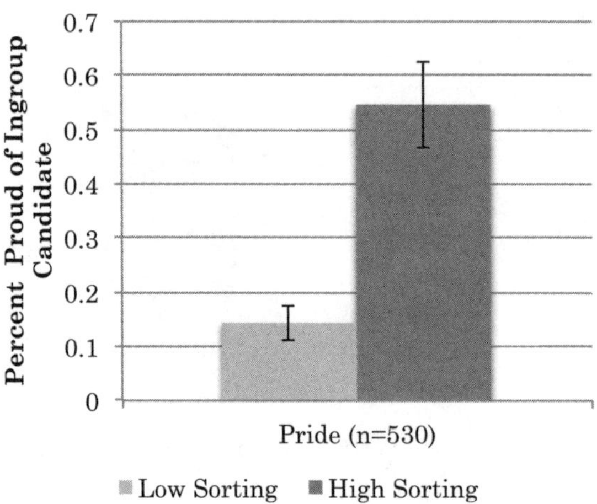

Figure 6.7. Percent proud of the ingroup candidate in matched sample
Note: Data drawn from ANES cumulative file through 2012. Ninety-five percent confidence intervals shown. Respondents matched on ideological identification, issue extremity, education, sex, race, age, southern location, and church attendance. Low sorting and high sorting are divided by cutting the sorting score at its median.

These differences are not only statistically and substantively significant, they are compelling because they occur among respondents that are as similar to one another as possible. Furthermore, though issue extremity is matched here, these models have been replicated using an issue-constraint measure instead, and the results support the same conclusions. Individuals who are similar on ideology and issue positions grow far more proud of their candidate when their party is well matched to their ideological identity, even though their beliefs do not differ. Partisan-ideological sorting is capable of encouraging an increasingly angry and enthusiastic electorate.

Evidence from an Experiment

Up until now, the effects of sorting on anger have only been demonstrated in the case of partisan-ideological sorting. Furthermore, all of the models presented above have measured anger as a simple yes/no response to a question regarding anger at the outgroup candidate, which a respondent must recall from memory. According to social identity theory and intergroup emotions theory, a threat is necessary for group identities to activate anger. The outgroup candidate is a good representation of a threat to group status. He or she is, after all, the embodiment of the party whose victory will mean an inevitable defeat for a partisan's own party. However, more precision in measuring both anger and threat is possible.

In the 2011 YouGov survey, I included an experiment in which respondents were randomly assigned to one of five conditions. Some respondents were asked to read a message that threatened their party. They were told it was taken from a political blog, but in fact I fabricated it based on a number of blog comments I had collected, in order to make the messages as comparable as possible. For Republicans, this message read:

> 2012 is going to be a great election for Democrats. Obama will easily win re-election against whatever lunatic the Republicans run, we are raising more money than Republicans, our Congressional candidates are in safer seats, and Republicans have obviously lost Americans' trust. Our current Congress is proving to Americans that Republicans do not deserve to be in the majority, and Americans will make sure they're gone in 2012. Finally, we'll take the Congress back and won't have to worry about the Republicans shutting down government anymore! I'm glad that Americans have finally returned to their senses. Republicans should get used to being the minority for the foreseeable future. Democrats will hold our central place in the leadership of the country. Obama 2012!!

For Democrats, the message read:

> 2012 is going to be a great election for Republicans. We're going to defeat the hardcore socialist Obama, we are raising more money than Democrats, our Congressional candidates are in safer seats, and Democrats have obviously lost Americans' trust. Our current Congress is proving to Americans that Democrats do not deserve to be in the majority, and Americans will make sure they're gone in 2012. Finally, we'll take the government back, and we won't have to worry about Democrats blocking us at every turn! I am so glad that Americans have finally returned to their senses. Democrats should not get used to running the government. Republicans will take back our central place in the leadership of the country. Defeat Obama in 2012!!

Other respondents were asked to read a "blog message" that threatened their party's cherished policy outcomes. For Republicans, this message read:

> 2012 is going to be a great election for responsible political ideas. After this election we can finally fix the economy using wise tax increases to pay for our indispensable social programs and infrastructure, so that we can create jobs instead of blindly throwing money to corporations and giving tax cuts to the millionaires who caused this mess. After this election we'll be able to improve the health care bill by adding a public option, make sure every woman has clear access to abortions, every child has a chance to learn evolutionary theory in school, and make it easier for all adults to get married if they want to, no matter who they are. Finally, our country will be on the right path again!

For Democrats, this message read:

> 2012 is going to be a great election for responsible political ideas. After this election we can finally fix the economy by enforcing personal responsibility, using a true free-market system to make sure people aren't handed more than they've earned. We'll be able to shrink the government and get it off our backs, and lower taxes so that hard-working people have a reason to work. After this election we'll be able to stop socialized medicine, prevent the abortions of innocent babies all over the country, bring God back into the public sphere, and make sure that we are a country that respects that marriage is between a man and a woman. Finally, our country will be on the right path again!

A fifth group did not read any message at all. The four messages were randomly assigned, so some Democrats would read the Republican threat message and some Republicans would read the Democratic threat message. When this occurred, I coded this as a message of support for the party.

After reading one of the messages, respondents were asked how the message had made them feel. They could answer A great deal, Somewhat, Very little, or Not at all to the following emotion items: Angry, Hostile, Nervous, Disgusted, Anxious, Afraid, Hopeful, Proud, and Enthusiastic. I combined their responses to the Angry, Hostile, and Disgusted items to form a scale of anger ($\alpha = 0.91$), and the Hopeful, Proud, and Enthusiastic responses to form a scale of enthusiasm ($\alpha = 0.93$). In comparison to the yes/no anger responses measured above, this measure created a scale of emotion that ranges relatively continuously from 0 to 1, creating much more variation in the amount of anger or enthusiasm a person could report.

Figure 6.8 illustrates the main effects of each experimental treatment on emotion. As expected, in the threat conditions, anger is substantially stronger than enthusiasm, and in the support conditions enthusiasm is the main result. The party-threat conditions included language that had the potential to generate stronger emotions than the issue conditions, but, as the data show, emotional reactions to the issue threats are relatively similar to the main emotional effects of party threats.

As in chapter 5, I measured sorting using the full social-sorting scale, including partisan, ideological, black, secular, evangelical, and Tea Party iden-

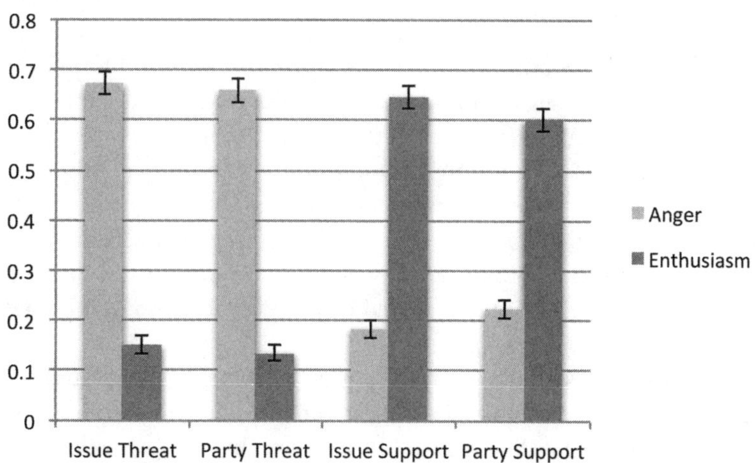

Figure 6.8. Main effects of experimental treatment
Note: Ninety-five percent confidence intervals shown. Bars represent mean levels of each emotion in each treatment, across the entire sample.

tities, measuring each, if present, using the four-item social-identification scale. This creates a much fuller measure of sorting by including multiple social identities that may come into play in determining how angry or enthusiastic each partisan can be.

I expected the most socially sorted partisans to be the most emotionally volatile. I thought they would react to the party-based threats with the most anger and to messages of support with the most enthusiasm. I also expected to find somewhat smaller results for partisan identity alone, and much smaller effects among those with the most extreme issue positions. In other words, I expected to see that a conglomeration of identities is most emotionally responsive to threat (particularly group-based threat), that one identity is slightly less so, and that a set of extreme issue positions generates the smallest emotional response to threat.

In order to give the issue positions a fair test, however, I included the threats that were devoid of partisan labels and only threatened policy outcomes. If anything were to anger those with strong issue positions, it should be these issue-based threats.[4] Furthermore, the issue measure used here accounts for not only issue extremity but also issue importance and issue constraint.[5] I refer to this measure as issue intensity, due to its inclusion of multiple elements of issue attitudes.[6]

Experimental Results

What I found was relatively consistent with expectations but also slightly surprising. The results are presented in figures 6.9 and 6.10. In short, the intensity of issue positions does, indeed, generate significant emotional reactions to issue-focused messages. When issue positions are threatened (fig. 6.9a) or reassured (fig. 6.10a), those with the most extreme, consistent, and salient issue positions respond by growing angrier and happier, respectively. However, when party defeat (fig. 6.9b) or victory (fig. 6.10b) is promised, issue extremity has no significant emotional effects. Issue-focused citizens are different from their issue-moderate counterparts in the degree to which they are angered and excited by practical goals but not by status threats regarding their own parties.

Partisanship has a different influence on emotion. Strong partisans are significantly angrier than weak partisans when the party is threatened (fig. 6.9b) but not when policy success is threatened (fig. 6.9a). They also grow significantly more enthusiastic than weak partisans when party victory is discussed (fig. 6.10b) but not when policy victory is promised (fig. 6.10a). It doesn't really matter to partisans whether their policy positions are threat-

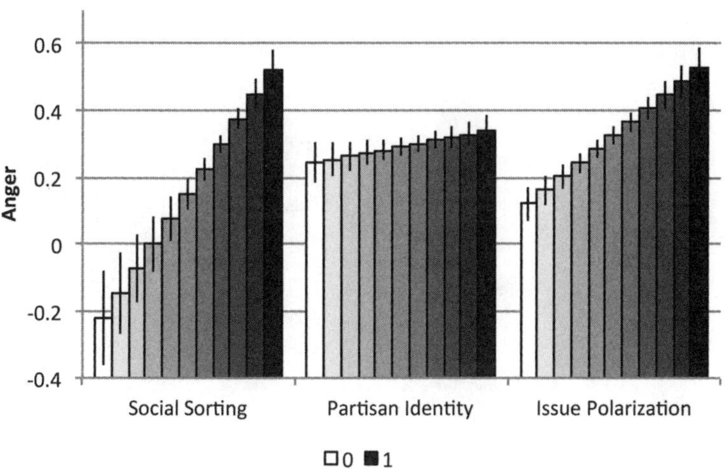

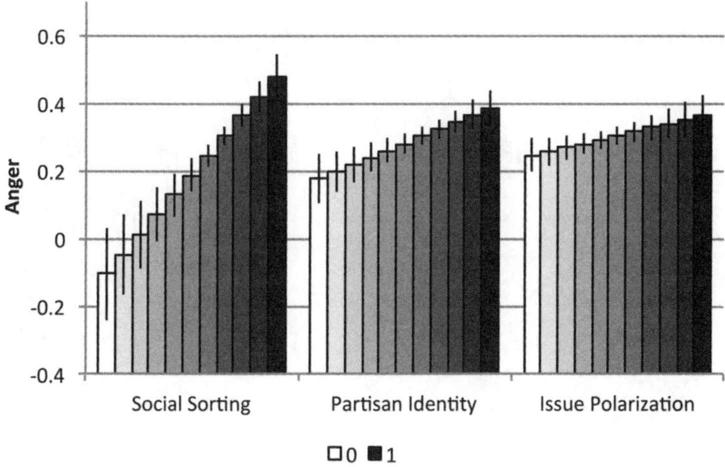

Figure 6.9. Predicted angry reactions to messages

Note: Bars represent the predicted values of anger at each level of issue extremity, partisan identity, or sorting. Originating regressions are shown in appendix table A.9. Ninety-five percent confidence intervals shown.

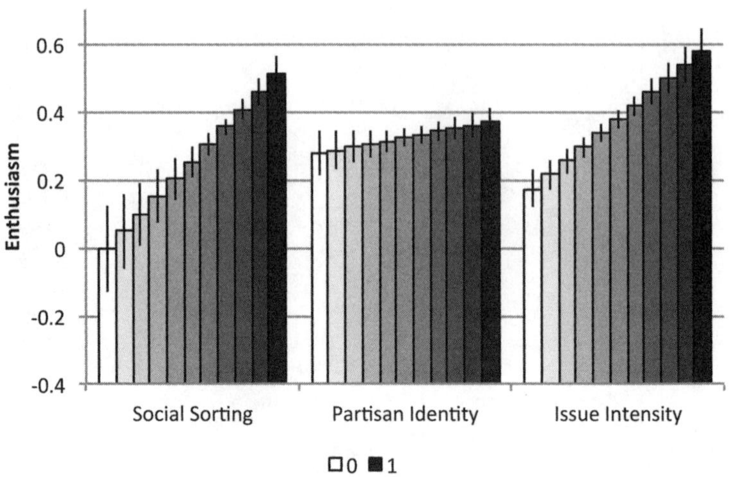

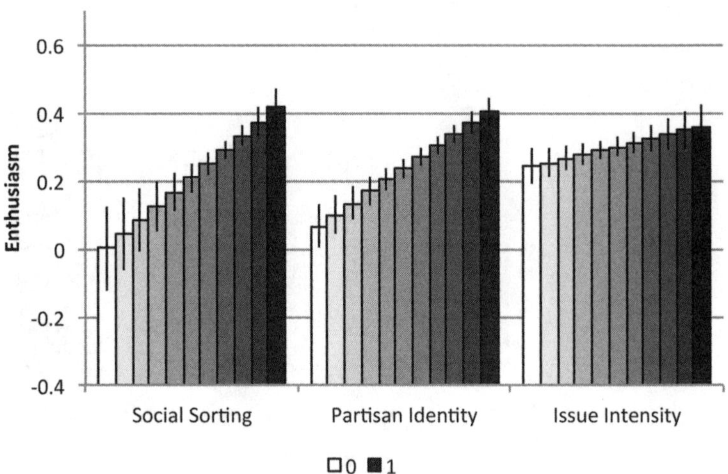

Figure 6.10. Predicted enthusiastic reactions to messages
Note: Bars represent the predicted values of enthusiasm at each level of issue extremity, partisan identity, or sorting. Originating regressions are shown in appendix table A.10. Ninety-five percent confidence intervals shown.

ened. Strong partisans are emotionally engaged by messages of support regarding their party's status—but not by the actual policy outcomes of that status.

Sorting is the unique variable in this sequence, in that it is capable of affecting emotion no matter what kind of message is presented. But this occurs in an interesting way. In figure 6.9, social sorting does affect angry reactions to both issue-based and party-based messages of threat. Unlike either issue intensity or partisan identity alone, the difference between cross-cutting and well-sorted identities is apparent in response to both messages. However, one important point to note is that, in the issue-based threat condition, the highest levels of sorting do not generate anger that is significantly higher than the anger produced among the most issue intense. Similarly, in the party-based threat condition, the highest levels of sorting do not generate anger that is significantly higher than the anger produced among the strongest partisans. The main difference between the effects of sorting versus issue intensity and partisanship is found at the *low* end of the scale.

The people with the most cross-cutting identities respond to both types of threat with significantly *less* anger than either the least issue-intense or the least partisan individuals. In fact, for both types of threat, the cross-cut individuals respond with no anger in the case of party threat and with *negative* anger in the case of issue threat. In other words, when these cross-cut individuals read a threatening political message, they remain impassive. These data suggest that Americans are not growing increasingly angry because the best-sorted identities drive the highest levels of anger. They are growing angrier because the people who tend to respond without anger (those with cross-cutting identities) are disappearing. As the sorting seen in chapter 3 continues, the people who have the best chance of remaining calm in the face of political conflict are shrinking as a proportion of the electorate.

A similar phenomenon is seen in the case of enthusiasm, shown in figure 6.10. In the presence of an issue-based message of victory (6.10a), the most socially sorted individuals are predicted to report no more enthusiasm than those who are the most issue intense. In this sense, sorting is not increasing enthusiasm beyond what it would already be among the most issue intense. However, at the low end of the spectrum, those with cross-cutting identities are significantly *less* enthusiastic than the least issue intense. The 95 percent confidence interval for the least-sorted group in figure 6.10a crosses zero, suggesting that, once again, those with cross-cutting identities have no emotional response whatsoever, even to a positive message.

In the case of party-based messages of victory, the same basic pattern arises. People who are highly socially sorted are no more enthusiastic after hearing a victory message than are the strongest partisans. In this one case, those with cross-cutting identities are statistically indistinguishable from very weak partisans. So the dampening effect of cross-cutting cleavages does not go beyond the dampening effect of simple weak partisanship. However, one difference does exist. The confidence interval around the predicted level of enthusiasm for those with the most cross-cutting identities includes zero, which means it is statistically probable that these people do not respond to encouraging messages with any enthusiasm at all. In comparison, the confidence interval for the weakest partisan's level of enthusiasm does *not* include zero (narrowly), and therefore, statistically speaking, a weak partisan is predicted to respond with some minimal level of enthusiasm.

Well-sorted citizens are broadly emotionally responsive. They get angry at any message of threat, and they get happy at any message of victory. Whether party-based or issue-based, highly sorted individuals react to political messages with emotional reactions that match those driven by the strongest partisans or the most issue-intense individuals. However, while the emotional reactions of highly sorted individuals match the maximum emotional reactions already found in the electorate, the reactions of cross-cut individuals are significantly less intense than the reactions of any other citizens measured here. Cross-cutting identities dampen emotional reactions to political messages, such that the most cross-cutting identities lead to a complete lack of emotional response. This lack of response exists only in the group of cross-cut citizens that are increasingly disappearing from the American electorate.

Obstructive Anger

Emotional reactivity is obviously important when we are trying to understand why certain partisans react to politics with anger or excitement and others respond less emotionally. The more sorted we become, the more emotionally we react to normal political events, and the more cross-cutting our identities, the more calmly we respond. The anger on display at Cliven Bundy's ranch, at the 2010 town hall meetings over Obamacare, at the Occupy Wall Street protests, and at Donald Trump's 2016 rallies is fueled by our increasing social and partisan isolation. As Americans continue to sort into partisan teams, we should expect to see more of this emotional reaction, no matter how much we may truly agree on specific policies.

In examining intergroup conflict in other nations, Kahn et al. (2016) found that "hatred and anger, and the absence of positive intergroup sentiments and moral sentiments of guilt or shame, may be an important obstacle both to the type of interest-based agreements that would benefit all concerned and to the type of relationship-building programs that can humanize adversaries and create the trust necessary for more comprehensive agreements. Indeed, trying to produce such agreement through careful crafting of efficient trades of concessions, without attending to relational barriers may be an exercise in futility" (83).

In other words, the anger that is driven by intergroup conflict and the gradual reduction of cross-cutting identities in the electorate is actively harming our ability to reasonably discuss the important issues at hand. The more people who feel angry, the less capable we are as a nation of finding common ground on policies, or even of treating our opponents like human beings. Our emotional relationships with our opponents must be addressed before we can hope to make the important policy compromises that are required for governing.

The increasingly prevalent well-sorted partisans are not only more intransigent in governing but also more active in politics, to make their intransigent inclinations known. Their emotional reactions to sorting can lead to a distinctly emotional type of political participation, in which partisans participate not only to make their policy positions known but, largely, because they're feeling particularly angry or elated.

SEVEN

Activism for the Wrong Reasons

> An important balance between action motivated by strong sentiments and action with little passion behind it is obtained by heterogeneity within the electorate. Balance of this sort is, in practice, met by a distribution of voters rather than by a homogenous collection of "ideal" citizens.
>
> —Bernard Berelson, Paul Lazarsfeld, and William McPhee, *Voting*

In their 1954 book, Berelson and colleagues made a relatively controversial claim. They suggested that an electorate composed entirely of "deeply concerned" voters would be unresponsive at the aggregate level and unsuitable to the needs of a changing nation. They pointed out that citizens who were "subjected to conflicting social pressures," such as those with cross-cutting identities, were necessary for providing the "inconsistent" preferences that lead to flexible voting records. These voters may be "erratic" in their voting patterns, but they would provide a net benefit to society, as the government could not change directions without them.

This chapter looks at the relationship between social sorting and political activism. As I explain below, there is a positive relationship between the two, with social sorting increasing levels of political activism. While most political scientists agree that political participation is a necessary ingredient of a functioning democracy, Berelson and colleagues pointed not to the value of participation itself but instead to the makeup of the electorate, and this is my focus as well. I do not argue that all political participation is bad for democracy. What I do argue is that the makeup of the electorate matters. If social sorting drives increased participation, the increasingly sorted electorate will be more homogeneously made up of the "deeply concerned" citizens. Highly sorted citizens, as seen in prior chapters, care more for party victory and therefore will be more consistently partisan in their voting than the "erratic," cross-cut voters. Cross-cutting identities provide some flexibility in voter preferences. Changing cross-cut voters into well-sorted voters is not necessarily a net good for a functioning democracy, particularly if the well-sorted are more likely to vote. The well-sorted voters are more likely to be active on behalf of their identities and emotions, which drive them consistently in the direction of voting that is less responsive to changing conditions and events.

A Brief History of Participation

Social identity theory would predict that an increase in political identity strength and sorting should increase political activism, but most of the stories we hear about the American electorate describe it as disengaged, uninformed, uninterested, and inactive. Robert Putnam, in his 2001 book *Bowling Alone*, paints a clear picture of an American public that is growing increasingly disconnected from one another on a civic and community-based level. As Americans become more isolated from each other, our engagement with politics is expected to go the way of our engagement with churches and civic organizations. We simply disconnect. In fact, Bill Bishop's 2009 book, *The Big Sort*, describing massive cultural and geographical partisan sorting relies on this process of disengagement to explain Americans' subsequent realignment along partisan lines.

So why isn't our narrative about activism the same as our narrative about polarization? Are we polarized and apathetic? Has our increasing sorting and polarization managed to keep us out of politics? The short answer is that, despite all of the lamentations about American political apathy, there has been an increase in activism to match our social sorting.

The traditional explanation for political participation in American politics is one of either socioeconomic status or resources. Brady, Verba, and Schlozman in 1995 elaborated a model of participation that relied on resources such as time, money, and civic skills. Those skills were learned in settings such as civic organizations and churches, exactly the type of organizations that Putnam saw Americans moving away from. As Americans abandoned these organizations and affiliations, they also avoided political participation. But Miller et al. (1981) pointed out that some groups in American politics have participated in politics at a higher rate than their socioeconomic resources alone could predict. They offered an early explanation that resonates today: people who are conscious of their group memberships are driven to participate in politics on behalf of their groups.

This is not always a normatively positive type of participation. A Pew study in 2016 found that "across most measures of political participation . . . individuals with no negative partisan stereotypes were less likely to participate in politics." This means that the active electorate is now more likely to include voters who hold negative partisan stereotypes, a result that matches an increasing identification with socially homogeneous parties.

Social psychology explains how political participation can be a direct outcome of our sense of feeling attached to others, not necessarily those that we see in distinctly community-based places but those with whom we simply feel socially connected. As Americans have rearranged their social affiliations, not around institutions but around socially similar others, they have laid the groundwork for getting involved in politics again. Work I did with Leonie Huddy and Lene Aarøe in 2015 explained how identifying with a political party in a social way can increase political participation, even more powerfully than partisans' issue positions. I therefore expect to find that, as levels of social sorting have increased, levels of activism have followed along.[1]

Although the changes over time have been small, political action has increased significantly in recent years. The cumulative ANES data through 2012 show rising levels of participation. Figure 7.1 presents the percentage of the American population who report that they have voted in each year. This measure is famous for false claims of voting due to social desirability

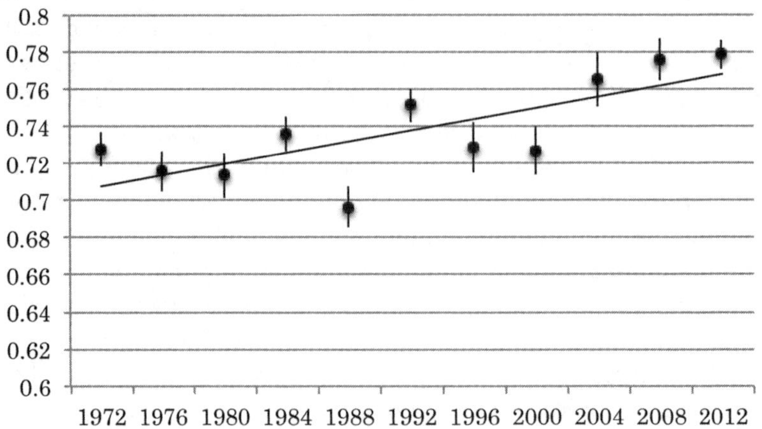

Figure 7.1. Percentage of US population reporting that they have voted
Note: Data drawn from the ANES cumulative file through 2012, weighted. Ninety-five percent confidence intervals shown. Linear trend line drawn for ease of interpretation.

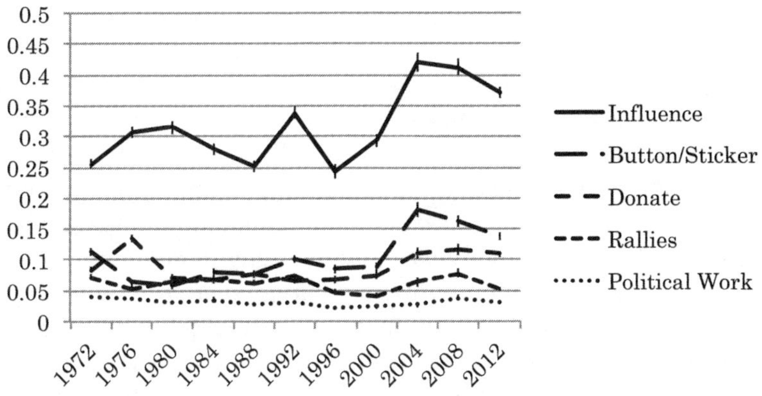

Figure 7.2. Percentage of US population reporting having participated in each political activity
Note: Data drawn from the ANES cumulative file through 2012, weighted. Ninety-five percent confidence intervals shown.

(Hanmer, Banks, and White 2014). However, even if we pretend that it is an entirely imaginary measure, always constructed from whole cloth by the respondents of the survey, it is clear that even the number of people who *wish to* have voted has increased. These are small total values, but between 1972 and 2012, the percentage of people who report having voted increased by about 5 percentage points.

Voting, of course, is not the only way to participate in politics. It is perhaps the most consequential, in terms of concrete electoral outcomes, but the ANES measures a series of other activities that certainly qualify as political activism, many of which require more commitment than simply casting a ballot (or reporting that you have done so, whether or not this is true). The ANES asks respondents whether they have tried to influence the vote of others, displayed a campaign button or bumper sticker or yard sign, attended a political rally, or done volunteer work for a political campaign.

Figure 7.2 lays out the trends in each of these types of political action between 1972 and 2012. By far the most popular, and the most rapidly increasing form of political activism is the simple act of speaking to another person and trying to convince them to vote for the candidate you support. Between 1972 and 2012, this very social form of activism increased by 11 percentage points. Levels have declined slightly since 2004, but even considering this decline, 2012 levels of political social contact are higher than they were in the 1970s, 1980s, and 1990s. It is also important to note that these measures do not account for Internet activism, which has been shown to have a mobilizing effect on voters (Settle et al. 2016).

Occupying a distant second place in popular political activism is wearing a button or putting a bumper sticker on your car or a sign in your yard. Though far fewer Americans engage in this type of public display of political affiliation, the number who have done so since 2000 has markedly increased. Between 2000 and 2004, the percentage of Americans who engaged in this public display increased by nearly 10 percentage points, with this increase declining to about 5 percentage points by 2012. However, since Bill Bishop, in his 2009 book, noted an increasing level of geographical polarization among American partisans, it is possible that, rather than indicating increasing partisanship, this increase simply indicates a more comfortable and nonconfrontational environment for public displays of partisanship.

To account for this possibility, I examined the button/sticker measure among those who never discuss politics with family and friends—indicating either an uncomfortable social environment for political engagement or a nonpolitical environment—and compared this against those who do discuss politics with family and friends. As figure 7.3 indicates, those who discuss politics with family and friends are significantly more likely to commit

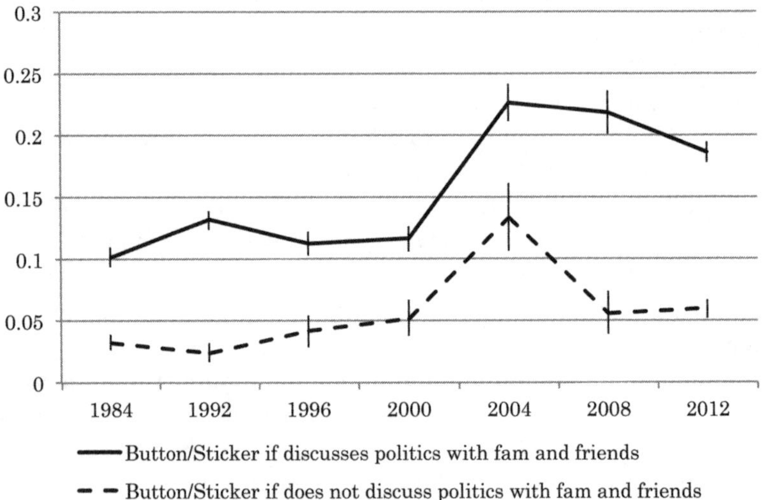

Figure 7.3. Percentage of US population reporting displaying a button, sticker, or sign, by level of political discussion

Note: Data drawn from the ANES cumulative file through 2012, weighted. Ninety-five percent confidence intervals shown.

one of these public acts of partisanship. Furthermore, although both groups of people grew more likely to engage in these displays in 2004, those who do not discuss politics fell back almost completely to pre-2004 levels in the 2008 election. Those who were socially engaged did not experience the same drop off. These partisans remained far more likely to engage in a public display of partisanship in the following elections. Though the percentage of Americans engaged in these displays declined, they remained significantly more publicly partisan than they had been in 2000. The trend shown in figure 7.2, then, is driven largely by people who are *socially* engaged in politics. The types of political engagement that are increasing are social engagements, and they occur most frequently among those who are in politically aware social networks.

Going back to figure 7.2, it is clear that donating to campaigns, attendance at political rallies, and volunteer work have not significantly increased, or have increased only modestly, during the last few decades. Most of the increase in political activism has been in the persuasion element, and in the public display of partisan attachments. These are certainly the least costly forms of engaging in politics, but their increase does indicate a meaningful change in the American electorate. Americans feel more compelled to report that they voted, they are more often attempting to convince others to vote for their preferred candidates, and they are more often publicly displaying signals indicating which candidate they prefer. All of this points to an electorate that finds political preferences to be a more social and public phenomenon than they were thirty years ago.

Identity-Driven Action

Social psychologists have already discovered that when people identify with a group of other people they are more likely to take political action on behalf of their group, particularly when that group is under threat. Kelly and Breinlinger (1996) found that identification as a woman increased the likelihood of participating in the women's movement. De Weerd and Klandermans (1999) discovered that social identification as a farmer increased action preparedness and farmers' protest participation. Ethier and Deaux (1994) observed that strongly identified Hispanic college students, when placed in an unfamiliar environment, engage more in group-based cultural activities than the less strongly identified. Huddy, Mason, and Aarøe (2015) demonstrated that a stronger partisan identity increased intentions to donate to and volunteer for a political campaign in the context of an election. Mackie, Devos, and Smith (2000) found that strong group identifiers were more likely to take action against a threatening outgroup.

It is tempting to argue that these actions are driven by self-interest (also called instrumental concerns) more than social identity. Group members take action because they will directly and individually benefit from the success of their group's objectives. But in most of these cases, the difference between the strong group identifier and the weak group identifier is simply the individual's psychological attachment to the group. A weakly identified farmer will reap the same benefits from political action as a strongly identified farmer, and yet only the strongly identified farmer takes action. The identification with the group drives the group member to take action to maintain positive group status, in line with the first imperative of a social identity—be victorious.

Partisans should be more likely to participate in politics not simply because the party holds sympathetic issue positions but also because the party is their team, it is under threat, and they are compelled to do something to maintain its status. As Klandermans (2003) explains, "People participate not so much because of the outcomes associated with participation but because they identify with the other participants . . . participation generated by the identity pathway is a form of automatic behavior, whereas participation brought forward by the instrumental pathway is a form of reasoned action" (687). Partisans are compelled to automatically participate in politics by social and psychological motivations. It should be noted that social and instrumental influences are never completely separate in a given individual. In most people, both types of motivations work simultaneously. The purpose here is to attempt to pull apart the effects of each so that the respective contributions of the two types of motivations can be more precisely seen.

In 2015, Leonie Huddy, Lene Aarøe, and I compared the effects of what we called an "expressive" partisan identity to the effects of an "instrumental" partisan identity. In other words, we measured whether social identification with a party drove more political action than issue-based identification with a party. We found that partisan identity was a significantly more powerful predictor of political action than an issue-based measure. We also found that the more social-identity-focused our measure was, the better the measure was at predicting activism. The traditional seven-point measure of partisan identification was less powerful than the four-item battery of social partisan identity. So, as we got closer to social identity, political action grew more likely. This is in line with what social psychology would have predicted. The same literature would predict that a set of highly aligned identities should have an even more powerful effect.

Partisan-Ideological Sorting

One way to begin finding effects of sorting on activism is to look at the simple alignment of partisan and ideological identities. If I look only at partisan-ideological sorting, I can use the fairly strong test of the matched sample that I examined in prior chapters. Again, in this sample, the full ANES cumulative file through 2012 is used to match respondents on ideological identification, issue extremity, education, sex, race, age, geographical location, and church attendance.[2] The only thing that moves in figure 7.4 is the extent to which partisanship lines up with ideological identification. When this very large set of data is combed to find people who are as similar as possible on many important traits, the effect of sorting on activism emerges as an important one. I put all of the five elements of activism from figure 7.2 into one combined measure, counting the number of activities that have been undertaken (and recoding this count to range from 0 to 1). The predicted levels of total activism in the presence of low and high levels of sorting are shown in figure 7.4. When a partisan identity is poorly aligned with an ideological identity, average levels of activism are significantly lower than when partisanship and ideology are well aligned. Again, the total effect size is small, as changes in activism over time also tend to be. However, there is a significant difference in political activism between the

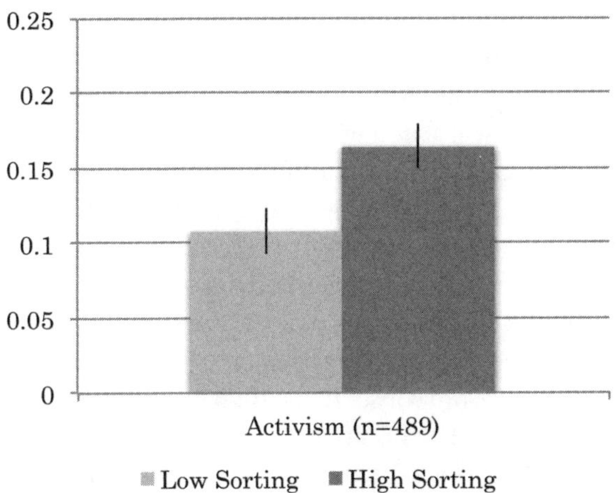

Figure 7.4. Mean activism: Matching on ideology and issue extremity
Note: Ninety-five percent confidence intervals shown. Data drawn from the ANES cumulative file through 2012. Samples are matched on ideology, issue extremity, education, sex, race, age, south/nonsouth location, and church attendance.

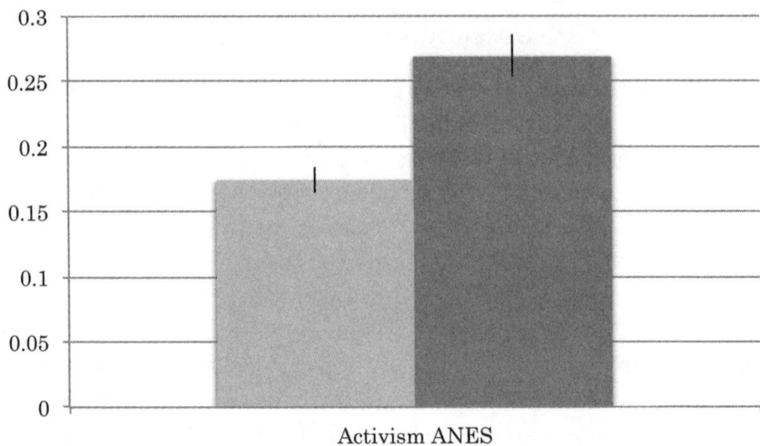

Figure 7.5. Predicted values of activism among strong partisans across levels of sorting
Note: Bars represent predicted values of activism at varying levels of partisan-ideological sorting controlling for a scale of issue extremity and issue constraint (and their interaction), political knowledge, race, sex, income, age, and church attendance. Originating regression is shown in appendix table A.11. Ninety-five percent confidence intervals are shown. This sample is fully weighted. The low sorting score is not zero, but 0.0857, the lowest sorting score possible given a strong partisan identity.

sorted and unsorted, even among people who are very similar, including in their political opinions.

These highly similar Americans are significantly more likely to participate in some form of political action when their partisan identities line up with their ideological ones. Even without the contribution of issue extremity—and in alternate models accounting for the constraint of issue positions—simple partisan-ideological sorting drives people to take political action. As seen above, this action is largely social in nature, like its motivations.

But do the effects of sorting surpass the effects of simple partisan identity? I look at this question by again examining partisan-ideological sorting while holding partisanship constant, looking only at strong partisans. As in prior chapters, this test again results in significant effects of sorting, this time on political action. Figure 7.5 uses the ANES cumulative sample through 2012 to present predicted values of the five-item activism scale, drawn from OLS regressions controlling for issue extremity, issue constraint, political knowledge, race, sex, income, age, and church attendance. While holding each of these variables constant, the predicted levels of activism among unsorted strong partisans is about 0.17, while the predicted level of activism among sorted partisans is 0.27, a significant 10 percentage point difference.

Once again, the difference between the sorted and unsorted partisans is significant, meaning that even among strong partisans a well-aligned ideological identity will generate more activism than a cross-cutting one. This model controls for issue extremity and constraint among other things. Therefore, the alignment of partisan and ideological identities is motivating increased political action even while issue positions are unchanging. American partisans are more willing to participate in politics when they are well sorted, no matter what their issue positions happen to be. This is political tribalism driving action. We are growing more politically engaged on behalf of our team spirit.

Social Sorting and Activism

If the alignment of the seven-point scales of partisanship and ideological identity can predict increasing activism, a more social-identity-based measure of partisanship and other social identities should have even more powerful effects. When the concept of social sorting is measured using multiple social identities and measures expressly designed to assess social identification, stronger effects do indeed result.

When looking at prior political activism, including working for a political party or candidate, engaging in political protest, writing a letter or email to a political official, and donating money to a political party or candidate (a count recoded to range from 0 to 1), social sorting indicates a much more engaged partisan. Figure 7.6 presents the predicted values of this activism scale, according to levels of social sorting. Importantly, these predicted values are generated from an OLS model that controls for a measure of issue positions including the extremity, constraint, and rated importance of five issues, as described in chapter 4. In this figure, when all other variables are held at their means or medians, the most cross-pressured partisan is predicted to rate an activism score of about 0.19. A partisan with very high levels of social sorting, however, is predicted to report an activism score of about 0.52. This is an increase of about 30 percent of the full range of activism, which corresponds to more than one additional political activity out of the full range of 4. Again, this is the relationship between social sorting and activism, holding issue positions constant. This is a powerful effect of the teaming up of social identities that drives people to engage in politics, even when their issue positions are no different than those of their fellow citizens who hold cross-cutting identities.

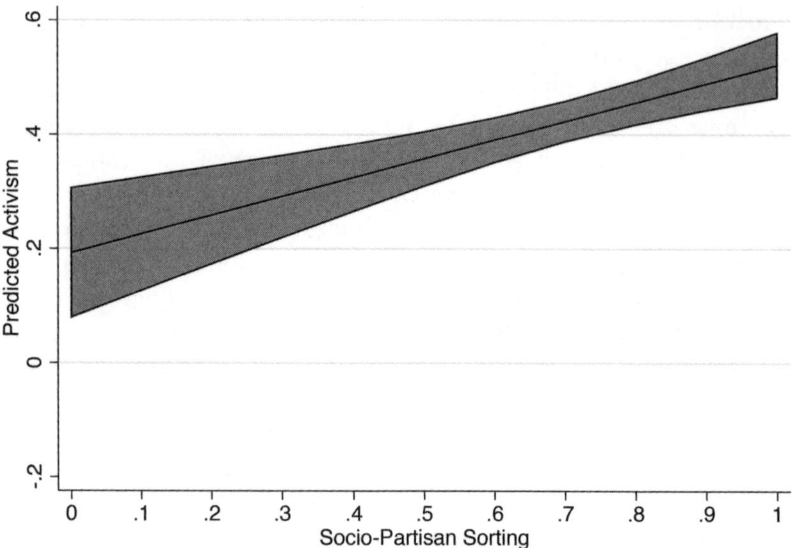

Figure 7.6. Predicted values of a scale of prior activism, by level of social sorting
Note: Predicted values drawn from OLS models shown in the appendix, controlling for issue extremity, constraint and rated importance, race, sex, income, age, political knowledge, and church attendance. Originating regression is shown in appendix table A.12. Ninety-five percent confidence intervals shown.

Predicting future or intended activism is slightly more problematic because there is no guarantee that these promises are fulfilled. However, figure 7.7 presents the predicted values of an index of intended activism in which people indicate whether they intend to (1) donate to or (2) volunteer for (3) candidates or (4) parties in the upcoming 2012 election. Remember, these data were collected a full year before the 2012 election, suggesting that the results should be taken with a grain of salt, as people engage less with elections so far away.

Still, these four possible activities are combined into a scale, again coded to range from 0 to 1. In figure 7.7, the promise of future political action is even more powerfully related to social sorting. Those with highly cross-cutting social identities are, in fact, predicted to participate in negative levels of activism, with a score of –0.07. The confidence interval is wide, however, and crosses zero, so it is fair to assume that these cross-cutting social identities essentially eliminate intentions to participate in politics. Those with very strong and well-aligned social identities are predicted to report an activism score of 0.36, a full 43 percentage points higher in the full range of intended

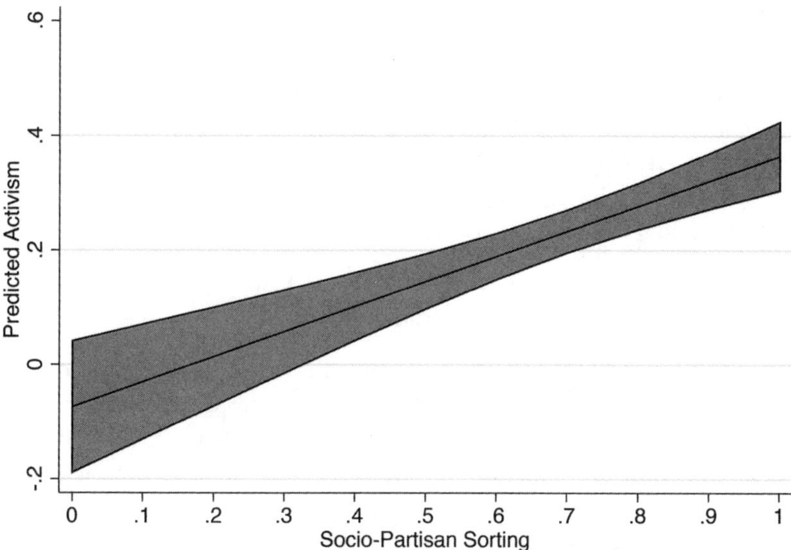

Figure 7.7. Predicted values of a scale of intended future activism, by level of social sorting
Note: Predicted values drawn from OLS models shown in the appendix, controlling for issue extremity, constraint and rated importance, race, sex, income, age, political knowledge, and church attendance. Originating regression is shown in appendix table A.12. Ninety-five percent confidence intervals shown.

activism than those with cross-cutting identities. With four activities in the scale, this increase in social sorting adds nearly two full activities. Even if this self-report of future behavior is inflated, the effect of social sorting is clearly large and powerful. People at least want to *say* that they will participate in politics far more strongly when their social identities line up with their partisanship.

Even when a host of highly salient issue positions are held constant, these large effects emerge. Social sorting is capable of making people want to participate in politics.

However, controlling for an index of issue positions perhaps does not provide a fair test of the potential impact of a truly extreme and salient issue position. What if someone cares mostly about one issue, for example? The five-issue index wouldn't account for the unique power of the single issue. Also, can an issue drive action not only from an instrumental motivation but also by generating an identity around itself? If instrumental concerns about single issues can motivate action, the evidence that I presented above doesn't allow that effect to come through.

Issue-Driven Action

One issue that tends to motivate single-issue voters is abortion. It is also a cause that has generated labels for the advocates of each side of the issue, potentially creating a social identity around issue advocacy. Pro-choice and pro-life opinions have produced potential political identities in a way that is distinct from the advocates of issues such as taxes or health-care reform.

The Case of Abortion Attitudes

Craig McGarty and his colleagues explained in 2009, "Merely holding the same opinion as others is not sufficient for such a group to be said to exist, rather the shared opinion needs to become part of that social identity. In this way, people can come to perceive and define themselves in terms of their opinion group membership in the same way as they would with any other psychologically meaningful social category or group" (846). The main incentive that drove McGarty et al. to identify such an issue-based identity was the distinctly activist outcomes that result directly from these identities.

A single issue for a voter who cares a great deal about it may generate a social identity, with both the issue and the identity driving the individual toward greater action. Klandermans (2014) has laid out a compelling case for the collective-action effects of group identities. When groups form around a particularly salient issue, they tend to lead to political action. In this sense, issue-based identity is potentially a unique motivator for political action, as it involves both issue opinions and a sense of group loyalty. It is this identification with the issue-based group that I expect to drive significant levels of activism and partisan bias, more powerfully than simply an extreme issue position.

Abortion attitude identities in particular—a sense of social connection to others who call themselves pro-choice or pro-life—seem to be a powerful example of this issue-based identity. Pro-choice and pro-life groups have undeniably engaged in group-based activism since the 1973 ruling in *Roe v. Wade* that legalized abortion. To this day, groups like Planned Parenthood and the National Right to Life Committee (NRLC) clash repeatedly over the legality and normative values at stake in abortion rights, with advocates on either side identifying with the issue-based labels "pro-choice" and "pro-life." I choose this topic mainly because of these preestablished and well-known names with which a person can identify to varying degrees. In fact, I specifically measured the social identity strength of affiliating with each side of the debate. I used the four-item scale of social identity[3] and applied it to the terms *pro-choice* and *pro-life*. The items for each label scaled together well, with both pro-life ($\alpha = 0.82$) and pro-choice ($\alpha = 0.80$) identities demonstrating a real identification with these labels. In fact, mean levels of identification with the pro-choice and pro-life labels was generally higher than partisan identification among partisans. Mean Democratic identity among Democrats (on a 0 to 1 scale) was 0.62 and Republican identity among Republicans was 0.60. But mean pro-choice identity among those who approved of abortion was 0.74, while mean pro-life identity among those who disapproved of abortion was 0.79.

In the sample used here, the issue of abortion was rated to be somewhat or extremely important by 87 percent of respondents, upholding its potential for representing issue-based identity.[4] I also looked at abortion issue extremity, operationalized as the abortion-opinion scale including the following four options: "By law, abortion should never be permitted," "The law should permit abortion only in case of rape, incest, or when the woman's life is in danger," "The law should permit abortion for reasons other than rape, incest, or when the woman's life is in danger," and "By law, a woman should always be able to obtain an abortion as a matter of personal choice." This scale was folded in half, so that abortion extremity is limited to a two-point measure, which can indicate either position in the middle of the scale (coded 0) or either position on the ends of the scale (coded 1). Finally, I looked at abortion issue importance, which was simply the follow-up importance item to the abortion-opinion prompt, asking "How important is this issue to you?" with the potential responses of Very important, Somewhat important, Not very important, and Not at all important. This four-point scale was recoded to range from 0 (not at all important) to 1 (very important). These alternate measures were used to determine which element of this issue most motivated political action. Is it the sense of being connected to like-minded others? Or is it the actual extremity of belief? Or is it instead a sense that the issue is important? As V. O. Key says in his 1961 book, "The more concerned a person is about an issue, the greater is the probability that his opinion will be intense" (219). I therefore compare the identity behind abortion attitudes with a combined effect of abortion extremity and importance.[5]

Key (1961) did not find a strong relationship between activism and issue intensity: "From our daily impressions of politics, we feel that persons who have opinions of high intensity are likely to seek energetically to achieve the ends in which they believe. . . . Little bands of dedicated souls leave their clear imprint on public policy" (229). However, in examining the data, he had to conclude that "under some circumstances persons have intense opinions that do not lead to heightened participation, although across the

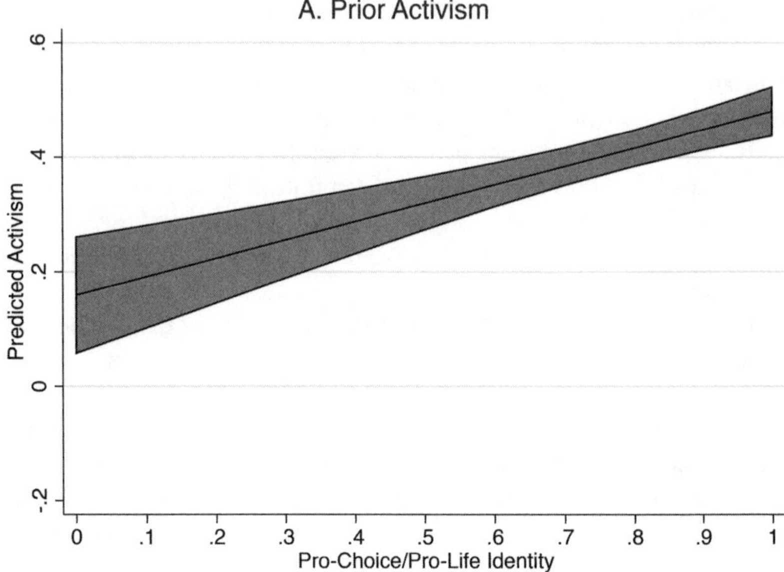

Figure 7.8. Predicted values of prior political engagement from abortion identity versus abortion extremity versus abortion extremity*importance

Note: Ninety-five percent confidence intervals shown. Identity measured from four items including (1) How important is being pro-choice/pro-life to you? (2) How well does the term *pro-choice/pro-life* describe you? (3) When talking about pro-choice/pro-life people how often do you use "we" instead of "they"? (4) To what extent do you think of yourself as pro-choice/pro-life? Prior political activism includes working for a political party or candidate, engaging in political protest, writing a letter or email to a political official, and donating money to a political party or candidate (a count recoded to range from 0 to 1). Panels A and C derive from a model including the interactive term between extremity and importance. Panel B only includes extremity and does not control for identity. All models control for race, sex, income, age, political knowledge, and church attendance. Originating regressions are shown in appendix table A.13.

electorate there seems to be a slight tendency for participation to increase with intensity of opinion" (230). Key blames these weak findings on the "crudeness of our measures of both intensity of opinion and participation" (230). Perhaps then a better measure, like the one that expressly gauges the social identity associated with an issue position, could do a better job explaining the link between issue position and political action.

Figure 7.8 shows that when looking at general political engagement, measured as the political activities a person has done, the identity associated with the abortion issue is better at driving activism than is the extremity of that abortion opinion, or even the extremity interacted with the rated importance of the issue. Figure 7.8a shows the predicted levels of activism at each level of

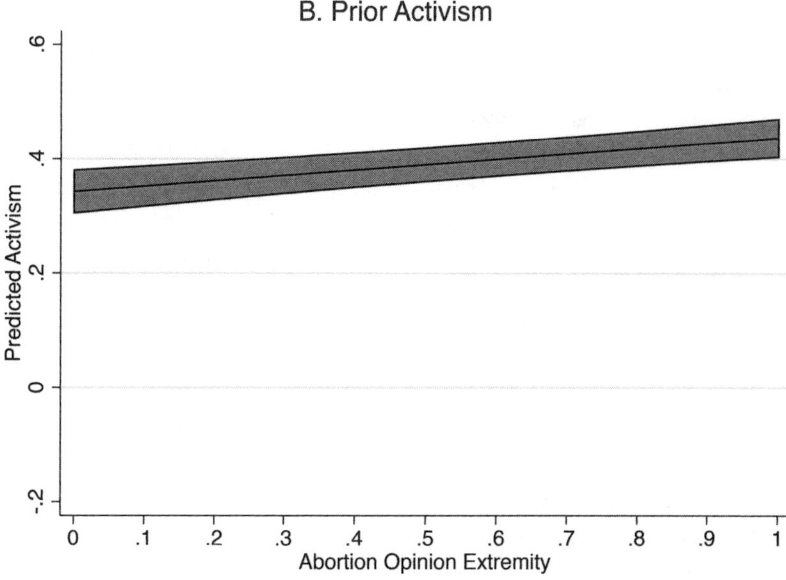

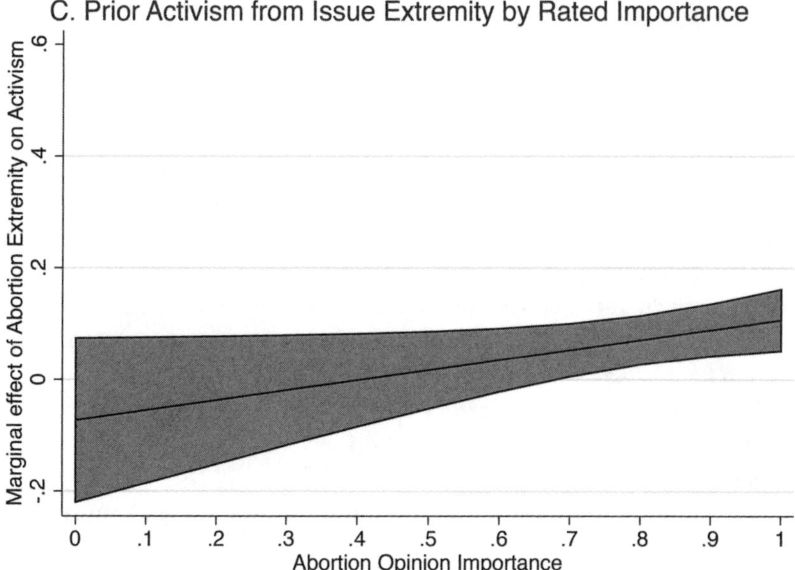

Figure 7.8. (continued)

social identification with the pro-choice or pro-life label. This identity has a significant effect. Those with the weakest attachments to the group labels are predicted to engage in 24 percent fewer political activities than those with the strongest attachments. This effect is controlling for the effect of both abortion-opinion extremity and importance, so these identity effects are occurring independent of a person's actual position on or passion about abortion.

In figure 7.8b, I look only at the effect of abortion-opinion extremity, not controlling for importance or the issue identity measured in 7.8a. As Key said, it is likely that importance and extremity go hand in hand, and this model is an attempt to see what power comes from allowing the extremity of the issue to account for all of the other issue-based influences. What I find, instead, is that the extremity of a person's position on abortion has some effect on general activism, but the effect is small—far smaller than the effect of abortion-opinion identity. The total effect of abortion-opinion extremity is less than half the size of the effect of identity, and this effect does not control for the effects of identifying with the abortion-opinion group. The best-case scenario for the motivating effects of extremism, therefore, is that it generates half the activism of the pro-choice or pro-life identity.

In figure 7.8c, I interact opinion extremity and importance to give issue intensity one last chance to prove its activating potential.[6] Figure 7.8c looks at the marginal effects of extremity (the effect of moving from lowest to highest extremity) on activism at varying levels of issue importance. This effect is technically significant but does not reach an actual positive effect on activism until the rated importance of the issue passes its midpoint. This means that the extremity of the abortion position has no effect on general activism unless the issue is rated by a person to be at least somewhat important. Even then, the effect increases activism by about only 10 percent of the total range of activism. In comparison with the 24 percentage point increase seen in figure 7.8a, abortion attitudes are doing something, but they are far from the most powerful motivator of political action. The social attachment to the pro-choice and pro-life groups drives twice as much action as the intensity of the attitudes themselves.

The same result appears, if not even more powerfully, in figures 7.9a, 7.9b, and 7.9c, which examine intentions to participate in future activism. In these models I asked people if they intended to participate in the upcoming 2012 election. In figure 7.9a, those who felt strongly socially connected to the pro-choice or pro-life group labels showed essentially the same reaction to that identity as they did in the case of prior activity. The most strongly socially connected are predicted to participate in about 25 percent more political actions (or to intend to do so) than those who feel only a

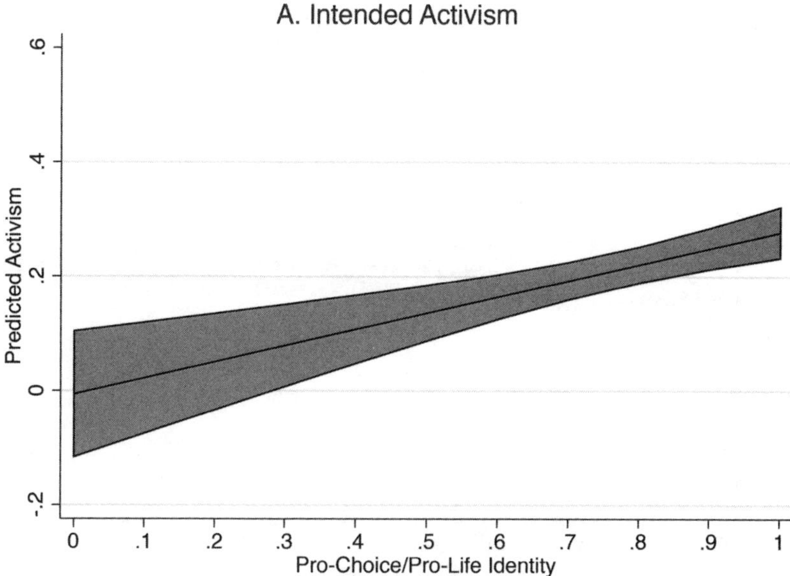

Figure 7.9. Predicted values of intended future political engagement from abortion identity versus abortion extremity versus abortion extremity*importance

Note: Ninety-five percent confidence intervals shown. Identity measured from four items including (1) How important is being pro-choice/pro-life to you? (2) How well does the term *pro-choice/pro-life* describe you? (3) When talking about pro-choice/pro-life people how often do you use "we" instead of "they"? (4) To what extent do you think of yourself as pro-choice/pro-life? Intended activism includes intention to (1) donate to or (2) volunteer for (3) candidates or (4) parties in the upcoming 2012 election. Panels A and C derive from a model including the interactive term between extremity and importance. Panel B only includes extremity and does not control for identity. All models control for race, sex, income, age, political knowledge, and church attendance. Originating regressions are shown in appendix table A.14.

weak social connection to these groups. Again, this is controlling for an interaction between abortion-opinion extremity and importance. So, without any change in beliefs about abortion, the people who feel socially connected to the pro-choice or pro-life groups are promising significantly more political activism than those who don't feel socially connected.

In comparison, in figure 7.9b, the effect of the extremity of the issue position alone (without even controlling for identity) is significant but quite small.[7] The difference between an extreme opinion and a moderate opinion generates 6 percent more intention to participate in the upcoming election. In figure 7.9c, when the extremity and importance are combined, the effect of issue intensity on intentions to participate in 2012 only rises above zero at the very highest levels of issue importance. Even then, it predicts an increase

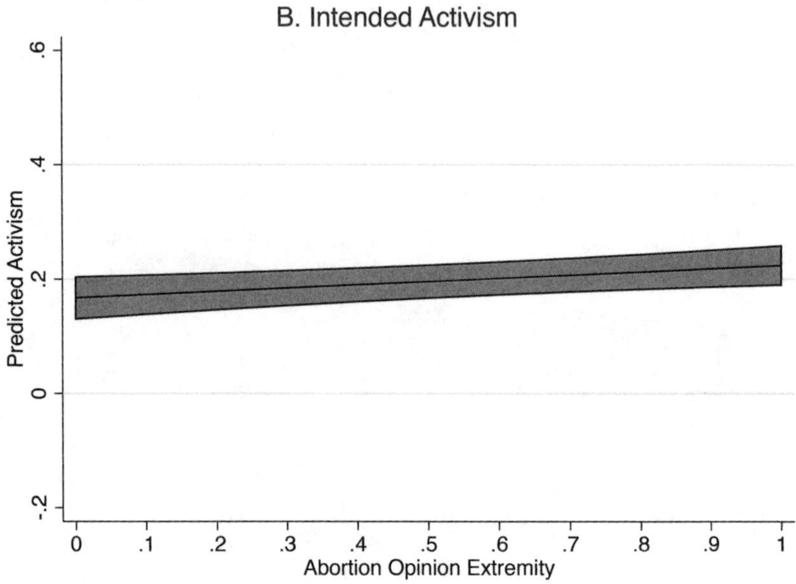

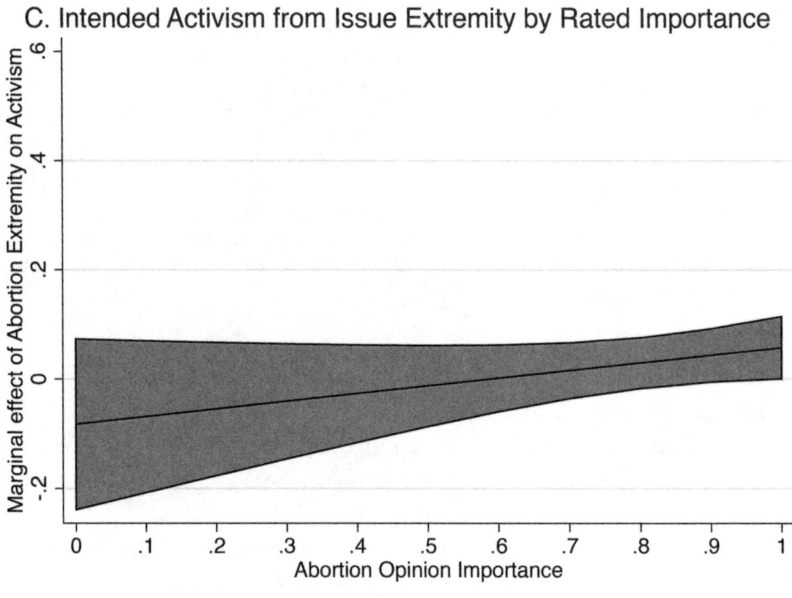

Figure 7.9. (continued)

in activist intentions of about only 6 percentage points, with a confidence interval that remains near zero.

When you ask people if they are planning to participate in the upcoming election, the intensity of their abortion opinion does very little to push them into action. However, their sense that they are socially connected to other people who call themselves pro-choice or pro-life is quite powerful. These single-issue activists are driven to act not by the intensity of their beliefs but by the sense that they are supported by like-minded others. Other people, not simple opinions, push activists into action.[8]

Even in looking at the effects of singularly powerful issues on political activism, the biggest motivator for political engagement is not the issue itself but the community around the issue. The extremity and importance of an issue is not what drives people to take political actions—to urge others to vote, to wear a button, to promise to donate to a cause. The thing that drives people into action on behalf on an individual issue is the sense that there are other people on their side. Their opinion on that issue generates an identity—a team—and their team spirit, just as in the case of partisan identity, is what makes them act. We are not observing a strongly outcome-oriented electorate. Even when looking directly at one single issue that people want to see changed or supported, it is group feelings that drive political action. Without team spirit, the extreme believers barely differ from the moderate believers. Political activism, then, is being driven by social cues, even when it is in service of a single issue.

Emotion-Driven Action

> Injustice, wrong, injury excites the feeling of resentment, as naturally and necessarily as frost and ice excite the feeling of cold, as fire excites heat, and as both excite pain. A man may have the faculty of concealing his resentment, or suppressing it, but he must and ought to feel it. Nay he ought to indulge it, to cultivate it. It is a duty. His person, his property, his liberty, his reputation are not safe without it. He ought, for his own security and honour, and for the public good, to punish those who injure him. . . . It is the same with communities. They ought to resent and to punish.
>
> —John Adams, diary entry of March 4, 1776, one month before Lexington and Concord (quoted in Philbrick 2013)

John Adams did not have a problem with action driven by resentment and anger. Be warned, however, that he was on the precipice of the Revolutionary War when he expressed this feeling.

The previous two chapters have demonstrated that social sorting and identity-based polarization have led not only to increased action but to prejudice and emotional volatility. If the American public was simply more biased and angry but did nothing about it, sorting would not necessarily have electoral effects. Unfortunately, sorting has driven American partisans to grow more biased and angry and to take more political action because of that bias and anger.

The motivating effects of emotion have been well studied. In chapter 6, social sorting was shown to be uniquely capable of driving angry and enthusiastic responses to political messages. These emotions are not only interesting in themselves. Emotions, particularly anger and enthusiasm, can change the way people think and analyze, and can drive them to action. In 2014, Eric Groenendyk and Antoine Banks found that "the emotions strong partisans experience help them to bypass individual-level utility calculations and take action on behalf of their party" (360). The emotions most often observed by Groenendyk and Banks among strong partisans were anger and enthusiasm. Psychologists have often discussed the particular power of these two emotions to drive action. They have been labeled "approach emotions" (Harmon-Jones, Harmon-Jones, and Price 2013). Both anger and enthusiasm tend to lead to more optimistic expectations for the future (Lerner and Keltner 2000). They are emotions that make you think that, if you get in the game, you are likely to win. These particular emotions are driving people toward action not because they have made a reasoned, utility-based calculation but because they are pushed by their feelings. Well-sorted people have more of these emotions, and they are more activist than those with cross-cutting identities.

When I look at the experimentally induced levels of anger and enthusiasm produced in the 2011 sample, these emotions have significant effects on people's intention to participate in the upcoming 2012 election. As a reminder, I had respondents read randomly assigned messages that were either threatening or supportive of groups (parties) or issues. For the purposes of simplification, the group- and issue-based messages are combined for this analysis. The activism questions were asked of the respondents after the experimental manipulations. As seen in chapter 6, the experimental messages generated significant anger and enthusiasm in the respondents, particularly among those with high levels of social sorting. These angry and enthusiastic responses significantly increased respondents' activism. Importantly, the results shown in figure 7.10 represent predicted values of activism drawn from an OLS regression that controls for issue-position extremity and constraint. So, just as Groenendyk and Banks (2014) found,

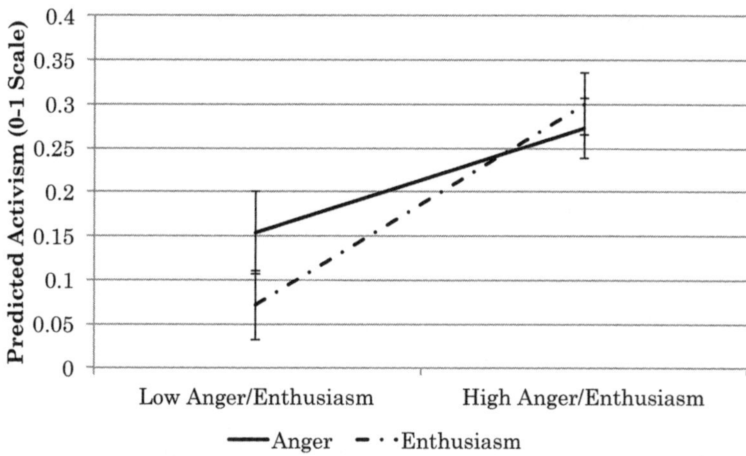

Figure 7.10. Predicted activism at low and high anger and enthusiasm
Note: Ninety-five percent confidence intervals shown. Model only includes those who were presented with a threatening or reassuring message. OLS model with robust standard errors controls for issue extremity and constraint, race, sex, income, age, political knowledge, and church attendance. Originating regressions are shown in appendix table A.15.

these emotions are driving people toward action, holding issue positions constant.

This effect is not due to issue positions, which are controlled, and it is not entirely due to the correlation between emotions and sorting because the effect remains (though it shrinks) when sorting is controlled. These emotional reactions drive people to want to act. When they have read a political message that makes them feel highly angry or enthusiastic, they want to jump into the ring. They want to get involved.

The experimental manipulations themselves had a significant effect on intended activism but only for threat-based messages. This is consistent with other research that has found stronger results in motivating activism via anger rather than enthusiasm (see Valentino et al. 2011). In figure 7.11, individuals who receive a threat-based message are significantly more likely to report that they intend to participate in the upcoming election than are those who receive no threat (including the control group and messages of support). These are simply mean levels of intended activism without any controls, which are comparable due to the randomization of the treatments.

A threatening message, in these data, does motivate increased intention to take political action. This is unique to the threatening message; the messages of support do not have the same power. This is, however, not surpris-

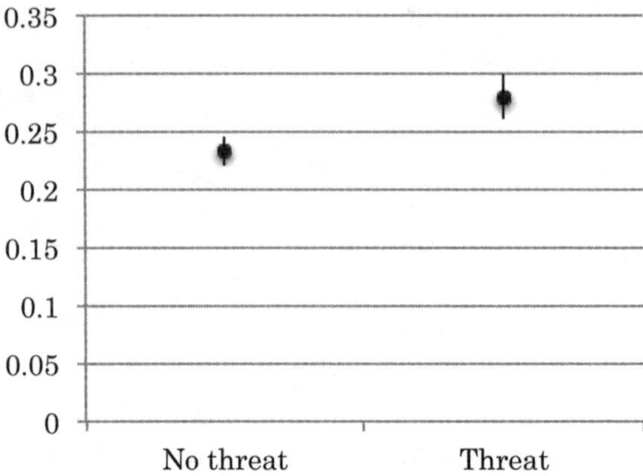

Figure 7.11. Mean levels of intended activism after threatening versus nonthreatening messages
Note: Ninety-five percent confidence intervals shown. Dots represent mean levels of intended activism in the presence of threatening or nonthreatening treatments. Data from 2011 YouGov sample.

ing, considering the importance of threat to activating social identity and group defense. Without a threat to a social group, members are less likely to derogate outgroups, and they have less of a motivation to improve the status of the group. Exposure to a threatening message does, overall, increase activism.

In 2011, Valentino and colleagues made the point that a simple resources-based model cannot account for the changes in activism that occur within individuals from year to year. Something else changes in each election that either motivates participation or depresses it. In 2001, psychologist Barbara Fredrickson explained that emotions, particularly positive emotions, lead people to engage in behavior that is not necessarily goal-oriented but, instead, rewarding in and of itself. The emotions that emerged in chapter 6, due largely to social sorting, guide people toward action because that action feels like the right thing to do. They are participating in politics, like Klandermans's farmers, because they feel connected to their groups, and that connection makes them feel more emotionally driven toward action. The highly sorted individuals don't necessarily hold more intense issue positions or stand to gain more tangible resources from a party victory, they act because it feels good to act.

But Don't We Want an Active Electorate?

> "I used to spend ninety per cent of my constituent response time on people who call, e-mail, or send a letter, such as, 'I really like this bill, H.R. 123,' and they really believe in it because they heard about it through one of the groups that they belong to, but their view was based on actual legislation," Nunes said. "Ten per cent were about 'Chemtrails from airplanes are poisoning me' to every other conspiracy theory that's out there. And that has essentially flipped on its head." The overwhelming majority of his constituent mail is now about the far-out ideas, and only a small portion is "based on something that is mostly true." He added, "It's dramatically changed politics and politicians, and what they're doing."
>
> —Devin Nunes, Republican congressman from California (quoted in Lizza 2015)

Activism may have increased over the last few decades, but this is not necessarily a responsible, outcome-based participation. As Republican congressman Devin Nunes told *New Yorker* reporter Ryan Lizza in 2015, the types of people who reach out to him (a form of participation) are increasingly ignorant of the actual policies they wish to see enacted. They are participating, but they are doing so on the basis of misinformation and ill-formed ideas. The findings of this chapter have shown that the most-sorted partisans are the most likely to take political action, regardless of their policy attitudes, particularly when they feel threatened and angry. In combination with the findings of chapter 3, this suggests that an increasing portion of the American electorate is driven to action by identity-centric motivations, while a decreasing portion of the population (those with cross-cutting identities) is relatively inactive.

The fact that action occurs because it simply feels good to act is not a great shining light of our contemporary democracy. Our political identities—partisan, ideological, racial, religious—and the alignment between them move us toward action without necessarily informing us about policy outcomes. We get up off of our sofas and put on buttons, talk to neighbors, go and vote, because it feels righteous. The bigger and more socially homogeneous the parties are, the more we have to fight for. We are only partially motivated by issue-based outcomes.

We are acting because our emotions and the self-esteem that is driven by our identities compel us to do something. We must defend our groups, and the larger and wider the group, the more necessary it is to defend it. When a threat to any of these party-related groups is perceived, political activism in defense of party status grows more likely. Even when we are acting in the pursuit of a single important issue, a large portion of that action is driven by our membership in a social group to which we feel socially and emotionally connected. Our actual opinions—the intensity of our attitudes—can't compel the same sort of political activism that our simple sense of social connection can. We take political action, potentially making real political changes, because we feel close to particular groups of people and want them (and therefore ourselves) to be winners.

This is partially why we see strong partisans out campaigning and voting even when they are nearly certain their candidate will win. They feel compelled to take political action not to achieve change but to express support for their team. It feels right to get out there and defend the team, even when the team is a guaranteed victor—possibly even more so when victory is imminent. There is a gleeful joy in participating in your own team's victory. The team doesn't need all of our votes and participation, but partisans gladly provide it anyway.

This group-based activism is unlikely to abate any time soon. Dinas (2014) found that not only does a strong partisan identity drive political action, including voting, but the act of voting also drives increasingly strong identification with the party. Therefore, the more we feel partisan, the more we vote, and the more we vote, the more partisan we feel. It is a self-reinforcing cycle. As our partisanship joins forces with many other social identities, this effect grows stronger. Our sense of social connection to other people is what drives us to take political action, not simply the intensity of our issue opinions.

While activism is generally a desirable element of a functioning democracy, blind activism is not. These results demonstrate that American partisans are working hard to participate in politics, but the ones who are most active tend to be those who cannot be convinced to change their minds. They react to threat, anger, and the strength of a whole cohort of identities that are increasingly harmonized. When individuals participate in politics driven by team spirit or anger, the responsiveness of the electorate is impaired. If their own party—linked with their race and religion—does something undesirable, they are less likely to seriously consider changing their vote in the ballot booth. As people grow more sorted, they are less likely to split their ballots or to vote for outgroup partisans in addition to ingroup partisans (Davis and Mason 2015). Without voters who may be cross-pressured or otherwise likely to allow their vote to respond to events on the ground, government has the potential to be too rigid to respond to modern changing conditions.

EIGHT

Can We Fix It?

> Identity is what gets the blood boiling, what makes people do unspeakable things to their neighbors. It is the fuel used by agitators to set whole countries on fire.
>
> —Ian Buruma, *The Blood Lust of Identity* (quoted in Kalyvas 2006)

How does American politics get back to the work of governing instead of focusing so much of our energy on partisan victory, conflict, and pride? Donald Trump won the presidential election of 2016. His ascent was bewildering to political scientists and pundits alike. One defining characteristic of his campaign was the effectiveness of his use of identity to anger and divide the electorate. By calling out distinct social groups, including women, Muslims, Mexicans, blacks, and a continuing list of others, Trump has made it clear that the American electorate can and should be divided into identity-based groups. While many conservatives lament his lack of consistently conservative policy positions, he remains remarkably popular with the base of the Republican Party to date, and this encourages establishment Republicans to fall in line behind him. This popularity does not come from his policy-based bona fides but from his use of the power of simple identity to rile up a significant portion of the American population.

Based on the research presented in this book, his success should not be surprising. Trump has taken advantage of a country whose parties have grown socially segregated. Threats to the status of any social group are linked to the status of other social groups as well, so that a single political threat has the ability to mobilize, anger, and bias large swaths of the electorate. The election of 2016 is the result of decades of social sorting, which has allowed a larger portion of the electorate to engage in politics out of defensiveness, judgment, anger, and a need to win. This is not a productive type of engagement, it is one that only deepens the divide between racial, religious, and partisan groups. The 2016 election is a perfect example of what happens to a nation that has seen its citizens gradually isolated from those who are socially unlike themselves.

What Happens to a Sorted Nation?

In the late eighteenth century, the term *party* was not meant to indicate the brittle, divided groups we have today. Robert Dahl describes the original concept of parties as "a current of political opinion, rather than an organized institution." As parties began to organize into more factional groups, Senator Hillhouse of Connecticut declared in 1808 that "party spirit is the demon which engendered the factions that have destroyed most free governments" (Dahl 1967, 207). In fact, it isn't only party spirit that can damage governments.

In political research outside of American politics, the alignment of multiple social identities has had some powerful and even dangerous outcomes. Selway (2011) finds that cross-cutting identities significantly reduce the risk of civil war in a country, while the alignment of ethnic and religious identities speeds the onset of civil war. He writes, "ethno-religious cross-cuttingness makes civil war less likely because it reduces the saliency of out-group differences and thus makes it harder for potential rebel leaders to recruit by appealing to ethnicity" (Selway 2011, 112). In a 2012 study, Gubler and Selway find that civil war is twelve times less probable in societies where ethnicity is cross-cut by another social identity such as class, geography, or religion. Kalyvas in his 2006 book writes, "The intuition is that if a population is clustered around a small number of distant but equally large poles, it is likely to undergo violent conflict. . . . The underlining mechanism is dislike so intense as to cancel even fraternal ties, imagined or real" (Kalyvas 2006, 64).

Even in the context of American politics, Dahl (1981) explained America's own civil war by stating, "Never before or since in American history has the pattern of moderate conflict with crosscutting divisions been so fully transformed into the pattern of severe conflict and polarization" (321). Fisher (1997) described the American civil war experienced in Tennessee as a distinctly social rupture: "Dedication to the cause and party consciousness broke former bonds of friendship and kinship; there was a tendency to greet and be friendly towards members of the same group, whilst systematically avoiding the others. Quarrels, rivalry and hatred developed out of these estrangements. Each group had its cafe, its meetings and even its feast days, religious on the one side and secular on the other" (Fisher 1997, 85).

The American electorate today is not engaged in a civil war. However, it is difficult to read Fisher's account and not feel echoes of contemporary American political culture. I do not argue here that the social sorting of the American electorate is inevitably leading to violent political conflict. After all, as Marilynn Brewer states, "In various contexts, groups have managed to live in a state of mutual contempt over long periods without going to war over their differences" (Brewer 2001a, 32). In fact, Scarcelli (2014) clarified that highly aligned identities don't always lead to civil war, and that catalysts such as economic decline or "adverse regime change" are often needed to exacerbate intergroup tensions to the point of organized violence. This is something to be wary of, but it is by no means unavoidable.

It should be emphasized, still, that increasing trends of social sorting are not simply benign, ignorable reorganizations. There can be real consequences when cross-cutting identities give way to orderly, segregated political teams. The question, then, becomes, is there a way to reduce or reverse the trends of social sorting or the sociological and emotional effects of this sorting?

Of course, some partisan conflict is necessary for any successful democracy. Parties should disagree about policy, and partisans should care which side wins. When the parties become socially isolated from one another, however, the conflict between them becomes less about governing and more about the conflict itself. This type of conflict is the one that needs to be addressed.

There are a number of ways to approach this problem, so I explore each strategy in turn, considering its usefulness for American polarization in particular. First, there is a broad literature that examines how to reduce intergroup conflict. This research was designed to reduce racial or religious group conflict, but in many cases it can be applied to partisan conflict as well. Second, some research in social psychology has begun looking at the effect of manipulating self-esteem and self-affirmation on political polarization, and this is another possible avenue for conflict reduction. Finally, there is a possibility for an unsorting or dealignment of our partisan and social identities. This could occur through demographic trends or by the reappearance of a major rift in one party.

In the end, none of these solutions may be effective or likely. However, each may provide some further insight into the depth and nature of the problem at hand.

How Social Science Deals with Intergroup Conflict

We do not need to disagree to feel connected to our social groups. The sense of well-being that we receive simply from being in the groups is reason enough to join them. And we do not need to dislike outgroups simply because we like our own group. It is possible to feel connected to social ingroups and not feel antagonism toward outgroups. In an ideal world, we would enjoy our own social-group identities without wishing harm upon others. Unfortunately, this is not how American politics works today.

Luckily, social scientists are not new to the concept of intergroup conflict. Since before the Rattlers and the Eagles set up camp, people have been trying to understand what makes us fight the people who aren't us. They have studied it in order to find ways to stop it. Considering the continuing existence of prejudice, none of these methods are absolutely effective. However, in the second half of the twentieth century there has at least been a reduction in the acceptability of expressing racial and religious prejudice in public, particularly among elected officials (with the troubling exception of Donald Trump). Perhaps some of these methods could prove useful in addressing the identity-fueled partisan prejudice that is currently so evident in American politics.

Contact Theory

> See that man over there?
>
> Yes.
>
> Well, I hate him.
>
> But you don't know him.
>
> That's why I hate him.
>
> —Gordon Allport, *The Nature of Prejudice*

The concept behind contact theory goes back to the work of Gordon Allport (1954) who specified that certain types of social contact can reduce prejudice between groups. This theory was so well accepted that it "provided the foundation for the Social Science Statement submitted to the U. S. Supreme Court in connection with the *Brown v. Board of Education* decision of 1954," desegregating public schools (Brewer and Kramer 1985, 232). Optimally, according to Allport, this contact would meet four conditions. It would occur (1) among groups of equal status who (2) have common goals, (3) no competition between them, and (4) the support of relevant authorities. The contact between opposing partisans is blatantly lacking conditions two and three. Luckily, later research by Pettigrew et al. (2011) found that Allport's conditions do help to reduce prejudice, but they aren't all absolutely necessary. They found that prejudice can be reduced in the presence of intergroup friendships, in the absence of anxiety, and in the presence of empathy. Even better, indirect contact can also reduce prejudice, such as contact through mass media or simply having a friend of a friend in the opposing group.

In terms of reducing American partisan prejudice, contact theory would send Democrats and Republicans into the same social arenas and ask them to simply see each other with a calm and friendly set of eyes. One way to accomplish this could be via media. Duckitt (1992) found that "the manner in which the media present and portray social and intergroup 'realities' can markedly influence the perceived salience of (a) intergroup distinctions, roles, and inequities; (b) negative stereotyping; (c) the social acceptability of prejudice; and (d) norms that govern intergroup behavior" (255). This approach would compel our partisan news media to present opposing partisans in more sympathetic ways, but would also add sympathetic partisans of both sides to simple entertainment-based television shows, including shows consumed mainly by partisans of each party. Recent research has shown that the gender roles portrayed in sitcoms have an effect on viewers' attitudes toward gender-based policies (Swigger 2017). Perhaps partisan portrayals could affect viewers' perceptions of who Democrats and Republicans are. In fact, since Democrats and Republicans reliably watch different types of television in a wide range of arenas, contact theory would suggest implanting sympathetic partisans of the opposing team into each party's television shows. Although this would be a welcome development, American partisans generally live in different social arenas and partisan television tends to pander to its own fans, making this development unlikely.

While exposure to opposing political ideas and individuals can moderate intolerance and polarization, this exposure is growing far less frequent. Furthermore, as Brewer and Kramer (1985) explain, attempts to locate the prejudice-reducing effects of contact have generated mixed results. In particular, when a group member comes into contact with a member of the opposing group, if she or he considers that member to be "atypical" of the opposing group the effects do not last beyond the moment of contact. Jacoby-Senghor, Sinclair, and Smith (2015) found that the people with the most bias against outgroups are not only less likely to have direct contact with outgroup members "but will also be less likely to have friends with outgroup friends." Therefore our most biased partisans will have little direct or even indirect contact with political opponents. In short, the amount of contact between Democrats and Republicans is decreasing, and it is quite unlikely that this trend will reverse without some larger outside influence.

Social Norms

> Don't boo. Vote.
>
> —President Barack Obama, 2016 Democratic National Convention

In 1994, Newt Gingrich sent members of the Republican Party a memo titled "Language: A Key Mechanism of Control." This memo came to be known as the GOPAC memo, and was meant to instruct Republicans on what types of words to use when describing their political opposition. As he wrote in the memo, "This list is prepared so that you might have a directory of words to use in writing literature and mail, in preparing speeches, and in producing electronic media. The words and phrases are powerful" (Gingrich 1994). Gingrich's list of recommended words to describe Democrats included betray, bizarre, decay, destroy, devour, greed, lie, pathetic, radical, selfish, shame, sick, steal, and traitors, among many others. To this day, this is the type of language used by party leaders to demonize opponents.

In 2015, Republican senator John McCain accused Democratic secretary of state John Kerry of being less trustworthy than the leaders of Iran, a known adversary of the United States. McCain and Kerry had once been friendly Senate colleagues. In response to McCain's comments, President Barack Obama announced, "That's an indication of the degree to which partisanship has crossed all boundaries. It needs to stop" (Coll 2015). Unfortunately, Obama was not the best person to make this argument. In fact, a prominent Republican would have presented the best chance for this message to have an effect, as the action that needed to be addressed came from within the Republican team.

One way that outright partisan prejudice may be addressed is for the parties themselves to establish new norms for partisan behavior. Putting aside for a moment how or why they would do this, scholars do know that "what group members think of what others are thinking may play a key role in influencing intergroup relations and perceptions" (Putra 2014). In other words, if group members believe that other ingroup members are tolerant of the outgroup, this can turn into a more broadly tolerant approach toward the opposing team.

In fact, Allport himself, back in 1954, argued that "the remedy for prejudiced opinion is not suppression, but rather a free-flowing counteraction by unprejudiced opinion" (469). If the parties themselves had any interest in reducing levels of partisan prejudice, they could likely do so simply by encouraging the prominent flag-bearers of the party to loudly and freely discuss partisan opponents in an unprejudiced way. According to Hogg (2001), group leaders have power to influence group members because group members "cognitively and behaviorally conform to the prototype" of the leader.

What if the leaders of the Democratic and Republican parties decided to take on a tolerant rhetoric toward the opposing team? What if party prototypes started discussing real differences rather than demonizing their opponents? What if party opinion leaders (of both parties) started talking about politics by commending compromise and acknowledging the humanity and validity of the opposing team? What if there were a new, opposite version of the GOPAC memo, in which the demonizing words were discouraged rather than encouraged?

There is no reason to believe that this will occur in the near term, particularly in the Republican Party. Trump supporters at the 2016 Republican National Convention repeatedly called for the imprisonment of Trump's Democratic opponent Hillary Clinton. Trump himself repeatedly encouraged bias and intolerance. Furthermore, party leaders are incentivized to maintain conflict and incivility. It draws attention and votes. But if for some reason both parties were to stand up for norms of civil partisan interaction, it could reduce partisan conflict and prejudice in American politics in general. This, however, is highly unlikely without some secondary intervention.

Superordinate Goals

Back in 1954, once the Rattlers and Eagles had reached a point of such violent conflict that they had to be separated, the experimenters decided to try to bring them back into friendly relations. They knew that superordinate goals, or goals that go beyond group boundaries and include both groups, had been theorized to help groups mend rifts between them. The experimenters presented the Rattlers and the Eagles with a number of challenges that could only be solved if the teams worked together. In one case, the experimenters cut off the water supply to the camp, and as the boys grew more and more thirsty, they were compelled to cooperate to find and solve the problem with the water supply. In a second case, the teams were asked to contribute money to fund a movie night at the camp. They were forced to decide together how much money each team would contribute to obtain this precious treat. Finally, a precariously angled tree that threatened the camp was chopped down and pulled away by both teams of boys working together. These superordinate goals allowed the boys a chance to see each other as human beings, and though they still identified as Rattlers and Eagles, the animosity between them began to subside. After these exercises, the boys remained partial to their own teams, but they did agree to ride home in the same bus at the end of camp. Prior to the exercises, both teams had refused to share a bus with the others.

A modern political example of this can be seen in the aftermath of the terrorist attacks of September 11. For a short time afterward, Democrats and Republicans came together, at least in their approval of the president, George W. Bush. However, the activation of a superordinate American identity did not heal the rift between the parties. In fact, the attacks spurred increasing disputes between the parties over how best to respond, and a drawn-out war further divided the parties. As of this writing, news of Russian tampering in the 2016 election may be another influence that can unite Democrats and Republicans in service to the same goal of protecting America, but already Republican public approval of Russian president Vladimir Putin has increased (Nussbaum and Oreskes 2016).

In the best case, as Bert Klandermans wrote in 2014, "superordinate identity makes it possible for people to accept disadvantages done to their subgroup in the interest of the larger community. People trust authorities to make sure that next time their group will benefit. This implies that superordinate identity and trust in authorities are intimately related" (14). Unfortunately, lack of trust in outgroup authorities does appear to be preventing at least some of the potential benefit of the common American identity. As Hetherington (2015) explains, "Trust among those who identify with the party outside the White House is much lower than historical norms and, indeed, almost completely evaporated among Republicans during Barack Obama's presidency" (446). With the decline in trust of outgroup partisans, superordinate goals are possibly no longer powerful enough to bring the parties together. Brewer (2001a) points out that "when intergroup attitudes and relations have moved into the realm of outgroup hate or overt conflict, . . . the prospect of superordinate common group identity may constitute a threat rather than a solution . . . when intense distrust has already developed, common group identities are likely to be seen as threats (or opportunities) for domination and absorption. In this case, the prescription for conflict reduction may first require protection of intergroup boundaries and distinctive identities" (36). Brewer adds that the best way to protect distinctive identities is for a society to be divided along multiple lines, in a cross-cutting pattern. Social sorting is a barrier to the possible solution of superordinate goals.

The challenge, then, is to find any goal that could unify Democrats and Republicans and not simply cause more harm than good. The magnitude of this challenge is, in fact, what has been revealed in the multiple models described in this book. Despite a large number of common goals and essentially American problems, partisans have yet to find a way to unite in defense of outcomes rather than lashing out with partisan rancor regardless of the consequences. So far, Democrats and Republicans still won't board the same bus to go home.

Self-Affirmation

> It is the frustration of basic needs by instigating conditions that leads group members, whose individual identity is shaken, to turn to the group for identity, to focus more on their social identity, or to "give themselves over" to an identity group. This frustration also leads to scapegoating and the creation of destructive ideologies (which identify enemies), that turns the group against another group.
>
> —Ervin Staub, "Individual and Group Identities in Genocide and Mass Killing"

A great deal of attention has been paid recently to uneducated, poor, white Americans, who are rising in prominence in American politics due to their increasingly visible racial prejudice, affiliation with Republican president Donald Trump, and their uniquely increasing rates of mortality due to drug and alcohol abuse (Case and Deaton 2015). Repeatedly, we see them described as feeling as if they have been left behind. As Trump reminded his supporters, "We got $18 trillion in debt. We got nothing but problems. . . . We're dying. We're dying. We need money. . . . We have losers. We have people that don't have it. We have people that are morally corrupt. We have people that are selling this country down the drain. . . . The American dream is dead" (Frum 2016). This is not an uplifting message. In fact, it is a message that explicitly reminds these Americans that they should have higher status but unfairly do not.

According to a theory from social psychology, there is good reason to believe that these voters are suffering from damaged self-esteem, driven by either a lack of economic opportunity, a fear of a culturally changing country, or some combination thereof. Those with damaged self-esteem normally look for a way to enhance their self-image. One powerful place to find such a thing is a person's group identity, which provides an alternate way for individuals to feel highly esteemed.

The study of self-esteem and self-uncertainty has been ongoing in the field of social psychology for some time. Recent research has examined the effects of self-esteem and self-affirmation on political variables. Self-esteem has been shown to affect ideological closed-mindedness (Cohen et al. 2007), American patriotism (Hohman and Hogg 2015), opinions about the Affordable Care Act (Bendersky 2014), evaluations of debate performances (Binning et al. 2010), and violence, extremism, and authoritarianism (Hogg, Kruglanksi, and van den Bos 2013), among other things.

Hogg (2014) has argued that uncertainty about a person's own status can lead them to identify with more extreme positions and groups, while Hogg, Adelman, and Blagg (2010) have shown that this same uncertainty can lead to stronger religious identification. Other work based in social identity theory finds that when self-esteem declines, people attempt to improve it by using the status of their social groups as a buttressing agent, privileging ingroups and derogating outgroups (Crocker et al. 1987). In essence, when people feel badly about themselves they turn to their groups for self-affirmation, becoming more strongly affiliated with the group.

Furthermore, when self-esteem is threatened, people tend to prefer their social groups to be increasingly homogeneous (Jetten, Hogg, and Mullin 2000). When people feel self-esteem declining, they not only cling more strongly to their group identities but they "circle the wagons" of social identity, a process very much like social sorting, in order to keep their multiple identities as aligned (and therefore impervious to outsiders) as possible.

In the realm of American politics, this leads to the social polarization that emerges out of strong and aligned political group identities, as well as the increasingly aggressive activism that arises from these strengthened identities.

The good news is that Cohen et al. (2007) have found that simply reminding a person of their own self-worth, a technique called self-affirmation, can significantly reduce extremism and ideological closed-mindedness. To date, very little research within political science has taken advantage of the self-esteem literature to explain political attachments and/or political polarization in American politics, but future research may be able to use this information in a way that can safeguard economically disadvantaged white Americans from using their group identities to soothe their own sense of inadequacy.

Alternatively, an economic upturn or change in economic status for these and other Americans could reduce the intensification of outgroup loathing that is currently occurring among American partisans.

Demographic Trends

Although we do not have reliable voter data from before the 1950s, McCarty, Poole, and Rosenthal (2008) have documented polarization in Congress going back to the Civil War. From these data, it is possible to see that the current levels of polarization, at least in Congress, are relatively close to what they were directly after the Civil War. So, considering that these levels of polarization significantly decreased between the Civil War and the 1950s, it may be possible to use some of the information from that period to help guide us toward a less polarized nation. In 2012, Hetherington and Haidt summarized for the *New York Times* multiple theories from political science that explain the depolarization period, including "shifts in the coalitions that composed each party, the shared experiences of war and economic calamity and very low levels of immigration, which allowed a stronger sense of national identity to form."

In all that this book has explored, it seems that the sense of national identity is one of the main victims of the social homogenization of the two parties. As the coalitions that make up Democrats and Republicans grow increasingly socially distant from one another, the superordinate identity of the nation grows less powerful and may even drive partisans apart.

In addition to this, we are witnessing a major change in the racial makeup of the American population. Ruy Teixeira, William Frey, and Robert Griffin predicted in February 2015 that the United States eligible voting population would reach majority-minority status in 2052. Some states, such as New Mexico, have already reached that status, while other states, like Colorado would have to wait until 2060. A number of Red states, however, would turn majority-minority even sooner. Texas is predicted to be majority-minority in 2019, Georgia in 2036, and Louisiana in 2048. Mississippi, Oklahoma, Virginia, and North Carolina are predicted to reach majority-minority status during the 2050 decade. Furthermore, Alabama, Arkansas, Kansas, Massachusetts, Michigan, Oregon, Pennsylvania, Rhode Island, South Carolina, and Utah are expected to reach at least 40 percent minority populations by 2060. They describe a "superdiversification" of American children, explaining, "In 1980, children were 25 percent minority; today, they are 46 percent minority. And diversification will not stop in the future: In 2040, children are projected to be 57 percent minority, and in 2060, children should be 65 percent minority" (Teixeira, Frey, and Griffin 2015, 11).

Unfortunately, decades of research, beginning with Allport, have found a positive relationship between the size of a minority group and levels of white prejudice against minorities. Craig and Richeson (2014) found that, when white respondents were presented with these statistics about the *projected* population breakdown, they more strongly preferred to spend time with other whites than did respondents who were told about current population statistics. Craig and Richeson found that concern about the status of white Americans drives this effect. This means that the changing demographics of the American population are not leading toward racial tolerance, at least not soon. Furthermore, recent research that I have done with Leonie Huddy and Nechama Horwitz has found that Latinos are increasingly identifying with the Democratic Party and that this is partially driven by their sense of general discrimination against Latinos (Huddy, Mason, and Horwitz 2016).

In terms of social sorting, racial minorities[1] tend to identify with the Democratic Party, while whites identify as Republicans. The changes in the makeup of the American electorate suggest that, should current alignments persist, the Democratic Party will gradually grow to win increasing numbers of local, state, and national elections, despite having lost the 2016 elections across the board. According to social identity theory, group status matters a great deal to group members. When a group's status is low, as would be the case if Republicans began to lose elections in a consistent manner, a group member has three choices. A group member can (1) exit the group, (2) grow increasingly creative about how to describe group status, or (3) fight to change the group's status in society. Currently, strongly identified Republicans have been fighting, via activism, to maintain their group's status, just as Democrats have. If, however, the status or coherence of the Republican Party declines in the next few years or decades, it may be the case that increasing numbers of Republicans will choose to exit the group (likely becoming independents). If that occurs, it is possible that American partisans will experience a new realignment, which would reduce party homogeneity and therefore reduce social polarization.

Rift in One Party: An Unsorting

> Should Mr. Trump clinch the presidential nomination, it would represent a rout of historic proportions for the institutional Republican Party, and could set off an internal rift unseen in either party for a half-century, since white Southerners abandoned the Democratic Party en masse during the civil rights movement.
>
> —Alexander Burns, Maggie Haberman, and Jonathan Martin, "Inside the Republican Party's Desperate Mission to Stop Donald Trump"

It is reasonable to argue that one major reason for the period of partisan dealignment in the 1970s and 1980s had a lot to do with the flight of southern conservatives from the Democratic Party. This era of dealignment, while messy, was also full of cross-cutting cleavages, which held levels of partisan rancor and social polarization lower than they are today. The Donald Trump phenomenon in 2016 was predicted by many to generate similar rifts in the Republican Party, though as of this writing few have appeared. Fred Malek, the finance chairman of the Republican Governors Association, was quoted by the *New York Times*: "There's no single leader and no single institution that can bring a diverse group called the Republican Party together, behind a single candidate. It just doesn't exist" (Burns, Haberman, and Martin 2016). Just as southern Democrats did not immediately join the Republican Party after 1964, it would take some time for any rifts in the Republican Party to realign into a new system of party coalitions. On the other hand, since the Republican victories in 2016, most party-infighting discussion has focused on the rifts within the Democratic Party.

Still, divisions in the Republican Party were emerging even before the appearance of Donald Trump. The rise of the Tea Party in 2010 and of the Freedom Caucus in the House of Representatives demonstrated genuine divisions between factions of the Republican Party. Ragusa and Gaspar (2016) found that the Tea Party and the Freedom Caucus have independently generated "party-like" effects in Congress, different from the Republican Party itself. Bode et al. (2015) analyzed Twitter posts and found that conservatives could be divided into three distinct groups. Since the widespread Republican victories in 2016, these various parts of the party must cooperate in governing. If the demographic trends toward racial diversity continue, and Republicans as a group begin to disagree on governing principles, it is distinctly possible that the party could reorganize itself into new sets of social groups. Social identities could be divided between factions of the party, which would generate the cross-cutting cleavages that suppress social polarization and social distance. This may be an unlikely scenario, but it is one way to imagine an unsorting of the American electorate, building, perhaps ironically, toward a more tolerant set of partisans on both sides.

Where Does This Leave Us?

Nothing in politics is forever, and party alignments change and move over time. It just so happens that the current alignment of social identities within the two parties is promoting a greater focus on partisan victory than on the good of the nation. This may be, in the context of the 2016 election, happening among Republicans more than Democrats. However, the social homogenization of the parties has made it difficult for partisans to learn to like, or even humanize, their partisan opponents. They are stereotyped, vilified, and rejected out of hand. The unfortunate truth of this, however, is that these deep social divisions are allowing opportunities for policy compromise to go unnoticed. A 2015 study found that there are multiple points of agreement across party lines, even on a polarizing topic like abortion (Vavreck 2016). Dozens of other studies have found the same regarding other issues, including gun control. Partisans of the two parties are capable of coming to agreement on many issues. But today, they will change their positions rather than agree with the other side.

As parties grow more sorted, the incentives for party identifiers to compromise with the opposition decline. As Tajfel found so many decades ago, when people are socially identified with a group, "it is the winning that seems more important to them." The social makeup of the two parties has real consequences for American politics. A more socially homogeneous set of parties generates an electorate that is unresponsive to external challenges. It reduces the portion of the population that can listen to political messages impassively. It generates prejudice between citizens who identify with differing parties but may otherwise get along.

Identity is a crucial component of American democracy. As I explain in chapter 2 and demonstrate in chapter 4, partisan identity can be separated from issue preferences, and the identity element can be a powerful motivator of human judgment, emotion, and behavior. Partisans have natural incentives to see the world through a partisan lens, and to privilege their own party over their opponents. They are naturally inclined to prefer to spend social time with members of their own party, and to interpret the actions and characteristics of the other party with bias.

Though political science has long understood the social power of partisan identity, or, separately, racial or religious identity, this book has shown that these identities are far more informative when they are examined in relation to one another. No single person holds one single identity. The convergence or divergence of multiple social identities has real consequences for political behavior, particularly when partisan identities are involved. As the Democratic and Republican parties have grown increasingly socially distinct from one another, as I document in chapter 3, the potential for compromise and cooperation have declined. In chapter 5, I describe the increased bias and social distance that is induced when partisan identities are aligned with other types of social identities. More than partisan identity alone, socially sorted parties motivate a preference for ingroup partisans and prejudice in evaluating national figures and conditions.

Social sorting also does another very important thing. When parties are socially divided, their members react emotionally to political messaging, leading to behavioral consequences elaborated in chapter 6. But when partisans hold cross-cutting social identities, their emotional reactions are dampened. These emotional reactions are partial drivers of political activism, as chapter 7 shows. Therefore, when a nation changes from one made up of many cross-cutting identities to one built on socially segregated parties, the result is an electorate that is, on average, more angry, excitable, and active than it was before the social shift.

I have taken the position that the social sorting of the American electorate has been, on balance, normatively bad for American democracy. Many may disagree, thinking that an engaged and excited electorate is desirable. I maintain that an electorate that is emotionally engaged and politically activated on behalf of prejudice and misunderstanding is not an electorate that produces positive outcomes. The social sorting of American partisans has changed the electorate into a group of voters who are relatively unresponsive to changing information or real national problems. The voting booths are increasingly occupied by those who fiercely want their side to win and consider the other party to be disastrous. This effect exceeds that of bias based on partisanship alone. As long as a social divide is maintained between the parties, the electorate will behave more like a pair of warring tribes than like the people of a single nation, caring for their shared future.

APPENDIX

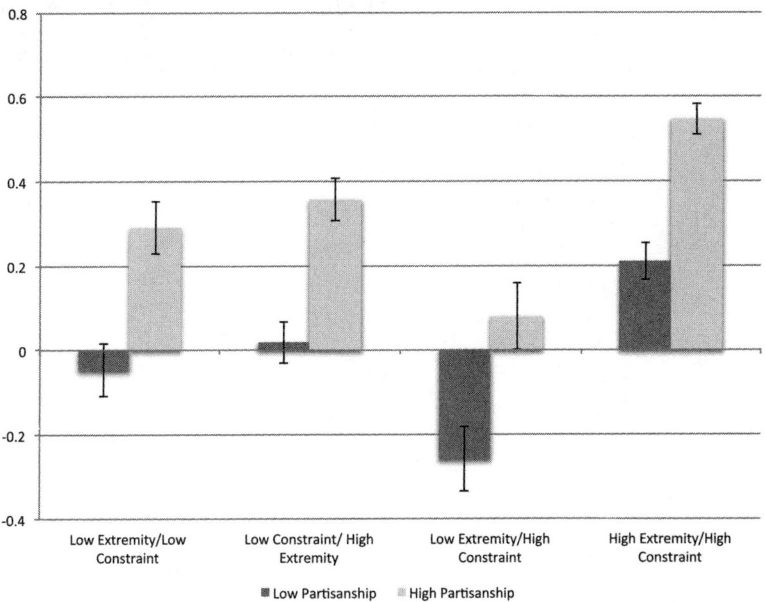

Figure A.1. Alternate to figure 4.5, varying issue extremity and constraint

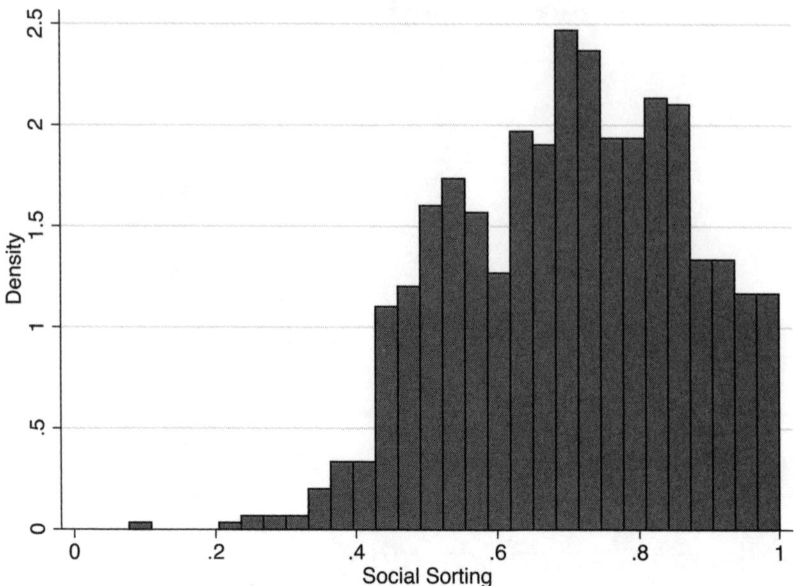

Figure A.2. Distribution of social-sorting score

Table A.1a Originating regressions for figure 4.2: Democratic feeling thermometer

	1980		1982		1984		1986		1988		1990		1992		1994	
Partisan identity (strong Democrat = high)	**0.37**	(.02)	**0.37**	(.01)	**0.35**	(.01)	**0.36**	(.01)	**0.37**	(.01)	**0.29**	(.01)	**0.35**	(.02)	**0.37**	(.02)
Issue scale (most liberal = high)	**0.09**	(.03)	**0.10**	(.03)	**0.10**	(.03)	**0.06**	(.03)	**0.10**	(.03)	**0.06**	(.03)	**0.16**	(.04)	**0.25**	(.04)
Education	**−0.12**	(.02)	**−0.10**	(.02)	**−0.08**	(.01)	**−0.08**	(.01)	**−0.08**	(.02)	**−0.09**	(.02)	**−0.12**	(.02)	**−0.05**	(.02)
Male	−0.01	(.01)	**−0.03**	(.01)	**−0.02**	(.01)	**−0.03**	(.01)	**−0.03**	(.01)	**−0.04**	(.01)	**−0.03**	(.01)	−0.02	(.01)
White	**−0.06**	(.01)	**−0.04**	(.01)	**−0.07**	(.01)	**−0.04**	(.01)	**−0.06**	(.01)	**−0.04**	(.01)	**−0.03**	(.01)	**−0.07**	(.02)
Age	**0.00**	(.00)	**0.00**	(.00)	**0.00**	(.00)	**0.00**	(.00)	**0.00**	(.00)	**0.00**	(.00)	**0.00**	(.00)	**0.00**	(.00)
South	**0.02**	(.01)	**0.03**	(.01)	0.00	(.01)	0.01	(.01)	0.00	(.01)	0.02	(.01)	**0.03**	(.01)	0.02	(.01)
Urban	0.00	(.01)	0.01	(.01)	0.00	(.01)	0.00	(.01)	0.01	(.01)	0.01	(.01)	**0.03**	(.01)	0.01	(.01)
Church attendance	**0.03**	(.01)	0.01	(.01)	0.01	(.01)	0.02	(.01)	0.00	(.01)	0.01	(.01)	−0.01	(.01)	−0.02	(.02)
Constant	**0.41**	(.03)	**0.42**	(.03)	**0.44**	(.02)	**0.45**	(.02)	**0.41**	(.03)	**0.47**	(.03)	**0.37**	(.04)	**0.27**	(.04)
R^2	0.38		0.46		0.41		0.38		0.39		0.29		0.42		0.51	
N	1580		1370		2198		2115		1977		1909		1077		991	

(continued)

Table A.1a (continued)

	1996		1998		2000		2004		2008		2012	
Partisan identity (strong Democrat = high)	**0.48**	(.03)	**0.34**	(.02)	**0.45**	(.02)	**0.42**	(.02)	**0.46**	(.02)	**0.49**	(.02)
Issue scale (most liberal = high)	−0.02	(.07)	**0.13**	(.03)	**0.05**	(.02)	**0.10**	(.04)	**0.11**	(.02)	**0.25**	(.03)
Education	0.01	(.04)	**−0.07**	(.02)	−0.03	(.02)	**−0.10**	(.02)	**−0.09**	(.02)	**−0.06**	(.02)
Male	**−0.07**	(.02)	**−0.03**	(.01)	**−0.03**	(.01)	−0.02	(.01)	**−0.03**	(.01)	−0.02	(.01)
White	**−0.08**	(.02)	**−0.09**	(.01)	**−0.05**	(.01)	**−0.05**	(.01)	**−0.05**	(.01)	**−0.07**	(.01)
Age	0.00	(.00)	**0.00**	(.00)	0.00	(.00)	**0.00**	(.00)	0.00	(.00)	0.01	(.02)
South	0.03	(.02)	0.01	(.01)	0.01	(.01)	0.02	(.01)	0.00	(.01)	0.00	(.01)
Urban	0.00	(.02)	−0.02	(.01)	**0.03**	(.01)	—		—		**0.03**	(.02)
Church attendance	−0.03	(.03)	0.01	(.01)	0.02	(.01)	−0.01	(.01)	0.01	(.01)	**−0.03**	(.01)
Constant	**0.37**	(.06)	**0.42**	(.03)	**0.34**	(.03)	**0.38**	(.03)	**0.38**	(.03)	**0.25**	(.02)
R^2	0.49		0.41		0.42		0.48		0.52		0.63	
N	395		1258		1754		1186		2030		3437	

Note: Coefficients indicate change in Democratic feeling thermometer. Bold coefficients are significant at the $p < .05$ level. Standard errors in parentheses. All models are OLS models with robust standard errors. All variables are coded to range from 0 to 1.

Table A.1b Originating regressions for figure 4.3: Republican feeling thermometer

	1980		1982		1984		1986		1988		1990		1992		1994	
Partisan identity (strong Democrat = high)	**−0.32**	(.02)	**−0.37**	(.02)	**−0.37**	(.01)	**−0.36**	(.01)	**−0.39**	(.01)	**−0.33**	(.02)	**−0.37**	(.02)	**−0.33**	(.02)
Issue scale (most liberal = high)	**−0.10**	(.03)	**−0.17**	(.03)	**−0.21**	(.03)	**−0.20**	(.03)	**−0.18**	(.03)	**−0.15**	(.03)	**−0.21**	(.04)	**−0.10**	(.05)
Education	**−0.08**	(.02)	−0.04	(.02)	**−0.06**	(.02)	−0.01	(.02)	**−0.04**	(.02)	**−0.06**	(.02)	**−0.12**	(.02)	−0.02	(.03)
Male	0.00	(.01)	−0.01	(.01)	−0.01	(.01)	−0.01	(.01)	0.00	(.01)	**−0.02**	(.01)	**−0.05**	(.01)	0.00	(.01)
White	−0.02	(.02)	0.03	(.02)	**−0.03**	(.01)	−0.02	(.01)	0.00	(.01)	−0.02	(.01)	0.00	(.02)	−0.03	(.02)
Age	**0.00**	(.00)	0.00	(.00)	**0.00**	(.00)	0.00	(.00)	**0.00**	(.00)	0.00	(.00)	0.00	(.00)	0.00	(.00)
South	0.01	(.01)	**0.03**	(.01)	**0.03**	(.01)	0.02	(.01)	**0.04**	(.01)	0.00	(.01)	**0.03**	(.01)	**0.05**	(.02)
Urban	−0.02	(.01)	0.01	(.01)	**−0.03**	(.01)	−0.02	(.01)	0.01	(.01)	0.01	(.01)	0.00	(.01)	−0.02	(.02)
Church attendance	**0.04**	(.01)	**0.04**	(.01)	**0.04**	(.01)	**0.03**	(.01)	**0.04**	(.01)	**0.05**	(.01)	0.02	(.02)	0.00	(.02)
Constant	**0.83**	(.03)	**0.81**	(.03)	**0.90**	(.03)	**0.90**	(.03)	**0.85**	(.03)	**0.86**	(.03)	**0.90**	(.04)	**0.81**	(.04)
R^2	0.24		0.33		0.35		0.29		0.33		0.25		0.33		0.29	
N	1580		1370		2198		2115		1977		1909		1077		991	

(continued)

Table A.1b (continued)

	1996		1998		2000		2004		2008		2012	
Partisan identity (strong Democrat = high)	**–0.38**	(.03)	**–0.40**	(.02)	**–0.38**	(.02)	**–0.46**	(.02)	**–0.49**	(.02)	**–0.45**	(.02)
Issue scale (most liberal = high)	–0.09	(.07)	–0.04	(.04)	**–0.05**	(.02)	**–0.20**	(.04)	**–0.07**	(.02)	**–0.25**	(.03)
Education	**–0.14**	(.05)	**–0.09**	(.02)	**–0.07**	(.02)	**–0.09**	(.03)	**–0.08**	(.02)	**–0.05**	(.02)
Male	–0.02	(.02)	0.00	(.01)	0.00	(.01)	–0.02	(.01)	**–0.04**	(.01)	**–0.02**	(.01)
White	0.02	(.03)	–0.02	(.02)	0.00	(.01)	**–0.04**	(.02)	**–0.03**	(.01)	0.02	(.01)
Age	0.00	(.00)	0.00	(.00)	0.00	(.00)	0.00	(.00)	0.00	(.00)	**0.06**	(.02)
South	0.00	(.02)	**0.04**	(.01)	0.00	(.01)	**0.03**	(.01)	**0.03**	(.01)	0.01	(.01)
Urban	0.01	(.03)	–0.02	(.01)	–0.01	(.02)	—		—		**0.04**	(.02)
Church attendance	**0.07**	(.03)	0.02	(.02)	**0.04**	(.01)	0.00	(.02)	**0.03**	(.01)	–0.01	(.01)
Constant	**0.86**	(.06)	**0.81**	(.03)	**0.78**	(.03)	**0.94**	(.04)	**0.83**	(.03)	**0.81**	(.02)
R^2	0.35		0.33		0.31		0.44		0.46		0.54	
N	395		1258		1754		1186		2030		3435	

Note: Coefficients indicate change in Republican feeling thermometer. Bold coefficients are significant at the $p < .05$ level. Standard errors in parentheses. All models are OLS models with robust standard errors. All variables are coded to range from 0 to 1.

Table A.2 Originating regression for figure 4.5

	Social-distance bias	
Partisan identity strength	**0.34**	(.04)
Issue extremity	0.07	(.10)
Issue constraint	−0.21	(.11)
Issue extremity*constraint	**0.40**	(.17)
Education	−0.01	(.01)
Sophistication	**0.11**	(.04)
White	0.02	(.04)
Hispanic	0.05	(.04)
Black	0.10	(.05)
Male	−0.02	(.02)
Income	**−0.09**	(.03)
Age (decades)	0.00	(.01)
Church attendance	**−0.05**	(.03)
Constant	−0.05	(.08)
R^2	0.20	
N	774	

Note: Coefficients indicate change in social-distance bias. Bold coefficients are significant at the $p <$ .05 level. Standard errors in parentheses. All models are OLS models with robust standard errors. All variables are coded to range from 0 to 1.

Explanation of the Social-Sorting Measure

The *social-sorting* scale begins with assessing the subjective strength of various political identities. It includes the *partisan-identity* and *ideological-identity* four-item scales described in the previous chapter, as well as identity scales created to measure the strength of evangelical, secular, African American, and Tea Party identities. These additional identity scales are created in the same manner as the partisan and ideological-identity measures and likewise form reliable scales: evangelical (α = 0.88), secular (α = 0.80), black (α = 0.78), and Tea Party (α = 0.90).

For ease of explanation, table A.3 presents two potential Republican subjects, one who scores the highest possible score on the sociopartisan sorting scale and another who receives the lowest possible score.

Individual A in this example would score highest on Republican identity, conservative identity, evangelical identity, and Tea Party identity. This score can rise no higher but could fall were she to identify less strongly with her party or any of her party-consistent groups. It could also fall were she to identify at all with any of the party-inconsistent groups. Individual B, still a Republican (because she chose to answer the traditional seven-point party-identification scale on the Republican end of the scale), holds the weakest possible Republican social identity, the strongest possible liberal identity, the strongest secular identity, and the strongest black identity. Her score can fall no lower, but it could increase were she to identify less strongly with a cross-cutting identity, or to identify at all with any of the party-consistent identities, or to identify more strongly with Republicans.

The distribution of this variable, after recoding, is presented below. Average score for Republicans is .72 and for Democrats is .68.

Table A.3 Example calculation of sociopartisan sorting scores

Individual A: Highest-score Republican	Individual B: Lowest-score Republican
Republican identity = 1	Republican identity = 0
Democratic identity = NA	Democratic identity = NA
Conservative identity = 1	Conservative identity = NA
Liberal identity = NA	Liberal identity = −1
Evangelical identity = 1	Evangelical identity = NA
Secular identity = NA	Secular identity = −1
Black identity = NA	Black identity = −1
Tea Party identity = 1	Tea Party identity = NA
Sorting score = (1 + 1 + 1 + 1)/4 = 1	Sorting score = (0 − 1 − 1 − 1)/4 = −0.75

Note: Sorting score rescaled to range from 0 to 1 by adding 0.75, then dividing by 1.75. No respondent rated the lowest sorting score. One Democrat scored −0.61 before recoding, and one Republican scored −0.27. The lowest recoded score is therefore 0.08. Nineteen respondents scored a perfect 1. All variables are coded to range between 0 and 1. Each identity score is generated from the four-item scale assessing social identification with the group. Party-inconsistent groups are reverse coded to range from −1 to 0. "NA" indicates a missing score.

Table A.4 Originating regressions for figure 5.1

	Cumulative ANES to 2012		2011 YouGov	
Partisan strength	**0.26**	(.02)	**0.31**	(.05)
Partisan-ideological sorting	**0.21**	(.03)		
Sociopartisan sorting			**0.36**	(.08)
Issue extremity	0.00	(.03)	**0.32**	(.13)
Issue constraint	−0.07	(.05)	0.14	(.13)
Issue extremity*constraint	**0.28**	(.08)	−0.21	(.20)
Political knowledge	0.00	(.02)	**0.14**	(.04)
Education	−0.03	(.02)	−0.01	(.01)
White	0.02	(.02)	0.04	(.04)
Hispanic	0.02	(.03)	0.03	(.04)
Black	**0.08**	(.03)	0.09	(.05)
Male	−0.02	(.01)	−0.03	(.02)
Income	−0.04	(.02)	0.00	(.00)
Age	0.00	(.00)	**0.01**	(.01)
Church attendance	0.00	(.00)	−0.04	(.03)
Constant	**0.07**	(.04)	**−0.26**	(.10)
R^2	0.26		0.25	
N	2147		775	

Note: Coefficients indicate change in partisan warmth bias. Bold coefficients are significant at the $p < .05$ level. Standard errors in parentheses. All models are OLS models with robust standard errors. All variables are coded to range from 0 to 1. Age is measured in ten-year increments. Coefficients should be interpreted with caution, as the partisan-identity and sorting measures are related by construction, so holding one constant while moving the other is not precisely possible. The predicted values take account of this problem by holding both variables constant at one value, but the regression coefficients do not.

Table A.5 Originating regression for figure 5.2

	Warmth bias	
Partisan identity	**0.31**	(.05)
Sociopartisan sorting	**0.36**	(.08)
Issue extremity (including importance)	**0.21**	(.07)
Issue constraint	−0.01	(.04)
Education	**−0.01**	(.01)
Sophistication	**0.14**	(.05)
White	0.04	(.04)
Hispanic	0.03	(.04)
Black	**0.09**	(.05)
Male	−0.03	(.02)
Income	**0.00**	(.00)
Age (decades)	**0.01**	(.01)
Church attendance	−0.04	(.03)
Constant	**−0.19**	(.07)
R^2	0.25	
N	775	

Note: Coefficients indicate change in partisan warmth bias. Bold coefficients are significant at the $p < .05$ level. Standard errors in parentheses. All models are OLS models with robust standard errors. All variables are coded to range from 0 to 1. Coefficients should be interpreted with caution, as the partisan-identity and sorting measures are related by construction, so holding one constant while moving the other is not precisely possible. The predicted values take account of this problem by holding both variables constant at one value, but the regression coefficients do not.

Table A.6 Originating regression for figure 5.4

	Social-distance bias	
Partisan identity	**0.25**	(.05)
Sociopartisan sorting	**0.27**	(.09)
Issue extremity	0.05	(.10)
Issue constraint	**−0.23**	(.11)
Issue extremity*constraint	**0.38**	(.16)
Education	−0.01	(.01)
Sophistication	0.06	(.04)
White	0.03	(.04)
Hispanic	0.05	(.04)
Black	**0.10**	(.05)
Male	−0.02	(.02)
Income	**−0.01**	(.00)
Age (decades)	0.00	(.01)
Church attendance	−0.05	(.03)
Constant	−0.14	(.09)
R^2	0.21	
N	774	

Note: Coefficients indicate change in social-distance bias. Bold coefficients are significant at the $p < .05$ level. Standard errors in parentheses. All models are OLS models with robust standard errors. All variables are coded to range from 0 to 1. Coefficients should be interpreted with caution, as the partisan-identity and sorting measures are related by construction, so holding one constant while moving the other is not precisely possible. The predicted values take account of this problem by holding both variables constant at one value, but the regression coefficients do not.

Table A.7 Originating regression for figure 5.5

	Warmth bias	
Partisan identity	**0.31**	(.05)
Sociopartisan sorting	**0.36**	(.08)
Issue extremity	**0.32**	(.13)
Issue constraint	0.14	(.13)
Issue extremity*constraint	−0.21	(.20)
Education	−0.01	(.01)
Sophistication	**0.14**	(.04)
White	0.04	(.04)
Hispanic	0.03	(.04)
Black	0.09	(.05)
Male	−0.03	(.02)
Income	0.00	(.00)
Age (decades)	**0.01**	(.01)
Church attendance	−0.04	(.03)
Constant	**−0.26**	(.10)
R^2	0.25	
N	775	

Note: Coefficients indicate change in partisan warmth bias. Bold coefficients are significant at the $p < .05$ level. Standard errors in parentheses. All models are OLS models with robust standard errors. All variables are coded to range from 0 to 1. Coefficients should be interpreted with caution, as the partisan-identity and sorting measures are related by construction, so holding one constant while moving the other is not precisely possible. The predicted values take account of this problem by holding both variables constant at one value, but the regression coefficients do not.

Table A.8 Originating regressions for figures 6.4 and 6.5

	Anger ANES		Pride ANES	
Sorting	**1.28**	(.24)	**0.85**	(.25)
Partisan strength	**1.54**	(.14)	**2.42**	(.14)
Issue extremity	−0.35	(.31)	−0.17	(.31)
Issue constraint	0.98	(.59)	0.64	(.60)
Issue extremity*constraint	0.93	(.90)	−0.42	(.87)
Education	**0.74**	(.15)	0.20	(.15)
Male	−0.03	(.08)	−0.08	(.08)
White	0.17	(.10)	−0.18	(.11)
Age	0.01	(.02)	0.04	(.02)
Southern location	**−0.20**	(.09)	**0.20**	(.09)
Urban	−0.19	(.11)	**−0.64**	(.12)
Church attendance	**−0.06**	(.03)	0.01	(.03)
Constant	**−1.67**	(.25)	**−1.43**	(.24)
Pseudo R^2 (from unweighted model)	0.13		0.15	
N	4395		4395	

Note: Dependent variables are coded 1 for reporting feeling angry/proud, and 0 for no report of this emotion. All variables are coded to range from 0 to 1. Bold coefficients are significant at the $p < .05$ level. Standard errors in parentheses. All models are logit models with sample weights.

Table A.9 Originating regressions for figure 6.9

	Issue polarization		Partisan identity		Sociopartisan sorting	
Angry responses to party-based threats						
Partisan identity			−0.08	(.04)		
Sociopartisan sorting					**−0.30**	(.12)
Group threat	**0.25**	(.05)	0.13	(.07)	−0.12	(.13)
Partisan identity × group threat			**0.24**	(.11)		
Sociopartisan sorting × group threat					**0.68**	(.23)
Issue polarization	0.03	(.05)	0.04	(.06)	0.09	(.06)
Issue polarization × group threat	0.12	(.10)	0.09	(.10)	−0.02	(.11)
White	0.01	(.04)	0.02	(.04)	**0.09**	(.03)
Black	**−0.15**	(.05)	**−0.14**	(.05)		
Male	0.00	(.02)	0.00	(.02)	0.01	(.03)
Income	0.00	(.00)	0.00	(.00)	0.00	(.00)
Age (decades)	**0.02**	(.01)	**0.02**	(.01)	**0.02**	(.01)
Sophistication	**0.14**	(.05)	**0.15**	(.05)	**0.13**	(.05)
Church attendance	0.04	(.03)	0.04	(.03)		
Constant	**0.14**	(.06)	**0.16**	(.06)	**0.22**	(.08)
R^2	0.16		0.17		0.18	
N	859		859		753	
Angry responses to issue-based threats						
Partisan identity			−0.03	(.04)		
Sociopartisan sorting					**−0.40**	0.12
Issue threat	**0.14**	(.05)	0.09	(.06)	**−0.27**	0.13
Partisan identity × issue threat			0.08	(.09)		
Sociopartisan sorting × issue threat					**0.70**	0.23
Issue polarization	−0.06	(.06)	−0.05	(.06)	0.00	0.07
Issue polarization × issue threat	**0.39**	(.10)	**0.38**	(.10)	**0.26**	0.12
White	0.01	(.04)	0.01	(.04)	0.09	0.03
Black	**−0.16**	(.05)	**−0.16**	(.05)	0.02	0.02
Male	0.01	(.02)	0.01	(.02)		
Income	0.00	(.00)	0.00	(.00)	0.00	0.00
Age (decades)	0.01	(.01)	0.01	(.01)	0.01	0.01
Sophistication	0.06	(.05)	0.06	(.05)	0.06	0.05
Church attendance	0.04	(.03)	0.04	(.03)		
Constant	**0.25**	(.06)	**0.27**	(.06)	**0.39**	0.08
R^2	0.17		0.17		0.19	
N	859		859		753	

Note: Coefficients represent changes in reported levels of anger. Bold coefficients are significant at the $p < .05$ level in a two-tailed test. Standard errors in parentheses. All models are OLS regressions with robust standard errors. All variables are coded to range from 0 to 1. Shaded cells represent marginal effects for ease of interpretation.

Table A.10 Originating regressions for figure 6.10

	Issue polarization		Partisan identity		Sociopartisan sorting	
Enthusiastic responses to party-based reassurances						
Partisan identity			**0.12**	(.04)		
Sociopartisan sorting					**0.30**	(.13)
Group support	**0.25**	0.05	0.03	(.07)	−0.06	(.13)
Partisan identity × group support			**0.34**	(.09)		
Sociopartisan sorting × group support					**0.54**	(.21)
Issue polarization	0.02	0.06	−0.01	(.06)	−0.04	(.06)
Issue polarization × group support	0.11	0.11	0.09	(.10)	0.01	(.11)
White	−0.02	0.04	−0.02	(.04)	**−0.07**	(.03)
Black	0.05	0.05	0.04	(.05)		
Male	0.02	0.02	0.03	(.02)	0.01	(.03)
Income	0.00	0.00	0.00	(.00)	0.00	(.00)
Age (decades)	0.00	0.01	0.00	(.01)	0.00	(.01)
Sophistication	−0.06	0.05	−0.08	(.05)	−0.10	(.06)
Church attendance	0.05	0.03	0.03	(.03)		
Constant	**0.36**	0.07	**0.33**	(.07)	**0.29**	(.08)
R^2	0.12		0.15		0.16	
N	859		859		753	
Enthusiastic responses to issue-based reassurances						
Partisan identity			**0.15**	(.04)		
Sociopartisan sorting					**0.28**	(.12)
Issue support	**0.17**	(.05)	0.12	(.07)	−0.09	(.14)
Partisan identity × issue support			0.08	(.10)		
Sociopartisan sorting × issue support					**0.51**	(.24)
Issue polarization	−0.04	(.06)	−0.07	(.06)	−0.10	(.06)
Issue polarization × issue support	**0.42**	(.11)	**0.39**	(.11)	**0.27**	(.13)
White	−0.04	(.04)	−0.04	(.04)	**−0.07**	(.03)
Black	0.03	(.05)	0.02	(.05)		
Male	0.01	(.02)	0.02	(.02)	0.01	(.02)
Income	−0.01	(.00)	0.00	(.00)	**−0.01**	(.00)
Age (decades)	0.00	(.01)	0.00	(.01)	0.00	(.01)
Sophistication	−0.07	(.05)	−0.08	(.05)	−0.09	(.05)
Church attendance	0.03	(.03)	0.02	(.03)		
Constant	**0.41**	(.06)	**0.37**	(.06)	**0.31**	(.08)
R^2	0.19		0.20		0.23	
N	859		859		753	

Note: Coefficients represent changes in reported levels of enthusiasm. Bold coefficients are significant at the $p < .05$ level in a two-tailed test. Standard errors in parentheses. All models are OLS regressions with robust standard errors. All variables are coded to range from 0 to 1. Shaded cells represent marginal effects for ease of interpretation.

Table A.11 Originating regression for figure 7.5

	Activism	
Partisan strength	**0.06**	(.01)
Partisan-ideological sorting	**0.10**	(.02)
Issue extremity	0.03	(.03)
Issue constraint	0.09	(.06)
Issue extremity*constraint	0.00	(.08)
Political knowledge	**0.08**	(.01)
White	0.00	(.01)
Black	**0.05**	(.02)
Male	0.01	(.01)
Income	**0.04**	(.02)
Age	**0.01**	(.00)
Church attendance	0.00	(.00)
Constant	−0.04	(.02)
R^2	0.11	
N	3426	

Note: Coefficients represent changes in levels of activism. Bold coefficients are significant at the $p < .05$ level. Standard errors in parentheses. All models are OLS models with robust standard errors. All variables are coded to range from 0 to 1. Coefficients should be interpreted with caution, as the partisan-identity and sorting measures are related by construction, so holding one constant while moving the other is not precisely possible. The predicted values take account of this problem by holding both variables constant at one value, but the regression coefficients do not. Data are weighted and drawn from the cumulative ANES file through 2012.

Table A.12 Originating regressions for figures 7.6 and 7.7

	Past activism		Intended activism	
Social sorting	**0.10**	(.02)	**0.44**	(0.08)
Issue extremity	0.03	(.03)	0.13	(0.14)
Issue constraint	0.09	(.06)	0.21	(0.18)
Issue extremity*constraint	0.00	(.08)	−0.14	(0.25)
White	0.00	(.01)	**−0.10**	(0.03)
Male	0.01	(.01)	**0.07**	(0.03)
Income	**0.04**	(.02)	**0.01**	(0.00)
Age	**0.01**	(.00)	0.02	(0.01)
Political knowledge	**0.08**	(.01)	**0.26**	(0.05)
Church attendance	0.00	(.00)	0.05	(0.04)
Constant	−0.04	(.02)	**−0.50**	(0.11)
R^2	0.19		0.17	
N	776		776	

Note: Coefficients represent changes in activism indices. Bold coefficients are significant at the $p < .05$ level. Standard errors in parentheses. All models are OLS models with robust standard errors. All variables are coded to range from 0 to 1.

Table A.13 Originating regressions for figure 7.8

	Prior activism	
Panels A and C		
Abortion social identity	**0.32**	(0.06)
Abortion issue extremity	−0.07	(0.07)
Abortion issue importance	**−0.17**	(0.07)
Abortion extremity*importance	**0.18**	(0.09)
White	0.00	(0.03)
Male	**0.06**	(0.02)
Income	**0.01**	(0.00)
Age	**0.03**	(0.01)
Political knowledge	**0.38**	(0.05)
Church attendance	0.01	(0.03)
Constant	**−0.27**	(0.08)
R^2	**0.20**	
N	**869**	
Panel B		
Abortion issue extremity	**0.09**	(0.02)
White	−0.01	(0.03)
Male	**0.05**	(0.02)
Income	**0.01**	(0.00)
Age	**0.03**	(0.01)
Political knowledge	**0.42**	(0.04)
Church attendance	0.04	(0.03)
Constant	**−0.19**	(0.05)
R^2	**0.18**	
N	**1041**	

Note: Coefficients represent changes in the four-item index of prior activism. Bold coefficients are significant at the $p < .05$ level. All models are OLS models with robust standard errors. All variables are coded to range from 0 to 1.

Table A.14 Originating regressions for figure 7.9

	Intended activism	
Panels A and C		
Abortion social identity	**0.28**	(0.07)
Abortion issue extremity	−0.08	(0.08)
Abortion issue importance	**−0.17**	(0.08)
Abortion extremity*importance	0.14	(0.09)
White	**−0.07**	(0.03)
Male	**0.07**	(0.02)
Income	**0.01**	(0.00)
Age	**0.02**	(0.01)
Political knowledge	**0.30**	(0.05)
Church attendance	**0.07**	(0.03)
Constant	**−0.29**	(0.08)
R^2	**0.14**	
N	**868**	
Panel B		
Abortion issue extremity	**0.06**	−(0.02)
White	**−0.07**	−(0.03)
Male	**0.08**	−(0.02)
Income	**0.01**	(0.00)
Age	**0.02**	−(0.01)
Political knowledge	**0.34**	−(0.04)
Church attendance	**0.09**	−(0.03)
Constant	**−0.24**	−(0.05)
R^2	**0.18**	
N	**1041**	

Note: Coefficients represent changes in the four-item index of intended activism. Bold coefficients are significant at the $p < .05$ level. All models are OLS models with robust standard errors. All variables are coded to range from 0 to 1.

Table A.15 Originating regressions for figure 7.10

	Intended activism		Intended activism	
Anger			**0.12**	(0.06)
Enthusiasm	**0.23**	(0.05)		
Issue extremity and constraint	**0.13**	(0.07)	**0.16**	(0.08)
White	−0.05	(0.07)	−0.01	(0.06)
Black	0.01	(0.09)	0.13	(0.08)
Male	0.05	(0.04)	**0.10**	(0.04)
Income	**0.01**	(0.00)	0.01	(0.00)
Age (decades)	0.00	(0.01)	**0.02**	(0.01)
Political knowledge	**0.36**	(0.08)	**0.21**	(0.08)
Church attendance	0.04	(0.05)	0.01	(0.05)
Constant	**−0.29**	(0.09)	**−0.25**	(0.10)
R^2	0.17		0.13	
N	366		376	

Note: Coefficients represent changes in the four-item index of intended activism. Bold coefficients are significant at the $p < .05$ level. Standard errors in parentheses. All models are OLS models with robust standard errors. All variables are coded to range from 0 to 1.

NOTES

CHAPTER ONE

1. According to the 2016 American National Election Study (ANES), with full sample weights, and independent "leaners" coded as partisans. The ANES is a series of election studies conducted by the ANES since 1948 to support analysis of public opinion and voting behavior in US presidential elections. The 2016 study features a dual-mode design with both face-to-face interviewing (n = 1,181) and surveys conducted on the Internet (n = 3,090), and a total sample size of 4,271. Respondents were interviewed in a pre-election survey between September 7 and November 7, 2016. The study reinterviewed as many as possible of the same respondents in a postelection survey between November 9 and January 8, 2017. The study was funded by the National Science Foundation via grants to the University of Michigan and Stanford University (grant nos. SES-1444721 and SES-1444910 respectively). The data were released by the ANES in April 2017. The data can be accessed at www.electionstudies.org.
2. This concept makes up the origin of social categorization theory and social identity theory, pioneered by Henri Tajfel and John Turner (1979).
3. For an early summary of these experiments, see Brewer (1979).
4. See Levendusky (2010) for this argument.
5. See Garner and Palmer (2011) for this argument.

CHAPTER TWO

1. Data drawn from a study by the author, funded by the National Science Foundation under grant no. SES-1065054 and fielded by Polimetrix, who collect an online sample of Americans and use matching techniques to construct a sample that is as similar as possible to a nationally representative sample.

CHAPTER THREE

1. South here is measured as what the ANES characterizes as the "political south," including only the eleven secession states: Alabama, Arkansas, Florida, Georgia, Louisiana, Mississippi, North Carolina, South Carolina, Tennessee, Texas, and Virginia.

CHAPTER FOUR

1. The issue extremity measure is an index of six issues: (1) The circumstances under which abortion should be allowed by law (four-point scale); (2) Whether to priori-

tize government services or spending (seven-point scale); (3) Whether government should have a role in health insurance (seven-point scale); (4) Whether government should provide aid to minorities/blacks (seven-point scale); (5) The extent to which defense spending should be increased or decreased (seven-point scale); and (6) Whether government should guarantee jobs to citizens (seven-point scale). Each issue is folded in half such that extreme liberal and conservative views are coded 1 and moderate views are coded 0. All of these folded issues are then combined into a scale. This is a well-differentiated measure—314 respondents or 3.16 percent of the sample score 0 on the scale, while 236 respondents or 2.37 percent of the sample score 1. The median score is 0.44 and the mean score is 0.45. The choice to measure issue extremity this way, without including any element of ideological constraint, was an intentional one. Broockman (2016) has found that "many Americans are not very ideologically consistent, [which] can lead summary measures that average individuals' positions across multiple issues to give the impression that these individuals support moderate policies 'on average' because they support some liberal policies and some conservative policies. An individual may well want policy to be very far left on one issue and very far right on another, but summarizing this individual's views as 'moderate' is misleading" (3). This extremity measure is examined here in order to account for an issue-based radicalization that can be seen to match the change in partisan feelings. An alternate measure that includes constraint (such as the one that Broockman argues can obscure issue extremism) does, in fact, increase somewhat over time, by nearly 10 points, while the warmth-bias measure increases by 15 points. An increase in constraint, however, does not necessarily mean that partisans are growing more radical in their issue positions, simply less conflicted. Extremity and constraint will be measured separately in later chapters.

2. Originating regressions can be found in the appendix.
3. The 1996 ANES, however, had a reduced sample size. For a comparable sample, the largest partisan difference was in 2000, in which the two cross-pressured partisans placed the Democratic Party 39 points apart.
4. 1980 is the first year that all six issues were included together in the ANES.
5. Eleven hundred respondents answered a web-based survey conducted by Polimetrix during November of 2011. Polimetrix maintains a panel of respondents, which it recruits through their polling website in return for incentives. Since recruitment into the panel is voluntary, the sample may be unrepresentative of the national population. However, sample matching was employed to draw a nearly nationally representative sample from the larger, nonrepresentative sample. The matching resulted in a sample with characteristics as similar as possible to the national population. This sample was balanced between Democrats and Republicans.
6. Responses included "I absolutely would do this," "I probably would do this," "I probably would not do this," and "I absolutely would not do this."
7. Items include the following: (1) How important is being a [identity] to you? [*Extremely important, Very important, Not very important, Not important at all*] (2) How well does the term [identity] describe you? [*Extremely well, Very well, Not very well, Not at all*] (3) When talking about [identity]s how often do you use "we" instead of "they"? [*All of the time, Most of the time, Some of the time, Rarely, Never*] (4) To what extent do you think of yourself as being a [identity]? [*A great deal, Somewhat, Very little, Not at all*]
8. The issues include the following: (1) Should the number of legally permitted immigrants be increased or decreased? (2) Do you support or oppose health care reforms

passed by Congress in 2010? (3) Should abortion be permitted? (4) Do you support or oppose same-sex marriage? (5) Which is more important—reducing the deficit or reducing unemployment? These items form a reliable scale ($\alpha = 0.78$). Each issue position is followed by an *issue-importance* item that asks, "How important is this issue to you?" Issue positions are measured using two separate scales, which are then interacted. First, each issue item is folded in half and coded to range from 0 (weakest issue position) to 1 (most extreme issue positions on either end of the spectrum). These folded items are then weighted by the issue importance items and combined to form a scale of *issue extremity*. The full weighted index is coded to range from 0 (weakest, least important issue positions) to 1 (strongest, most important issue positions) on both ends of the spectrum. A second measure assesses *issue constraint*, or how well these issue positions align on the liberal or conservative end of the ideological spectrum. This is measured by counting the percentage of answers on the liberal side of the issues and the percentage of answers on the conservative side of the issues. The difference between these two numbers is used to represent constraint.

In OLS models, these two measures, extremity and constraint, are interacted in order to account for separate variations in each type of issue polarization. The predicted values set the two measures of issue positions at either their minimum or maximum values.

9. For the curious reader, various combinations are presented in appendix figure A.1. The general picture is that no combination of extremity and constraint does anything to increase social-identity bias without the addition of partisan identity, with the exception of the strongest levels of both extremity and constraint.

CHAPTER FIVE

1. These predicted values are based on regressions that can be found in the appendix.
2. This is the interaction of the extremity and constraint measures explained in chapter 4.
3. I also examined an interaction between partisan identity and sorting and found no significant results. For example, in looking at the predicted values of the YouGov data in figure 5.1, weak partisans with cross-cutting identities are still significantly less biased than weak partisans with more highly sorted identities.
4. Also controlled for here is political knowledge, education, race, sex, income, age, and church attendance.
5. Tea Party identity is significantly correlated (in pairwise correlations) with Republican Party identity ($r = 0.34$), conservative social identity ($r = 0.65$), evangelical identity ($r = 0.34$), issue polarization ($r = 0.59$), and black identity ($r = -0.17$). Although it is strongly related to conservative social identity and conservative issue positions, I treat it here as a separate social identity as it does appear to be an identity of its own, related to evangelical, Republican, and white social identities, and not simply an ideology.
6. By including religion, race, and political-movement identities in addition to ideological identities (all measured using a four-item scale of social identification), this measure of sorting should drive higher levels of partisan prejudice. It accounts for the powerful combination of all of these social identities with partisanship. This data set, however, also includes a far more powerful measure of partisan identity (a four-item scale of social identification), which could make a more difficult test for the added effect of sorting.
7. For a practical example of coding the social-sorting scale, see appendix table A.3.

8. I manipulate only issue extremity, rather than constraint, as the extremity variable was the only one to have a significant effect in the originating regression. The interaction with constraint was not significant, so these models are run simply controlling for constraint rather than including the interaction, which would complicate predicted values.
9. Only partisan-ideological sorting is examined here, because it is the only sorting measure available in the ANES cumulative data file.
10. Because a number of the key variables are continuous, coarsened exact matching is used to make the matches more feasible (Iacus et al. 2012). The univariate imbalance in means is below 0.00001 for all covariates. This indicates that the samples are very well balanced and thus require no statistical model to account for any remaining imbalance. The ANES cumulative data file (through 2012) is used to provide as large a sample as possible for the matching process, with standard errors clustered by year. Matching on year was not feasible as the sample size was too severely restricted.
11. In an alternate model not shown here, issue constraint rather than extremity is matched (matching on both too severely restricted the sample size). In this model, almost identical results were obtained.
12. See, to begin, Converse (1964).
13. Extremity and constraint are interacted in this model, though the interaction term is not significant. However, both variables are set to minimum, mean, and maximum levels in producing predicted values.

CHAPTER SIX

1. In other analyses not shown, levels of anger toward the ingroup candidate have been decreasing over the same period. For more information on these trends, see Mason (2016).
2. For the purposes of this figure, issue extremity and constraint are combined into one measure that I am calling issue intensity. This measure is coded by creating a scale of issues ranging from most extremely and consistently liberal to most extremely and consistently conservative (by averaging the six issue positions). The entire scale is then folded in half so that 0 represents the most moderate/conflicted positions and 1 represents the most extreme/constrained positions.
3. In a separate model, in which an interaction between partisanship and sorting is included, this interaction is, in fact, significant. Predicted probabilities taken from this model still reveal significant differences between strong partisans with cross-cutting identities (67 percent probability) and strong partisans with well-aligned identities (76 percent probability). The interactive model is, however, very difficult to interpret, as the partisanship and sorting measures are related by construction.
4. I included each type of threat separately in a regression, controlling for demographic variables (race, gender, political knowledge, age, income, and church attendance), and included interactions between each variable of interest (sorting, partisan identity, issue extremity) and either party-based or issue-based threats. The interactions showed the effect of each of these variables only when the respondent had read a threatening message. In the sorting and partisan-identity models, issue extremity is also interacted with threat in order to control for the effects of issue extremity more fairly. All other variables are held at their means or modes. Modes in this sample for the dichotomous variables are female and white. See originating regressions in the appendix.
5. The full set of issue positions is combined into a scale ranging from most liberal on

all issues to most conservative on all issues. Each issue in the scale is weighted by its importance, as rated by the respondent. This full weighted scale is then folded in half, to range from the most conflicted/moderate/unimportant issues to the most consistent/extreme/important issue positions on either end of the ideological spectrum. This measure proved to generate the most powerful emotional results for issue positions and is therefore used here so as not to undersell the impact of issue positions. As noted in chapter 4, Broockman (2016) has argued that including constraint in the measure obscures important heterogeneity in extreme responses across ideological boundaries. This is true. However, the current measure is theoretically appropriate in the case of this particular experiment, as the models here are run under the assumption that issue positions are constrained. The issue threats are full of party-consistent issue positions. Furthermore, parties constrain issues, and partisanship is a key element of the models. An unconstrained set of issues, for the purposes of this particular model, should be expected to reduce emotional reactivity due to their cross-cutting effects. Including constraint in the issue-polarization measure is therefore a decision that is intentional.

6. It should also be noted that in all the following models, those that examine the effects of sorting or partisan identity control for issue intensity. The issue-intensity models do not control for partisanship or sorting. These models therefore provide a particularly generous test of the effects of issue polarization. Also controlled for in all models are white race, sex, income, age, political knowledge, and church attendance. In the issue-intensity and partisanship models, black race is also controlled for, but, as it is included in the sociopartisan sorting measure, it is not separately controlled in the social-sorting models.

CHAPTER SEVEN

1. Political engagement is obviously not entirely driven by sorting, but sorting is one contributor. This section establishes the context of political engagement; subsequent sections look more directly at causality.
2. An alternate model with samples matched on issue constraint provides nearly identical results. Including both extremity and constraint in the matching severely reduced the sample size.
3. The items, again, are (1) How important is being a [insert identity] to you? (2) How well does the term [insert identity] describe you? (3) When talking about [insert identity]s how often do you use "we" instead of "they"? (4) To what extent do you think of yourself as being a [insert identity]?
4. The issue that was rated as somewhat or extremely important by the most respondents was whether we should focus on reducing the deficit or unemployment (98.3 percent of respondents). In future research, it may be interesting to examine the potential for issue-based identities around these economic concerns, but the group labels on either side do not naturally come to mind.
5. The extremity and importance were interacted, and the interactive effect is presented.
6. Models including only abortion importance provided weaker results than those including opinion extremity.
7. Models including only abortion importance provided weaker results than those including opinion extremity.
8. For those who are wondering what type of people are moderate on the issue but identify strongly with the group, a few answers exist. The whole sample includes only fifty-four of them (with the absolute strongest social connection to the abortion-

group label and a moderate position on abortion). Of these fifty-four, about 91 percent are pro-life, 80 percent are Republicans, 90 percent are white, half are male, they earn $50,000 to $70,000 per year, they are about fifty-seven years old, and they go to church almost weekly. So, at least in this sample, the respondents who identify strongly with the pro-life social identity but can bend on the actual issue are middle-aged, middle-class, churchgoing, white Republicans.

CHAPTER EIGHT

1. It should be noted that, as social groups, racial minorities are not monolithic. This partially explains the higher prevalence of sorting-related behavior among Republicans, who do not have multiple racial groups associated with the party.

REFERENCES

Abramowitz, Alan I. 2011. *The Disappearing Center: Engaged Citizens, Polarization, and American Democracy*. New Haven, CT: Yale University Press.

Achen, Christopher H., and Larry M. Bartels. 2016a. *Democracy for Realists: Why Elections Do Not Produce Responsive Government*. Princeton, NJ: Princeton University Press.

———. 2016b. "Do Sanders Supporters Favor His Policies?" *New York Times*, May 23. http://www.nytimes.com/2016/05/23/opinion/campaign-stops/do-sanders-supporters-favor-his-policies.html?nytmobile=0.

Ahler, Douglas, and Gaurav Sood. 2016. "The Parties in Our Heads: Misperceptions about Party Composition and Their Consequences." Working paper. http://www.dougahler.com/uploads/2/4/6/9/24697799/ahlersood_partycomposition.pdf.

Albertson, Bethany, and Shana Kushner Gadarian. 2015. *Anxious Politics: Democratic Citizenship in a Threatening World*. New York: Cambridge University Press.

All In with Chris Hayes. 2013. NBC News, October 16. http://www.nbcnews.com/id/53307558/ns/msnbc-all_in_with_chris_hayes/.

Allport, Gordon. (1954) 1979. *The Nature of Prejudice: 25th Anniversary Edition*. Reading, MA: Addison Wesley Publishing Company.

American Political Science Association. 1950. "A Report of the Committee on Political Parties: Toward a More Responsible Two-Party System." *American Political Science Review* 44 (3): part 2.

Arceneaux, Kevin, and Martin Johnson. 2013. *Changing Minds or Changing Channels? Partisan News in an Age of Choice*. Chicago: University of Chicago Press.

Avenanti, Alessio, Angela Sirigu, and Salvatore M. Aglioti. 2010. "Racial Bias Reduces Empathic Sensorimotor Resonance with Other-Race Pain." *Current Biology* 20 (11): 1018–22. doi:10.1016/j.cub.2010.03.071.

Banks, Antoine J. 2016. *Anger and Racial Politics: The Emotional Foundation of Racial Attitudes in America*. New York: Cambridge University Press.

Bartels, Larry M. 2002. "Beyond the Running Tally: Partisan Bias in Political Perceptions." *Political Behavior* 24:117–50.

Bendersky, Corinne. 2014. "Resolving Ideological Conflicts by Affirming Opponents' Status: The Tea Party, Obamacare and the 2013 Government Shutdown." *Journal of Experimental Social Psychology* 53 (July): 163–68.

Berelson, Bernard R., Paul F. Lazarsfeld, and William N. McPhee. 1954. *Voting*. Chicago: University of Chicago Press.

Bertrand, Marianne, and Sendhil Mullainathan. 2003. "Are Emily and Greg More Employable than Lakisha and Jamal? A Field Experiment on Labor Market Discrimination." Working Paper 9873. National Bureau of Economic Research. http://www.nber.org/papers/w9873.

Billig, Michael, and Henri Tajfel. 1973. "Social Categorization and Similarity in Intergroup Behaviour." *European Journal of Social Psychology* 3 (1): 27–52.

Binning, Kevin R., David K. Sherman, Geoffrey L. Cohen, and Kirsten Heitland. 2010. "Seeing the Other Side: Reducing Political Partisanship via Self-Affirmation in the 2008 Presidential Election." *Analyses of Social Issues and Public Policy* 10:276–92.

Bishop, Bill. 2009. *The Big Sort: Why the Clustering of Like-Minded America Is Tearing Us Apart*. New York: First Mariner Books.

Bode, Leticia, Alexander Hanna, Junghwan Yang, and Dhavan V. Shah. 2015. "Candidate Networks, Citizen Clusters, and Political Expression Strategic Hashtag Use in the 2010 Midterms." *ANNALS of the American Academy of Political and Social Science* 659 (1): 149–65. doi:10.1177/0002716214563923.

Bogardus, E. S. 1925. "Measuring Social Distance." *Journal of Applied Sociology* 9 (2): 299–308.

Bonica, Adam, Nolan McCarty, Keith Poole, and Howard Rosenthal. 2013. "Why Hasn't Democracy Slowed Rising Inequality?" *Journal of Economic Perspectives* 27:103–24.

Brady, Henry E., Sidney Verba, and Kay Lehman Schlozman. 1995. "Beyond SES: A Resource Model of Political Participation." *American Political Science Review* 89 (2): 271.

Branscombe, Nyla R., and Daniel L. Wann. 1994. "Collective Self-Esteem Consequences of Outgroup Derogation When a Valued Social Identity Is on Trial." *European Journal of Social Psychology* 24 (6): 641–57.

Brewer, Marilynn B. 1979. "In-group Bias in the Minimal Intergroup Situation: A Cognitive-Motivational Analysis." *Psychological Bulletin* 86 (2): 307–24.

———. 1991. "The Social Self: On Being the Same and Different at the Same Time." *Personality and Social Psychology Bulletin* 17 (5): 475–82.

———. 2001a. "Ingroup Identification and Intergroup Conflict." In *Social Identity, Intergroup Conflict, and Conflict Reduction*, edited by Richard Ashmore, Lee Jussim, and David Wilder, 17–41. New York: Oxford University Press.

———. 2001b. "The Many Faces of Social Identity: Implications for Political Psychology." *Political Psychology* 22 (1): 115–25.

Brewer, M. B., and R. M. Kramer. 1985. "The Psychology of Intergroup Attitudes and Behavior." *Annual Review of Psychology* 36 (1): 219–43.

Broockman, David. 2016. "Approaches to Studying Policy Representation." *Legislative Studies Quarterly* 41 (1): 181–215.

Brooks, David. 2012. "Poll Addict Confesses." *New York Times*, October 22. http://www.nytimes.com/2012/10/23/opinion/books-poll-addict-confesses.html.

Bullock, John G. 2011. "Elite Influence on Public Opinion in an Informed Electorate." *American Political Science Review* 105 (3): 496–515.

Burnham, Walter Dean. 1969. "The End of American Party Politics." *Trans-action* 7 (2): 12–22.

Burns, Alexander, Maggie Haberman, and Jonathan Martin. 2016. "Inside the Republican Party's Desperate Mission to Stop Donald Trump" *New York Times*, February 27. http://www.nytimes.com/2016/02/28/us/politics/donald-trump-republican-party.html?nytmobile=0.

Buruma, Ian. 2002. "The Blood Lust of Identity." *New York Review of Books*, April 11. http://www.nybooks.com/articles/2002/04/11/the-blood-lust-of-identity/.

Cahn, Naomi, and June Carbone. 2010. *Red Families v. Blue Families: Legal Polarization and the Creation of Culture*. New York: Oxford University Press

Campbell, Angus, Philip E. Converse, Warren E. Miller, and Donald Stokes. 1960. *The American Voter*. Chicago: University of Chicago Press.

Carmines, Edward G., and Harold W. Stanley. 1992. "The Transformation of the New Deal Party System: Social Groups, Political Ideology, and Changing Partisanship Among Northern Whites, 1972–1988." *Political Behavior* 14 (3): 213–37.

Carmines, Edward G., and James A. Stimson. 1982. "Racial Issues and the Structure of Mass Belief Systems." *Journal of Politics* 44 (1): 2–20.

Carsey, Thomas M., and Geoffrey C. Layman. 2006. "Changing Sides or Changing Minds? Party Identification and Policy Preferences in the American Electorate." *American Journal of Political Science* 50 (2): 464–77.

Carter, Bill. 2012. "Republicans Like Golf, Democrats Prefer Cartoons, TV Research Suggests." *Media Decoder* [*New York Times* blog], October 11. http://mediadecoder.blogs.nytimes.com/2012/10/11/republicans-like-golf-democrats-prefer-cartoons-tv-research-suggests/.

Case, Anne, and Angus Deaton. 2015. "Rising Morbidity and Mortality in Midlife among White Non-Hispanic Americans in the 21st Century." *Proceedings of the National Academy of Sciences*, November. http://www.pnas.org/content/112/49/15078.full.

Cohen, Geoffrey L. 2003. "Party over Policy: The Dominating Impact of Group Influence on Political Beliefs." *Journal of Personality and Social Psychology* 85 (5): 808–22.

Cohen, Geoffrey L., David K. Sherman, Anthony Bastardi, Lillian Hsu, Michelle McGoey, and Lee Ross. 2007. "Bridging the Partisan Divide: Self-Affirmation Reduces Ideological Closed-Mindedness and Inflexibility in Negotiation." *Journal of Personality and Social Psychology* 93 (3): 415.

Coll, Steve. 2015. "Talk of the Town: Dangerous Gamesmanship." *New Yorker*, April 27.

Conover, Pamela Johnston. 1984. "The Influence of Group Identifications on Political Perception and Evaluation." *Journal of Politics* 46 (3): 760.

Conover, Pamela Johnston, and Stanley Feldman. 1981. "The Origins and Meaning of Liberal/Conservative Self-Identifications." *American Journal of Political Science* 25 (4): 617–45.

Converse, Philip E. 2006. "The Nature of Belief Systems in Mass Publics (1964)." *Critical Review* 18 (1–3): 1–74.

Craig, Maureen A., and Jennifer A. Richeson. 2014. "More Diverse yet Less Tolerant? How the Increasingly Diverse Racial Landscape Affects White Americans' Racial Attitudes." *Personality and Social Psychology Bulletin* 40 (6): 750–61.

Crocker, Jennifer, Riia Luhtanen, Bruce Blaine, and Stephanie Broadnax. 1994. "Collective Self-Esteem and Psychological Well-Being among White, Black, and Asian College Students." *Personality and Social Psychology Bulletin* 20 (5): 503–13. doi:10.1177/0146167294205007.

Crocker, Jennifer, Leigh L. Thompson, Kathleen M. McGraw, and Cindy Ingerman. 1987. "Downward Comparison, Prejudice, and Evaluations of Others: Effects of Self-Esteem and Threat." *Journal of Personality and Social Psychology* 52 (5): 907–16.

Dahl, Robert. 1967. *Pluralist Democracy in the United States: Conflict and Constant*. Chicago: Rand McNally Political Science Series.

———. 1981. *Democracy in the United States: Promise and Performance*. Boston: Houghton Mifflin.

Davis, Nicholas T., and Lilliana Mason. 2015. "Sorting and the Split-Ticket: Evidence from Presidential and Subpresidential Elections." *Political Behavior* 38 (2): 337–54.

Davis, Otto A., Melvin J. Hinich, and Peter C. Ordeshook. 1970. "An Expository Development of a Mathematical Model of the Electoral Process." *American Political Science Review* 64 (2): 426–48.

de Weerd, Marga, and Bert Klandermans. 1999. "Group Identification and Political Protest: Farmers' Protest in the Netherlands." *European Journal of Social Psychology* 29 (8): 1073–95.

Dinas, Elias. 2014. "Does Choice Bring Loyalty? Electoral Participation and the Development of Party Identification." *American Journal of Political Science* 58 (2): 449–65.

Downs, Anthony. 1957. *An Economic Theory of Democracy*. New York: Harper & Row.

Druckman, James N., Erik Peterson, and Rune Slothuus. 2013. "How Elite Partisan Polarization Affects Public Opinion Formation." *American Political Science Review* 107 (1): 57–79.

Duckitt, John H. 1992. *The Social Psychology of Prejudice*, vol. 8. Westport, CT: Praeger.

Edsall, Thomas B. 2012. "Let the Nanotargeting Begin." *Campaign Stops* [*New York Times* blog], April 15. http://campaignstops.blogs.nytimes.com/2012/04/15/let-the-nanotargeting-begin/.

Ellis, Christopher, and James A. Stimson. 2012. *Ideology in America*. 1st ed. New York: Cambridge University Press.

Enns, Peter K., and Gregory E. McAvoy. 2012. "The Role of Partisanship in Aggregate Opinion." *Political Behavior* 34 (4): 627–51.

Ethier, Kathleen A., and Kay Deaux. 1994. "Negotiating Social Identity When Contexts Change: Maintaining Identification and Responding to Threat." *Journal of Personality and Social Psychology* 67 (2): 243–51.

Fiorina, Morris P. 1977. "An Outline for a Model of Party Choice." *American Journal of Political Science* 21 (3): 601–25.

———. 1981. *Retrospective Voting in American National Elections*. New Haven, CT: Yale University Press.

Fiorina, Morris P., Samuel J. Abrams, and Jeremy Pope. 2005. *Culture War? The Myth of a Polarized America*. New York: PearsonLongman.

Fisher, Noel C. 2001. *War at Every Door: Partisan Politics and Guerrilla Violence in East Tennessee, 1860–1869*. Raleigh: University of North Carolina Press.

Fredrickson, Barbara L. 2001. "The Role of Positive Emotions in Positive Psychology: The Broaden-and-Build Theory of Positive Emotions." *American Psychologist* 56 (3): 218–26.

Frey, William H. 1979. "Central City White Flight: Racial and Nonracial Causes." *American Sociological Review* 44 (3): 425–48.

Frum, David. 2016. "The Great Republican Revolt." *Atlantic*, February. http://www.theatlantic.com/magazine/archive/2016/01/the-great-republican-revolt/419118/.

Fuller, Jaime. 2014. "Everything You Need to Know about the Long Fight Between Cliven Bundy and the Federal Government." *Washington Post*, April 15. http://www.washingtonpost.com/blogs/the-fix/wp/2014/04/15/everything-you-need-to-know-about-the-long-fight-between-cliven-bundy-and-the-federal-government/.

Gallup, Inc. 2016. "U.S. Economic Confidence Surges after Election." *Gallup.com*, November 15. http://www.gallup.com/poll/197474/economic-confidence-surges-election.aspx.

Garner, Andrew, and Harvey Palmer. 2011. "Polarization and Issue Consistency over Time." *Political Behavior* 33 (2): 225–46.

Giles, Michael W., and Kaenan Hertz. 1994. "Racial Threat and Partisan Identification." *American Political Science Review* 88 (2): 317–26.

Gingrich, Newt. 1994. "Language: A Key Mechanism of Control." GOPAC Memo. http://www.informationclearinghouse.info/article4443.htm.

Goldmacher, Shane. 2016. "Trump Shatters the Republican Party." *Politico*, February 24. http://politi.co/1KJyp0T.

Green, Donald, Bradley Palmquist, and Eric Schickler. 2002. *Partisan Hearts and Minds: Political Parties and the Social Identity of Voters*. New Haven, CT: Yale University Press.

Greene, Joshua David. 2013. *Moral Tribes: Emotion, Reason, and the Gap between Us and Them*. New York: Penguin.

Greene, Steven. 1999. "Understanding Party Identification: A Social Identity Approach." *Political Psychology* 20:393–403.

———. 2002. "The Social-Psychological Measurement of Partisanship," *Political Behavior* 24 (3): 171–97.

———. 2004. "Social Identity Theory and Political Identification," *Social Science Quarterly* 85 (1): 138–53.

Groenendyk, Eric. 2013. *Competing Motives in the Partisan Mind: How Loyalty and Responsiveness Shape Party Identification and Democracy*. New York: Oxford University Press.

Groenendyk, Eric W., and Antoine J. Banks. 2014. "Emotional Rescue: How Affect Helps Partisans Overcome Collective Action Problems." *Political Psychology* 35 (3): 359–78.

Gubler, Joshua R., and Joel Sawat Selway. 2012. "Horizontal Inequality, Crosscutting Cleavages, and Civil War." *Journal of Conflict Resolution* 56 (2): 206–32.

Hanmer, Michael J., Antoine J. Banks, and Ismail K. White. 2014. "Experiments to Reduce the Over-Reporting of Voting: A Pipeline to the Truth." *Political Analysis* 22 (1): 130–41.

Harmon-Jones, Eddie, Cindy Harmon-Jones, and Tom F. Price. 2013. "What Is Approach Motivation?" *Emotion Review* 5 (3): 291–95.

Healy, Andrew, and Neil Malhotra. 2014. "Partisan Bias among Interviewers." *Public Opinion Quarterly* 78 (2): 485–99.

Hetherington, Marc. 2015. "'Why Polarized Trust Matters.'" *Forum* 13 (3): 445–58.

Hetherington, Marc J., and Jonathan Haidt. 2012. "Look How Far We've Come Apart." *Campaign Stops* [*New York Times* blog], September 17. http://campaignstops.blogs.nytimes.com/2012/09/17/look-how-far-weve-come-apart/.

Hobson, Nicholas M., and Michael Inzlicht. 2016. "The Mere Presence of an Outgroup Member Disrupts the Brain's Feedback-Monitoring System." *Social Cognitive and Affective Neuroscience*, 11 (11): 1698–1706.

Hogg, Michael A. 2001. "A Social Identity Theory of Leadership." *Personality and Social Psychology Review* 5 (3): 184–200.

———. 2014. "From Uncertainty to Extremism Social Categorization and Identity Processes." *Current Directions in Psychological Science* 23 (5): 338–42.

Hogg, Michael A., Janice R. Adelman, and Robert D. Blagg. 2010. "Religion in the Face of Uncertainty: An Uncertainty-Identity Theory Account of Religiousness." *Personality and Social Psychology Review* 14 (1): 72–83.

Hogg, Michael A., Arie Kruglanski, and Kees van den Bos. 2013. "Uncertainty and the Roots of Extremism." *Journal of Social Issues* 69 (3): 407–18.

Hohman, Zachary P., and Michael A. Hogg. 2015. "Mortality Salience, Self-Esteem, and Defense of the Group: Mediating Role of In-Group Identification." *Journal of Applied Social Psychology* 45 (2): 80–89.

Huddy, Leonie. 2001. "From Social to Political Identity: A Critical Examination of Social Identity Theory." *Political Psychology* 22 (1): 127–56.

Huddy, Leonie, Lilliana Mason, and Lene Aarøe. 2015. "Expressive Partisanship: Campaign

Involvement, Political Emotion, and Partisan Identity." *American Political Science Review* 109 (1): 1–17.

Huddy, Leonie, Lilliana Mason, and S. Nechama Horwitz. 2016. "Political Identity Convergence: On Being Latino, Becoming a Democrat, and Getting Active." *RSF: The Russell Sage Foundation Journal of the Social Sciences* 2 (3): 205–28.

Hui, Iris. 2013. "Who Is Your Preferred Neighbor? Partisan Residential Preferences and Neighborhood Satisfaction." *American Politics Research* 41 (6): 997–1021.

Iacus, Stefano M., Gary King, Giuseppe Porro, and Jonathan N. Katz. 2012. "Causal Inference without Balance Checking: Coarsened Exact Matching." *Political Analysis* 20 (1): 1–24.

Isenstadt, Alex. 2009. "Town Halls Gone Wild." *Politico*, July 31. http://www.politico.com/news/stories/0709/25646.html.

Iyengar, Shanto, Gaurav Sood, and Yphtach Lelkes. 2012. "Affect, Not Ideology A Social Identity Perspective on Polarization." *Public Opinion Quarterly* 76 (3): 405–31. doi:10.1093/poq/nfs038.

Jacobson, Gary C. 2012. "The Electoral Origins of Polarized Politics: Evidence from the 2010 Cooperative Congressional Election Study." *American Behavioral Scientist* 56 (12): 1612–30.

Jacoby-Senghor, Drew S., Stacey Sinclair, and Colin Tucker Smith. 2015. "When Bias Binds: Effect of Implicit Outgroup Bias on Ingroup Affiliation." *Journal of Personality and Social Psychology* 109 (3): 415–33.

Jetten, Jolanda, Michael A. Hogg, and Barbara-Ann Mullin. 2000. "In-Group Variability and Motivation to Reduce Subjective Uncertainty." *Group Dynamics: Theory, Research, and Practice* 4 (2): 184–98.

Kagan, Robert. 2016. "This Is How Fascism Comes to America." *Washington Post*, May 17. https://www.washingtonpost.com/opinions/this-is-how-fascism-comes-to-america/2016/05/17/c4e32c58-1c47-11e6-8c7b-6931e66333e7_story.html?wpmm=1&wpisrc=nl_opinions.

Kahn, Dennis T., Varda Liberman, Eran Halperin, and Lee Ross. 2016. "Intergroup Sentiments, Political Identity, and Their Influence on Responses to Potentially Ameliorative Proposals in the Context of an Intractable Conflict." *Journal of Conflict Resolution* 60 (1): 61–88.

Kalyvas, Stathis. 2006. *The Logic of Violence in Civil War*. Cambridge Studies in Comparative Politics. New York: Cambridge University Press.

Katz, Josh. 2016. "'Duck Dynasty' vs. 'Modern Family': 50 Maps of the U.S. Cultural Divide." *New York Times*, December 27. http://www.nytimes.com/interactive/2016/12/26/upshot/duck-dynasty-vs-modern-family-television-maps.html.

Kelly, Caroline, and Sara Breinlinger. 1996. *The Social Psychology of Collective Action: Identity, Injustice and Gender*. European Monographs in Social Psychology. Philadelphia, PA: Taylor & Francis.

Key, Valdimer Orlando. 1961. *Public Opinion and American Democracy*. New York: Knopf.

Key, Valdimer O., and Milton Cummings. 1966. *The Responsible Electorate: Rationality in Presidential Voting: 1936–1960*. New York: Vintage.

Klandermans, Bert. 2003. "Collective Political Action." In *Oxford Handbook of Political Psychology*, edited by David O. Sears, Leonie Huddy, Robert Jervis, 670–709. Oxford: Oxford University Press.

Klandermans, P. G. 2014. "Identity Politics and Politicized Identities: Identity Processes and the Dynamics of Protest." *Political Psychology* 35 (1): 1–22.

Klar, Samara. 2014. "Partisanship in a Social Setting." *American Journal of Political Science* 58 (3): 687–704.

Klar, Samara, and Yanna Krupnikov. 2016. *Independent Politics: How American Disdain for Parties Leads to Political Inaction*. New York: Cambridge University Press.

Klayman, Larry. 2014. "Mounting Government Tyranny Furthers Revolution." *World Net Daily*, April 18. http://www.wnd.com/2014/04/mounting-government-tyranny-furthers-revolution/#U4rjwj22IBqS0qsr.99.

Lacey, Marc. 2011. "Countless Grievances, One Thread: We're Angry." *New York Times*, October 17. http://www.nytimes.com/2011/10/18/us/the-occupy-movements-common-thread-is-anger.html?pagewanted=all.

Lavine, Howard G., Christopher D. Johnston, and Marco R. Steenbergen. 2012. *The Ambivalent Partisan: How Critical Loyalty Promotes Democracy*. New York: Oxford University Press.

Layman, Geoffrey. 2001. *The Great Divide: Religious and Cultural Conflict in American Party Politics*. New York: Columbia University Press.

Lazarsfeld, Paul F., Bernard Berelson, and Hazel Gaudet. 1944. *The People's Choice: How the Voter Makes Up His Mind in a Presidential Campaign*. New York: Duell, Sloan & Pearce.

Lee, Frances E. 2009. *Beyond Ideology: Politics, Principles, and Partisanship in the US Senate*. Chicago: University of Chicago Press.

Lerner, Jennifer S., and Dacher Keltner. 2000. "Beyond Valence: Toward a Model of Emotion-Specific Influences on Judgement and Choice." *Cognition & Emotion* 14 (4): 473–93.

Lesthaeghe, Ron J., and Lisa Neidert. 2006. "The Second Demographic Transition in the United States: Exception or Textbook Example?" *Population and Development Review* 32 (4): 669–98.

Levendusky, Matthew. 2009. *The Partisan Sort: How Liberals Became Democrats and Conservatives Became Republicans*. Chicago: University of Chicago Press.

———. 2010. "Clearer Cues, More Consistent Voters: A Benefit of Elite Polarization." *Political Behavior* 32 (1): 111–31. doi:10.1007/s11109-009-9094-0.

———. 2013. *How Partisan Media Polarize America*. Chicago: University of Chicago Press.

Lipset, Seymour Martin. (1960) 1963. *Political Man: The Social Bases of Politics*. New York: Doubleday. Reprint, New York: Anchor. Citations refer to the Anchor edition.

Lizza, Ryan. 2015. "A House Divided." *New Yorker*, December 14. http://www.newyorker.com/magazine/2015/12/14/a-house-divided.

Lodge, Milton, and Charles S. Taber. 2013. *The Rationalizing Voter*. Cambridge: Cambridge University Press.

Luhtanen, Riia, and Jennifer Crocker. 1992. "A Collective Self-Esteem Scale: Self-Evaluation of One's Social Identity." *Personality and Social Psychology Bulletin* 18 (3): 302–18.

Mackie, D. M., T. Devos, and E. R. Smith. 2000. "Intergroup Emotions: Explaining Offensive Action Tendencies in an Intergroup Context." *Journal of Personality and Social Psychology* 79 (4): 602–16.

MacNab, J. J. 2014. "Context Matters: The Cliven Bundy Standoff—Part 3." *Forbes*, May 6. http://www.forbes.com/sites/jjmacnab/2014/05/06/context-matters-the-cliven-bundy-standoff-part-3/.

Mangum, Maruice. 2013. "The Racial Underpinnings of Party Identification and Political Ideology." *Social Science Quarterly* 94 (5): 1222–44.

Marcus, George E., W. Russell Neuman, and Michael MacKuen. 2000. *Affective Intelligence and Political Judgment*. Chicago: University of Chicago Press.

Masket, Seth. 2016. "The Toughest Death of 2016: The Democratic Norms That (Used

To) Guide Our Political System." *Pacific Standard*, December 27. https://psmag.com/the-toughest-death-of-2016-the-democratic-norms-that-used-to-guide-our-political-system-cc7f6b4361fa.

Mason, Lilliana. 2016. "A Cross-Cutting Calm: How Social Sorting Drives Affective Polarization." *Public Opinion Quarterly* 80 (S1): 351–77.

Mason, Lilliana, and Nick Davis. 2016. "Trump Attracts Poor Voters with Multiple Republican Social Identities." *Vox*, March 9. http://www.vox.com/mischiefs-of-faction/2016/3/9/11186314/trump-voters-identities.

McCarty, Nolan, Keith T. Poole, and Howard Rosenthal. 2008. *Polarized America: The Dance of Ideology and Unequal Riches*. Cambridge, MA: MIT Press.

McConnell, Christopher, Yotam Margalit, Neil Malhotra, and Matthew Levendusky. 2016. "The Economic Consequences of Partisanship in a Polarized Era." Working paper. http://web.stanford.edu/~neilm/Economic_Consequences_Final_Identified.pdf.

McGarty, Craig, Ana-Maria Bliuc, Emma F. Thomas, and Renata Bongiorno. 2009. "Collective Action as the Material Expression of Opinion-Based Group Membership." *Journal of Social Issues* 65 (4): 839–57.

Miller, Arthur H., Patricia Gurin, Gerald Gurin, and Oksana Malanchuk. 1981. "Group Consciousness and Political Participation." *American Journal of Political Science* 25 (3): 494–511.

Munro, Geoffrey D., Terell P. Lasane, and Scott P. Leary. 2010. "Political Partisan Prejudice: Selective Distortion and Weighting of Evaluative Categories in College Admissions Applications." *Journal of Applied Social Psychology* 40 (9): 2434–62.

Musgrave, Paul, and Mark Rom. 2015. "Fair and Balanced? Experimental Evidence on Partisan Bias in Grading." *American Politics Research* 43 (3): 536–54. doi:10.1177/1532673X14561655.

Mutz, Diana C. 2002. "Cross-Cutting Social Networks: Testing Democratic Theory in Practice." *American Political Science Review* 96 (1): 111–26.

Nadeau, Richard, Richard G. Niemi, Harold W. Stanley, and Jean-François Godbout. 2004. "Class, Party, and South/Non-South Differences: An Update." *American Politics Research* 32 (1): 52–67.

Nadeau, Richard, and Harold W. Stanley. 1993. "Class Polarization in Partisanship among Native Southern Whites, 1952–90." *American Journal of Political Science* 37 (3): 900–919.

Nordlinger, Eric A. 1972. *Conflict Regulation in Divided Societies*. Cambridge, MA: Center for International Affairs, Harvard University.

Nussbaum, Matthew, and Benjamin Oreskes. 2016. "More Republicans Viewing Putin Favorably." *Politico*, December 16. http://politi.co/2h6BgU7.

Office of Management and Budget. 2013. "Impacts and Costs of the October 2013 Federal Government Shutdown." https://www.whitehouse.gov/sites/default/files/omb/reports/impacts-and-costs-of-october-2013-federal-government-shutdown-report.pdf.

Pettigrew, Thomas F., Linda R. Tropp, Ulrich Wagner, and Oliver Christ. 2011. "Recent Advances in Intergroup Contact Theory." *International Journal of Intercultural Relations* 35 (3): 271–80.

Pew Research Center for the People and the Press. 2013a. "Broad Support for Renewed Background Checks Bill, Skepticism about Its Chances." http://www.people-press.org/2013/05/23/broad-support-for-renewed-background-checks-bill-skepticism-about-its-chances/.

———. 2013b. "Majority Views NSA Phone Tracking as Acceptable Anti-terror Tactic." June 10. http://www.people-press.org/2013/06/10/majority-views-nsa-phone-tracking-as-acceptable-anti-terror-tactic/.

———. 2014. "Few See Quick Cure for Nation's Political Divisions." December 11. http://www.people-press.org/2014/12/11/few-see-quick-cure-for-nations-political-divisions/.

———. 2016. "Partisanship and Political Animosity in 2016." June 22. http://www.people-press.org/2016/06/22/partisanship-and-political-animosity-in-2016/.

Philbrick, Nathaniel. 2013. *Bunker Hill: A City, a Siege, a Revolution*. New York: Penguin.

Pierce, Lamar, Todd Rogers, and Jason A. Snyder. 2016. "Losing Hurts: The Happiness Impact of Partisan Electoral Loss." *Journal of Experimental Political Science* 3 (1): 44–59.

Powell, G. Bingham, Jr. 1976. "Political Cleavage Structure, Cross-Pressure Processes, and Partisanship: An Empirical Test of the Theory." *American Journal of Political Science* 20 (1): 1–23.

Putnam, Robert. 2001. *Bowling Alone: The Collapse and Revival of American Community*. New York: Simon & Schuster.

Putra, Idhamsyah Eka. 2014. "The Role of Ingroup and Outgroup Metaprejudice in Predicting Prejudice and Identity Undermining." *Peace and Conflict: Journal of Peace Psychology* 20 (4): 574–79.

Ragusa, Jordan M., and Anthony Gaspar. 2016. "Where's the Tea Party? An Examination of the Tea Party's Voting Behavior in the House of Representatives." *Political Research Quarterly* 69 (2): 361–72.

Roccas, Sonia, and Marilynn Brewer. 2002. "Social Identity Complexity." *Personality and Social Psychology Review* 6 (2): 88–106.

Roof, Wade Clark, and William McKinney. 1987. *American Mainline Religion: Its Changing Shape and Future*. New Brunswick, NJ: Rutgers University Press.

Ross, Edward Alsworth. 1920. *The Principles of Sociology*. New York: The Century Co.

Rucker, Philip, and Dan Balz. 2016. "Trump's Growing List of Apostasies Puts Him at Odds with Decades of Republican Beliefs." *Washington Post*, March 22. https://www.washingtonpost.com/politics/trump-seeks-a-gop-platform-more-in-his-common-sense-image/2016/03/22/0389d688-f046-11e5-89c3-a647fcce95e0_story.html.

Sampasivam, Sinthujaa, Katherine Anne Collins, Catherine Bielajew, and Richard Clément. 2016. "The Effects of Outgroup Threat and Opportunity to Derogate on Salivary Cortisol Levels." *International Journal of Environmental Research and Public Health* 13 (6): 616.

Saunders, Kyle L., and Alan I. Abramowitz. 2004. "Ideological Realignment and Active Partisans in the American Electorate." *American Politics Research* 32 (3): 285–309. doi:10.1177/1532673X03259195.

Scarcelli, Marc. 2014. "Social Cleavages and Civil War Onset." *Ethnopolitics* 13 (2): 181–202.

Schattschneider, Elmer Eric. 1942. *Party Government*. New York: Holt Rinehart and Winston.

———. (1960) 1975. *The Semisovereign People: A Realist's View of Democracy in America*. Hinsdale, IL: Dryden Press.

Scheepers, Daan, and Belle Derks. 2016. "Revisiting Social Identity Theory from a Neuroscience Perspective." *Current Opinion in Psychology* 11 (October): 74–78.

Schnabel, Landon Paul. 2013. "When Fringe Goes Mainstream: A Sociohistorical Content Analysis of the Christian Coalition's Contract with the American Family and the Republican Party Platform." *Politics, Religion & Ideology* 14 (1): 94–113.

Schwartz, Ian. 2015. "Trump: 'We Will Have So Much Winning If I Get Elected That You May Get Bored with Winning.'" *Real Clear Politics*, September 9. http://www.realclearpolitics.com/video/2015/09/09/trump_we_will_have_so_much_winning_if_i_get_elected_that_you_may_get_bored_with_winning.html.

Selway, Joel Sawat. 2011. "Cross-Cuttingness, Cleavage Structures and Civil War Onset." *British Journal of Political Science* 41 (1): 111–38.

Settle, Jaime E., Robert M. Bond, Lorenzo Coviello, Christopher J. Fariss, James H. Fowler, and Jason J. Jones. 2016. "From Posting to Voting: The Effects of Political Competition on Online Political Engagement." *Political Science Research and Methods* 4 (2): 361–78.

Sherif, Muzafer, O. J. Harvey, B. Jack White, William R. Hood, and Carolyn W. Sherif. 1988. *The Robbers Cave Experiment: Intergroup Conflict and Cooperation*. Middletown, CT: Wesleyan University Press.

Sinclair, Betsy. 2012. *The Social Citizen: Peer Networks and Political Behavior*. Chicago Studies in American Politics. Chicago: University Of Chicago Press.

Stanley, Harold W., William T. Bianco, and Richard G. Niemi. 1986. "Partisanship and Group Support over Time: A Multivariate Analysis." *American Political Science Review* 80 (3): 969–76.

Staub, Ervin. 2001. "Individual and Group Identities in Genocide and Mass Killing." In *Social Identity, Intergroup Conflict, and Conflict Reduction*, edited by Richard D. Ashmore, Lee Jussim, and David Wilder, 159–84. New York: Oxford University Press.

Sundquist, James L. 1983. *Dynamics of the Party System: Alignment and Realignment of Political Parties in the United States*. Washington, DC: Brookings Institution.

Sunstein, Cass R. 2015. "Partyism." *University of Chicago Legal Forum* 2015 (1): 1–27.

Swigger, Nathaniel. 2017. "The Effect of Gender Norms in Sitcoms on Support for Access to Abortion and Contraception." *American Politics Research* 45 (1): 109–27.

Sykes, Charles J. 2016. "Charlie Sykes on Where the Right Went Wrong." *New York Times*, December 15. http://www.nytimes.com/2016/12/15/opinion/sunday/charlie-sykes-on-where-the-right-went-wrong.html?nytmobile=0.

Tajfel, Henri, M. G. Billig, R. P. Bundy, and Claude Flament. 1971. "Social Categorization and Intergroup Behaviour." *European Journal of Social Psychology* 1 (2): 149–78.

Tajfel, Henri, and John Turner. 1979. "An Integrative Theory of Intergroup Conflict." In *The Social Psychology of Intergroup Relations*, edited by W. G. Austin and S. Worchel. Monterey, CA: Brooks/Cole.

Teixeira, Ruy, William H. Frey, Robert Griffin. 2015. "States of Change." Center for American Progress, February 24. https://www.americanprogress.org/issues/progressive-movement/report/2015/02/24/107261/states-of-change/.

Theriault, Sean M. 2008. *Party Polarization in Congress*. Cambridge: Cambridge University Press.

Triandis, C. H., and L. M. Triandis. 1960. "Race, Social Class, Religion, and Nationality as Determinants of Social Distance." *Journal of Abnormal and Social Psychology* 61 (1): 110–18.

Turner, John. 1996. "Henri Tajfel: An Introduction." In *Social Groups and Identities: Developing the Legacy of Henri Tajfel*, edited by William Peter Robinson, 1–24. Oxford: Butterworth-Heinemann.

Valentino, Nicholas A., Ted Brader, Eric W. Groenendyk, Krysha Gregorowicz, and Vincent L. Hutchings. 2011. "Election Night's Alright for Fighting: The Role of Emotions in Political Participation." *Journal of Politics* 73 (01): 156–70.

Van Zomeren, Martijn, Russell Spears, and Colin Wayne Leach. 2008. "Exploring Psychological Mechanisms of Collective Action: Does Relevance of Group Identity Influence How People Cope with Collective Disadvantage?" *British Journal of Social Psychology* 47 (2): 353–72.

Vavreck, Lynn. 2016. "Candidates Fight over Abortion, but Public Has Surprising Level of Harmony." *New York Times*, May 6. http://www.nytimes.com/2015/05/06

/upshot/candidates-disagree-on-abortion-but-public-is-in-surprising-harmony.html ?nytmobile=0.

Vyan. 2014. "Cliven Bundy Is a Big Fat Million Dollar Welfare Dead Beat!" *Dailykos.com,* April 14. http://www.dailykos.com/story/2014/04/13/1291642/-Cliven-Bundy-is-a-Big-Fat-Million-Dollar-Welfare-Dead-Beat.

Waldman, Paul. 2014. "Cliven Bundy and the Perils of Identity Politics." *Washington Post,* April 24. http://www.washingtonpost.com/blogs/plum-line/wp/2014/04/24/cliven-bundy-and-the-perils-of-identity-politics/.

Washington, George. (1796) 2016. "Transcript of President George Washington's Farewell Address (1796)." Our Documents. https://www.ourdocuments.gov/doc.php?doc=15&page=transcript.

Wolf, Michael R., J. Cherie Strachan, and Daniel M. Shea. 2012. "Forget the Good of the Game: Political Incivility and Lack of Compromise as a Second Layer of Party Polarization." *American Behavioral Scientist* 56 (12): 1677–95.

INDEX